THE COOMBS

A House of Memories

A House of Memories

Editors: Brij V. Lal, Allison Ley

Published by ANU eView
The Australian National University
Canberra ACT 0200, Australia
Email: enquiries.eview@anu.edu.au
This title is also available online at http://eview.anu.edu.au

---

National Library of Australia Cataloguing-in-Publication entry

Title: The Coombs: a house of memories
         2nd edition

Bibliography
Includes index

ISBN: 9781921934179 (pbk) 9781921934186 (online)

Subjects: Coombs Building (Canberra, ACT) - History - Anecdotes.
          Australian National University - History - Anecdotes.
          Australian National University - Alumni and alumnae.
          Universities and Colleges - Australian Capital Territory - Canberra - History.

Dewey Number: 378.947

All rights reserved. No part of this publication may be reproduced, stored in a retrieval system or transmitted in any form or by any means, electronic, mechanical, photocopying or otherwise, without the prior permission of the publisher.

Cover design by Nic Welbourn and layout by ANU eView

Cover image: Matcham Skipper's wrought iron frieze, photo courtesy of Coombs Photography

Previous edition © 2006 Research School of Pacific and Asian Studies, The Australian National University

This edition © 2014 ANU eView

This book can be purchased from http://eview.anu.edu.au

for

the people of Coombs
past, present and future

Table of Contents

	Acknowledgements	ix
	Foreword: The Coombs Building *William C. Clarke*	xiii
	Preface *Brij V Lal*	xvii
Part I	*The Coombs: A Portrait*	
1	The Coombs: Journeys and Transformations *Brij V. Lal*	1
Part II	*A Room at the Top*	
2	Salad Days *Oskar Spate*	23
3	An OHB Beginner *Anthony Low*	35
4	People and the Coombs Effect *Wang Gungwu*	43
5	In the Room at the Top *R. Gerard Ward*	47
6	Coombs Reflections *Merle Ricklefs*	55
7	Turn Right at the Buddha *James J. Fox*	61
Part III	*Coombs Journeys*	
8	Hexagonal Reflections on Pacific History *Niel Gunson*	69
9	Seriously but not Solemnly *Bryant Allen*	79
10	A Wurm Turned in Coombs *Darrell Tryon*	87
11	Northern Exposure: The New Guinea Research Unit *R.J. May*	95
12	On the Wrong Side of Coombs? *John Ravenhill*	101
13	Prehistory: A Late Arrival *Jack Golson*	109
14	We, the Ethnographers *Kathryn Robinson*	117
15	Real Australians in Economics *Ross Garnaut*	125
16	Reflections of a Defence Intellectual *Desmond Ball*	149
17	Political and Social Change: Not the Research School of Politics and Sociology *R.J. May*	159

Part IV	Running the Coombs	
18	Sue's Story *Sue Lawrence*	171
19	PAMBU, the Islands and the Coombs *Ewan Maidment*	179
20	EWG and me *Claire Smith*	189
21	Editing Reflections *Maxine McArthur*	193
22	Finding Nuggets in Coombs *Allison Ley*	199
23	A Fly on the Wall of Room 4225 *Jude Shanahan and Julie Gordon*	207
24	Fieldwork and Fireworks: A Lab Assistant's Tales *Gillian Atkin*	213
25	Coombs Administration *Ann Buller*	221
26	At the Leading Edge: Computer Technology in Coombs *Allison Ley*	227
Part V	Across Coombs	
27	Have You Got a Title? Seminar Daze *Hank Nelson*	235
28	Space Wars *Colin Filer*	243
29	Dark Side of the Coombs *Allison Ley*	251
30	All Corridors Lead to the Tea Room *Sophie Vilaythong and Lisa (Alicia) Dal Molin with Maxine McArthur*	259
Part VI	Coombs Memories	
31	Work and Play in the Coombs Building 1967–73 *Peter Corris*	265
32	Recalling the Coombs – Pacific History 1970–73 *Kerry Howe*	269
33	1970s Coombs Dramas *Grant McCall*	273
34	The 'Catacoombs' *Michael R. Godley*	279
35	The Old Hospital Building *Anton Ploeg*	285
Part VII	Corridors of Coombs *Tessa Morris-Suzuki*	291
	List of Contributors	293
	Index	295

ACKNOWLEDGEMENTS

Our grateful thanks go to many people who helped us bring this project to fruition. Jim Fox provided the initial support and encouragement which Robin Jeffrey, his successor as the Director of the Research School of Pacific and Asian Studies, continued. Pennie Pemberton at the ANU Archives provided assistance with the documentary material, and Doug Munro, F.B. (Barry) Smith, Anthony Low, Stephen Foster, Hugh Laracy and Hank Nelson helped with recollections and pointers for further work. Paul D'Arcy read the entire manuscript with care. We are grateful to Darren Boyd and the Noel Butlin Archives Centre for the photographs. Maxine McArthur both edited the volume and prepared the index with exemplary care and speed. Oanh Collins, of the Division of Pacific and Asian History, prepared the manuscript for publication with her legendary generosity and efficiency. Lorena Kanellopoulos, Duncan Beard and Jude Shanahan gave wise advice during the production stage. Our greatest debt is, of course, to our contributors without whom this book would not exist. Their warm support and affection for the project, despite its somewhat eccentric character—an anthology on a building rather than an institution or a discipline—made our task as editors very agreeable. But then Coombs people are an unconventional lot, and this is appropriately and unapologetically an unconventional book. Our pleasure at completing this project is tinged only with the regret that we were not able to include more contributions from colleagues both inside and outside Coombs. We hope nonethelss that they will recognize markers of their own special moments and echoes of their individual footsteps in the recollections here.

Brij V. Lal
Allison Ley

Copyright Permissions

A photographic representation of the statue of 'Meditating Buddha sheltered by the Naga King' by Matthew Harding and Nath Chun Pok by permission Matthew Harding; a photographic representation of Clifton Pugh's portrait of H.C. Coombs by permission Shane Pugh; an aerial photograph of Coombs Building courtesy of Jeremy Clarke, SJ. Editors' photo by Darren Boyd, Coombs Photography.

Clifton Pugh's portrait of H.C. Coombs

FOREWORD

The Coombs Building

William C. Clarke

> Any discipline can be the starting point for an education which is culturally rich, provided its formal content is regarded as a starting point and not as an end and provided that the scholar is in one way or another brought into contact with the developing fringes of his subject.
>
> —H.C. ("Nugget") Coombs, *Other People's Money*,
> ANU Press, 1971:180

I couldn't write a poem about the building
without going back to the man it honours.
Australian-born, Nugget would have known the native silky oaks,
kangaroo paws, and *Eriostemon* now gracing the main entrance,
whose outer doors open outward to the world, as did his mind.

Adviser to seven Prime Ministers, a principled economist,
governor of the central bank, the best of public administrators,
first chairman of the Council for the Arts, Chancellor of the ANU—
the university he helped to found—supporter of environmental causes,
but to go on with the accolade would affront the memory of a modest man.

Modest but passionate, ready to use his influence into old old age
in a crusade for the dignity and better treatment
of Australia's aboriginal peoples, titling a book on that cause
and other matters of importance to his country
Shame on Us! Essays on a Future Australia.

But what of the building that bears his name?
Was it dreamed into existence?
For some it is an Escher image made real.
For others, a labyrinthine puzzle, "the Catacoombs",
as with growing desperation they seek Seminar Room E—or B.

And often we Coombs dwellers meet lost souls
peering this way and that who beg with some chagrin
"Please, how do I get out?" having become lost in the building's
straight corridors (I calculate there are 51), all of which lead
to non-right-angle turns and often to a branching of the ways,

and at times to levels at slightly different heights calling for
short links on longer stairs, some of which go straight
while other grander ones circle gently in wells of iridescent tesserae.
The building's brickwork puts to shame most current craft.
Less precise but very human are the nooks and crannies

used in different ways by the denizens in their locale—
some filled with a photocopier and sorting table, others have a pretty rug
between a few chairs, a cubby for chats, for drinking tea,
or at times champagne. The courtyards and the birds
also merit words. Three linked hexagonal buildings contain three hexagons

open to the sky, each with its own character,
all planted with Australian shrubs and trees, one with splendid banksias,
another favoured for bar-b-ques is graced with a handsome argyle apple
and other eucalypts, the third offers capacious paths to the tea room. To enter
any of them is to find a tranquil haven from the disordered world.

Nor are we alone in our appreciation of the courtyards.
Magpies and currawongs brandish their intensity of white against black,
colour comes with the sulphur crests of raucous white cockatoos,
the crimson rosellas chime from balcony rails like tiny glass bells,
and we are further blessed by the scarlet and green of genteel king parrots.

Aside from the birds, another presence other than human
dwells within the building—brushtail possums,
which the Field Guide to Mammals describes as a cat-sized
terrestrial and arboreal possum that in cities commonly dens
in building roofs. And in the Coombs Building,

in the women's loo near the Coombs Theatre, where a mother possum
was accustomed to rear her young, which led a concerned soul
to put a notice on the door requesting visitors to the loo to please
not disturb the mother and babies. Many other possum
tales could be told but it's time to turn to ourselves.

Within the building's congenially complex architecture
dwells a hive of academic pursuits and scholarly devotions
too intricate by far to spell out here but ranging from philosophy

through archaeology, linguistics, history, and anthropology
to the Australian Centre for Population Research, and much left unnamed.

Within the programs, centres, departments, and projects work
an even greater medley of people of many nations and ages,
some struggling for seven years to gain a PhD, others with scores
of publications and many honours. There are those who are gregarious,
door open, ready for any joust or game, loud with ideas at seminars.

Others slip along the walls between entrance and office,
working behind closed doors with prodigious scholarship on obscure topics.
Some offices are bedecked with rug and armchair, others clotted with books;
Doors may be decorated with rude political cartoons or esoteric art—all this
somehow fitting easily within the walls of Mother Coombs.

To end by turning back to Nugget, I can't remember now the story's source
but heard it said that in his later years once walking by the Coombs Building
on his way to lunch he gave the building's entrance a sidelong glance,
remarking "They told me I'd have an office in there." He never did,
but can it not be hoped the building's people and its geometry
resonate still with his intellect, his ethics, and his passionate tenacity.

PREFACE

Brij V Lal

The Coombs: A House of Memories was first published in 2006 and sold out within months. The book's appeal both surprised and delighted us. Former students, now widely scattered across the globe, re-visited through its pages their youthful years spent in the building, the interesting characters they encountered, the pranks they played on fellow students, and the heady optimism about the future that lay before them. Others perused the book to find out 'what else' went on in the building during the day and at night. Quite a bit, as it turns out. Everyone was grateful for the time they spent here and for the enduring friendships they made. Some, full of nostalgia, regretted the passing of the old ways when scholars could chew the cud of research in quiet, uninterrupted contemplation with scant thought for notions of accountability and outcomes so commonplace now. Scholars knew the value and importance of what they were doing and that, as far as they were concerned, was that. We are delighted that the book will be available again, now in an electronic form to a much larger audience. Our joy though is tinged with the sadness that many of our senior contributors have passed on and others have retired. Their names will mean little to our newer colleagues, but they live on fondly in the memories of the old denizens of Coombs.

The Coombs Building still retains its unique, and to some (luckily very few!) baffling, and allegedly disorienting architectural features, heritage-listed invitingly as 'an innovative trio-hexagonal labyrinth of six hundred rooms on nineteen different levels'[1] Canberra satirist and one-time resident of Coombs Ian Warden writes: 'It is an only-in Canberra building. The architect surely had a sense of humour. It is indescribable really but inside is like a very complex system of wombat burrows arranged to give wombats stimulating intellectual challenges in finding their way about.' Ian quotes a poem about Coombs sent to him by Reg Naulty, another Coombs scholar and a philosophy tutor at John XXIII in 1969:

---

[1] Warden, Ian. *Canberra Times*, 3 January 2013.

The Coombs

> *Iridescent mosaics flash knowledge's*
> *Occasional lustre*
> *Around the spiral staircases of the Coombs*
> *Scholars, hunched over dormant ideas,*
> *Advance*
> *To the tea room; in the queue they open*
> *into smiles;*
> *The conversations of the Coombs*
> *brighten. When walking encyclopaedias*
> *Meet*
> *They don't neglect truth, they enlighten.*
> *Some, even,*
> *with beneficent intent, find the person*
> *In abstract argument. Until eleven ten*
> *Adventurous minds contend and diffident*
> *Ones suspend*
> *Judgement, when scholars return to their*
> *rooms*
> *down the angled corridors of the Coombs* [2]

Alas, things are not now what they were thirty, or even ten, years ago. The Coombs Tearoom which once bustled with animated conversation at morning and afternoon tea about the most serious issues of the day, about war and peace and footy results and cricket scores, is now an abandoned place, forlorn, the venue for occasional celebrations and solitary lunches. It could not compete with more popular upmarket coffee outlets elsewhere around the building, and the old culture of collegiality and conversation is now largely a vanishing memory.

---

[2] Ibid.

The Research School of Pacific and Asian Studies (RSPAS) is no longer a bricks-and-mortar institution, but rebranded as the Research School of Asia and the Pacific (RSAP), a cyber-reality. On earth, RSPAS has been replaced by the College of Asia and the Pacific, comprising the School of Culture, History and Language, the School of International and Political Studies, and the Crawford School of Public Policy. The new outfit has dynamics of its own whose distinctive cultural pattern and profile will emerge in time. It is now in its teething stages. But for someone who has spent a quarter of a century in Coombs, it is clear that the sense of a cohesive community, with a collective identity and a common purpose marked by care and concern that transcended the normal routine of academic life, is fragmented, possibly beyond repair.

The intensely competitive environment in which universities function today makes inordinate demands on its staff – to get grants, for example, to publish incessantly in peer-reviewed journals, to be mindful of the mysterious arithmetic of international ranking systems – though whether these make much substantial difference to the broad quantum and quality of human knowledge is not always certain. Vice-Chancellor Ian Young's exhortation that academics should produce first class research and earn money for the university would sound incongruous to our forebears in Coombs: produce lasting research, yes; but to be revenue earners as well? Sadly, Young is not the only university leader to think about money and international competitiveness.

This book is published in its original form. We have refused the temptation to fatten it with new contributions. That will be the task for another day, for someone else. For now, we invite you to enter its pages to glimpse a world that once was but no longer is, to share the passions and predilections of an earlier generation, our forebears, on whose shoulders we proudly stand as they 'quietly savour their accomplishments and recall the failings and foibles of the past with a kindly tolerance.' For me, now on my way out after nearly half a lifetime in the Coombs Building: It is not now as it hath been of yore / the things I have seen I can see no more. [3]

Brij V Lal

College of Culture, History and Language
College of Asia and the Pacific

---

[3] Wordsworth, William. 'Intimations of Immortality from Recollections of Early Childhood'.

PART I

The Coombs: A Portrait

The Coombs: View from a hot air balloon, 2006

CHAPTER 1

The Coombs:
Journeys and Transformations

Brij V. Lal

The Coombs Building is a Canberra icon. Ask any taxi driver at the airport. They are not likely to know the location of Fellows Road or Liversidge and East Streets which frame the building, but they will all know where the Coombs is. On the campus itself, the Coombs stands out for its distinctive hexagonal shape, so unlike the bland concrete multi-story structures that began to dot the Australian university landscape from the 1960s. Visitors comment wryly on its seemingly disorientating sets of spiralling staircases on three levels—split levels at that—making seminar rooms difficult to find, and offices even harder to locate, their occupants busily filling blinking screens behind shelves creaking with books and papers. New research scholars sometimes express bemused surprise at the ancient, yellowing name plates they see on the doors of people they thought were, or should have been, long dead. Jokes abound about skeletons behind book cases (entomed, as some say), and about the daily routine organized around the leisurely morning and afternoon tea and long (in the past liquid) lunches, with a few hours of work thrown in between. Envy and admiration, sometimes pity and exasperation is what most people feel about the lives (and deaths) inside the Coombs—or 'Tombs', according to some.

It is true that in the Coombs work does not follow the normal rhythm of a teaching university where life begins wearily on Monday morning and ends with a collective sigh on Friday. Among teachers, things have to be done whether ready or not: lectures delivered, tutorials conducted, assignments marked, exam papers corrected, grades allocated, department meetings attended, leaving precious little time for research—or anything else. Coombs inhabitants are spared the tyranny of the didactic clock—or denied the pleasure of the change of seasons, if you like—but those who want have their own punishing rhythm and pattern of work which are intense and relentless in their own way. Hardly a day goes by without a seminar or workshop being held in the building on topics ranging from the prehistoric agriculture in the New Guinea Highlands, 19th century resistance movements in New Caledonia, to the latest political developments in Indonesia. On any given day you are likely to see a diplomatic car parked in front of the Coombs while dignitaries consult a world expert on the Australian economy and population trends, the East Timor elections, the Bougainville peace process, or the Fijian constitution. On your evening news, you are likely to see the face of a Coombs scholar enlightening the world about dating the first human settlement of Australia or the likelihood of a terrorist attack in the Asia-Pacific region.

The Coombs Building is all this and more. For over forty years, it has housed the Research School of Social Sciences (RSSS) and the Research School of Pacific Studies (RSPacS). These were two of the ANU's original four research schools, the other two being the John Curtin School of Medical Research (JCSMR) and the Research School of Physical Sciences (RSPhyS). As well as research, the academics engaged in postgraduate supervision but were free from undergraduate teaching. In 1960, under federal government duress, ANU amalgamated with the contiguous Canberra University College (previously associated with the University of Melbourne). The original ANU was then referred to as the Institute of Advanced Studies and the former Canberra University College as the School of General Studies (later renamed The Faculties). New research schools were gradually added or modified; in 1994, RSPacS was renamed the Research School of Pacific and Asian Studies and was duly abbreviated to RSPAS.

This book of recollections is about RSPacS/RSPAS. It is not about RSSS, the other half of the Siamese twin, whose intellectual concerns and interests are essentially discipline-based (with some excursions into cross-disciplinary research such as history of ideas and restorative justice) and whose geographical focus largely excludes Asia-Pacific. In RSPAS, research is also organised along disciplinary lines, but an overarching awareness of a larger Asian and Pacific region, with its connections and continuities, and its importance to Australia, informs its research enquiry. RSPAS's intellectual and practical engagement with the region through research, consultancy and graduate training provides its scholars with common points of reference, a shared intellectual space and a unity of purpose.

The profound contribution RSPAS scholars have made to graduate training and scholarship on the Asia Pacific is beyond question, and it is no surprise that the School is universally esteemed. But this book is not about celebrating our accomplishments, all there in prizes, honorary degrees, membership of the learned academies and frequent mention in citation indices. Neither is this an institutional history designed to offer a scrupulously balanced (and suitably bland) coverage of every discipline, every field of enquiry, every major development in the School. Rather, its purpose is to reflect partially and anecdotally on the personal journeys and transformations of the Coombs community over the past half century. 'One does not have to be solemn to be serious,' O.H.K. Spate, one of the Coombs' more illustrious denizens, was fond of saying. This volume is conceived in that vein, looking at life in the Coombs through the prism of personal experience and happenstance. What we have here are the recollections of both 'sahibs' and 'subalterns,' old timers and newcomers, insiders and outsiders, the lost and the discovered. How does Coombs look from the room at the top? At night? From the desk of the divisional administrator and the research assistant? From its former students and present inhabitants? From the seminar rooms and academic offices? From the vantage point of the 'tea ladies?' Stories have a curious way of capturing elusive human truths and illuminating patterns, touching you in ways that self-conscious scholarship often cannot. So this book, part memoir, part biography, and part celebration, is about us, the people of the Coombs, past and present. And about time too.

The Coombs Building was officially opened on 11 September 1964 although staff had begun to move in from 29 July, even as tiles and carpet were being laid. But the idea of a national university dedicated, in part, to studying Australia's regional neighbourhood had been canvassed before the end of World War Two, the brainchild of an exceptional group of public-minded intellectuals and large-hearted public servants. A Pacific School was included in the 1945 cabinet submission, and the 1946 Act was piloted through the House by J.J. Dedman who had the distinction, as Oskar Spate recalled, of receiving an Honorary ANU LLD while he was still one of its undergraduates—in political science, of all subjects! Planning began soon afterwards. In March 1948, a small committee led by H.C. Coombs, who would play a central role in the creation of the ANU and after whom the new building would be named, made some preliminary suggestions about the new school tentatively titled 'School of Pacific and Asiatic Studies.' The War had starkly exposed Australia's ignorance of its neighbours in the region, and the new School was expected to fill that gap.

Once the idea of a research university had been accepted, the next stage was its detailed planning. The university appointed four distinguished Academic Advisors: Howard Florey for the medical school, Sir Mark Oliphant for the physical sciences, Sir Keith Hancock for social sciences and Raymond Firth for Pacific studies. A New Zealand-born anthropologist at the London School of Economics, Firth was well known for his Pacific research, especially on the island of Tikopia. All the Academic Advisors were expected to take up directorships of their respective schools. Two of them did, Oliphant with alacrity and Hancock eventually. Firth told the university he was reluctant to give up his European cultural and intellectual interests even for a research-only career in Australia, and returned to London with his English wife. Florey too was reluctant to leave Oxford for the new university, with the University Council appointing the incumbent caretaker.

Firth submitted his report in June 1948. 'Asiatic' was dropped from the title, but without serious loss: the Pacific was defined to include South, East and Southeast Asia. 'The pursuit of science as such,' he wrote, 'has no boundaries and any scientist who engaged to work in the Pacific School should be free to give the most liberal interpretation to the regional limits of his enquiry.' A fine sentiment on paper, but it complicated relations with the Social Sciences which cavilled at such a wide definition that intruded upon their own areas of enquiry and interest. Only by the most liberal stretch of the imagination—and even then—could India, for instance, be said to have some connection with New Guinea, or with Samoa or Kiribati. These disputes were not satisfactorily resolved, the Joint Faculty Board opting not for a fixed boundary but a 'march' in which the important spheres of interest of the two schools were recognised, but left enough room for some departments in the two Schools—Geography and Demography, for instance—to work cooperatively.

The early research focus of the School dismayed some, including Coombs, who in 1958 complained to Pacific historian J.W. (Jim) Davidson about the 'unduly Pacific Islands emphasis.' 'The basic purpose of the School,' noted Coombs, 'is to provide an increasing body of knowledge necessary to the conduct of the Australian affairs regionally considered. The development of Australia as an outpost of European civilisation has left us appallingly ignorant of the region of which we are suddenly conscious, and whose affairs daily assume greater practical significance for us.' And he wanted more coordinated, multi-disciplinary, problem-solving, outcome-oriented research, especially on New Guinea.

To meet Coombs' New Guinea concern, the School created the New Guinea Research Unit in 1961. The Unit was based in Port Moresby and coordinated applied social science research. David Bettison was its first executive director. It was formally handed over to Papua New Guinea after independence, acquiring new life first as the Institute of Applied Economic and Social Research and later as the National Research Institute. Davidson also pointed out that wherever possible or appropriate, scholars with Asian interests were being appointed to broaden the scope of the School's work. Paul van de Veur, John

Bastin and Emily Sadka were just three examples from his own department. And he promised that work on India and Indonesia would be given due attention in future appointments. But in 1957, Davidson wanted to incorporate Indian history into his Department, as per the promise in his 1954 inaugural lecture. He ran up against Hancock who wrote him a memo that contained a hint of menace: 'Some day you will please tell me why you think that Indian history falls within the sphere of the Department of Pacific History, and then I shall tell you why it falls within the sphere of the Department of History.' By the late 1960s, Davidson had changed his views about the place of South Asia in the School. He (and Spate) initially opposed Anthony Low's appointment as director because his interests (Africa and South Asia) were outside the research interests of the School, and relented only when reassured that the status quo regarding the Pacific islands would remain.

The foundational departments of the School were Pacific History, Geography, Anthropology and Sociology and International Relations, with Far Eastern History joining amicably after a brief location in Pacific History. Within a few years, other disciplines or sub-disciplines emerged: Linguistics, Biogeography and Geomorphology (this was the physical geographers from Oskar Spate's Department of Geography heading off on their own, with the original Department being renamed the Department of Human Geography, leading Oskar to light-heartedly comment that he had at last parted company with his 'inhuman' colleagues), Economics, and Political and Social Change. The broad thrust was the social sciences and to a lesser extent the humanities, although Firth had pushed hard for work on ecology and the environment (which closely anticipate more recent developments).

Individual research was vital to the production of sound scholarship, but Firth feared that 'the energies of the research workers may go into projects so individual and unrelated that no advantage is derived from the presence of these people together under one roof.' To avoid that, Firth recommended collaborative research on a common set of problems on which different disciplines might work together. The New Guinea Research Unit was an early example, but too many scholars had settled comfortably into their accustomed habit of solitary research, as academics in the humanities and the social sciences often do. Over the years, there have been some notable examples of cross-disciplinary research carried out in the School. These include the Austronesian Project, the Economic History of Southeast Asia Project, the Transformation in Communist Regimes Project, Resource Management in Asia Pacific, and State, Society and Governance in Melanesia Project. But they are exceptions rather than the rule.

By the late fifties, the urge to individualistic, interest-driven research was on the ascendancy, and Coombs was starting to worry that his creation was moving away from the path laid out for it. In his ABC Radio Boyer lectures in 1970, as ANU historians Stephen Foster and Margaret Varghese report, Coombs noted ruefully that the ANU had become 'a university of quality and distinction, but bearing little resemblance to the ante-natal image of its parents.' Social engineering of the Keynesian type he had in mind when he had mooted the idea of a national university had given way to work of creative imagination. Scholars, Coombs continued, 'were disinclined to direct their labours to policy objectives, which they felt to be parochial and earthbound; the problems which excited their curiosity and imagination were intellectually rather than practically motivated; they were anxious to establish their identity with their colleagues in other places and in other times rather than with the eager re-builders of contemporary society.' But what goes around comes around, as the saying goes. By the 1990s, as Foster and Varghese themselves point out, a new system was in place that compelled universities (the ANU included) to 'respond to the government's assessment of national needs' and to bow to 'unprecedented levels of government regulation'.

Firth and other Academic Advisors saw a strong leadership role for the directors of the research schools in shaping vigorous and integrated research projects. The would-be directors themselves had the same view. Hancock wrote to Vice-Chancellor Douglas Copland on 6 September 1949: 'If I can recruit a strong professoriate, I shall come to Canberra. If I fail to do so, I shall not come.' That kind of ultimatum speaks to the scholarly culture of another era: of the god professors who expected compliance, not questions. But the Pacific School resisted the appointment of a director. Instead, it opted for the position of Dean. Davidson, the *enfant terrible* of the School and an adept bureaucratic in-fighter, distrusted hierarchy and concentration of power and wanted the School run by a succession of rotating deanships, in effect by a committee—so that he could continue to exercise influence from behind the scenes, some colleagues remarked sceptically.

Davidson himself argued that ANU's practice of appointing directors for a five-year term effectively meant taking a senior academic out of research work for five years, with the very great risk that he would never be able to return to his academic work again. Davidson was being slightly disingenuous, for in the fifties, even without overly demanding administrative duties, he was not one of the more productive members of RSPacS (and Hancock published far more as director of the Research School of Social Sciences than Davidson did as dean of the Pacific School). Like most historians, Davidson was also more suited to individual and not team research, and wanted to be left alone to get on with it. Direction was the last thing he needed or gave: as Dorothy Shineberg recalled, 'the good thing about Davidson's direction was the lack of it. He quite simply believed that people would do better research if they studied what interested *them*, rather than what appealed to him, or the powers-that-be, or the general public.'

It was not until 1961 that the School had simultaneously its first director and its first professor of Economics in Sir John Crawford. By wide consensus, Crawford was an academic administrator *par excellence*. Bruce Miller, the International Relations professor, recalled that Crawford 'endeared himself to those with whom he worked because he seemed moderate in opinion though extreme in concentration; because he was essentially fair-minded in his approach to problems; because he liked to help lame dogs over stiles; and because, when roused, he could speak boldly and with much effect.' 'I have been lucky in my life in usually having first class people to work under,' recalled Ron Crocombe, who left the New Guinea Research Unit to become professor of Pacific Studies at the University of the South Pacific in Suva, 'but none came anywhere near the class of Crawford. He was a [source of] constant inspiration although he kept right off your back and left you to run your own show. You just knew by feel that he was supportive.' Oskar Spate paid Crawford the supreme compliment with the words '*Suavita in modo, fortiter in re*' (gentle in manner, resolute in deed). Crawford was one of the 'seven dwarfs'—a reference to their short stature—who helped shape post-war Australia. 'Nugget' Coombs was another.

For the appointment of the academic staff, the hiring practice of those times now strains belief. Few advertisements, no precisely formulated selection criteria. The Advisors 'knew' the right people for the job or enquired discreetly from colleagues who might be available. Jim Davidson was recommended by Firth on the strength of his personal knowledge of him as a scholar and as co-editor of the British Naval Handbooks on the Pacific. Oskar Spate wrote his own resume, sent it to Firth and was appointed, he recalled, 'without interview or further correspondence.' S.F. Nadel, W.E.H. Stanner and W.R. Crocker were also Firth nominees.

Anthony Low's coming to Canberra had a great deal to do with Hancock. Sir Keith wanted him, and that was that. Wang Gungwu remembers his own surprise when he was offered the chair of Far Eastern History (at Jim Davidson's suggestion) to succeed C.P. Fitzgerald. Bruce Miller thought Sir John Crawford had gone to Leicester to talk to economists, while in fact 'it turned out that he wanted to see whether I would be suitable to invite to be Professor International Relations in the Research School of which he had recently become Director.' When Crawford left the School for the Chancelry, he wrote about his successor to the Vice-Chancellor Sir Leonard Huxley: 'I could name a person, I believe.' He did indeed. That person was Heinz Arndt, who was duly appointed professor and head of economics. Many appointees of the early generation recall how they were 'tapped on the shoulder' for a job. The academic world was a much smaller place then, more incestuous, very Oxbridge, and the 'Old Boys' Network,' powerful and intimate, decided destinies. Some outsiders think it still does.

Nonetheless, the early choices were outstanding; the names of those who were 'present at creation' are worth recalling, most men, most larger than life, legends in their own lifetime, or so at least some of them thought. From 1949 to1966, the senior academic staff of the School included: *Anthropology:* W.E.H. 'Bill' Stanner, Siegfried 'Fred' Nadel, Derek Freeman, A.L. 'Bill' Epstein, Stephen Wurm (who later established the department of linguistics), Jack Golson (who was subsequently appointed foundation professor of prehistory); *Far Eastern History*: C.P. 'Patrick' Fitzgerald, Wang Ling (Wang Gungwu joined in 1968); *Pacific History*: Jim Davidson, Harry Maude, Richard 'Dick' Gilson, Francis West; *International Relations*: W.R. 'Bill' Crocker, Arthur Burns (from the Social Sciences briefly), J.A. Modelski, Lord Lindsay and J.D.B. 'Bruce' Miller (Hedley Bull joined in 1967); *Geography*: O.H.K. 'Oskar' Spate, J.N. 'Joe' Jennings, Harold Brookfield and Donald Walker (who later developed the Department of Biogeography and Geomorphology); *Economics*: Sir John Crawford, T. Scarlett Epstein, D.M. Bensusan-Butt, W. Max Corden, Heinz Arndt, C.A. Blyth, E.K. 'Fred' Fisk (1967); *New Guinea Research Unit*: David Bettison, Ron Crocombe, Marion Ward and Ron May.

An impressive list, to be sure, but it also indicates the gender imbalance in the Coombs Building which, in fairness, was not of as much concern then than it became later. The academics were overwhelmingly males and the secretaries and research assistants were females. Ann Moyal, who worked with the historian Laurie Fitzhardinge, has written of those days that: 'Academic men— with few exceptions were adroit at marginalising women colleagues and devaluing their work.' She continues:

> Certainly there was a prevailing tendency to silence us. Norma McArthur [demographer] and I compared notes on the patriarchal procedures of the Research School of Social Sciences' Faculty meetings. There, truly female and anxious not to take up too

much time, we would make a succinct point; the point would be ignored, but later it would be taken up, elaborated at length by a male colleague, and listened to with attentive respect. Academia was fraternal, and the silencing we experienced had a disempowering effect.

The record of research and academic leadership of the School's founding scholars need not detain us here. It has its own public eloquence. But what is not readily available in the historical memory of the School, or in its annual reports, is the texture of intellectual and social life of the early days. Recollections of that vanished era leave a firm impression of the early scholars' wide ranging intellectual interests and skills. Oskar Spate, Hancock wrote, 'would have been just as much at home in any Chair of English Literature as he was in our Chair of Geography.' Oskar must have been hired on the strength of his massive geographical study of India, but he was not all that long at the ANU before producing his classic report on the social and economic problems of the Fijian people and serving on the Currie Commission, which was instrumental in the formation of the University of Papua New Guinea, not to mention a steady stream of journal articles which were gathered together in *Let Me Enjoy*.

Another impression of those times is its intimacy. Virtually everyone knew everyone else and often socialised with one another (or, occasionally, got tired of each other and became bitter life-long enemies). Serious scholars wrote and recited (sometimes wicked) poetry, acted in impromptu plays, played music, engaged in verbal jousts over suitably lubricated lunches and late dinners when 'sometimes the logic of the argument became a little blurred as the level in the bottles fell,' as Perc Partridge, professor of philosophy and later director of the Research School of Social Sciences, recalled; regular sherry in the office in the afternoons and occasional late night whisky and rum punch parties with students, as geographer Tom Perry has recalled on another occasion; and long breaks at the coast to 'finish off' *the* book whose completion kept getting delayed and sometimes never got written.

'Publish or perish' was then a phrase reserved for American universities of inferior quality. A doctorate was desirable, but not a requirement for an academic appointment. 'I repudiate the argument that academic qualifications are the only matter which is relevant when academic appointments are made,' Hancock wrote. An 'impressive list of publications' had to be weighed against other criteria. 'It is entirely proper to take into account, when reliable evidence is forthcoming, not only the academic qualification of applicants but also their reliability as colleagues.' Reliability: interesting word that, open to multiple meanings; but that was how things were done in those days. Whether or not someone was 'clubbable' was a related consideration. Many academics genuinely believed that they had a noble role to play in society and that the world owed them a living. There was no doubt whatsoever in their minds about their purpose and mission. The life of the mind was lived in the fullest sense of the phrase, without apology or embarrassment or 'accountability'.

Of course, there were the non-producers who failed to live up to expectations. Considerable resentment has been directed at the occupants of the Coombs Building over the years, and indeed of the ANU Research Schools generally, who have enjoyed freedom from the treadmill of undergraduate teaching. That resentment has intensified at the spectacle of people who have not made the most of their opportunities. Patrick O'Farrell, an ANU Research Scholar in the late 1950s, told Doug Munro, Davidson's biographer, in 2000 that 'ANU is a bit of a sad story—bright promise not achieved, talent and money squandered ...I regard the ANU—however grateful to it I am personally—as a marvellous opportunity lost'. The occupants of the Coombs Building were sometimes derided as 'Academic Remainders', the name of a suburban outlet for remaindered books. All that said, it remains beyond question that the laggards were few, counted on the fingers of one hand. Most RSPAS academics wrote and researched with extraordinary fecundity, and were (and are) world leaders in their fields. For most of them, scholarship is not merely a profession but a cherished way of life, a labour of love.

At first the two 'social science' Schools were housed in the Old Hospital Building—OHB as Anthony Low has characterised it affectionately. But it was always intended to be temporary. In 1955, as university development plans began to crystallise and as departments expanded, the search for a permanent building began. Departments were asked to specify their space requirements. Protocols were observed, hierarchies maintained. Professors' offices had to be 220 square foot per head, for Senior Fellows and Fellows 150, for non-permanent academic and visiting staff and for secretaries 150, and for research and departmental assistants 120. Professorial tables had to have three drawers, one more than those below that rank. The quality of the furniture in the Tea Room occupied the attention of some.

The founding fathers wanted to establish a senior common room and a junior common room along the Oxbridge model, the former to be located where the present Tea Room is. (By the same token, University House was on the Oxbridge style with a High Table and grace before dinner spoken in Latin.) But the plan was abandoned on the grounds that it would restrict the exchange of views between students and staff, defeating a central purpose of a research university. Others rejected the class distinction of the Old World implied in the archaic demarcation.

A small committee headed by Jim Davidson and Keith Hancock, the Dean and Director respectively of the two Schools, was asked to find out from colleagues what kind of building would be appropriate and to commission architectural plans. These two men, a complete contrast in many respects—Hancock, very Oxbridge, pukka, puffing a pipe, dressed like a don in somewhat ill-fitting suits, prompt and organised, and Davidson, affecting socialist mannerisms but privately wealthy, always in his ultra-brief, crumpled and scruffy white and coloured shorts, always predictably late, supremely confident of his ability to talk his way out of tight situations, cigarette ash everywhere—were appropriately chosen: both had advanced taste in art, architecture, music and the aesthetic life generally.

Here are some views they received: 'We shall be doing our work in studies—in the old fashioned sense of that word. When we enter our rooms, we shall want to feel that we enjoy scholarly seclusion,' 'places [where] we can think and write peaceably and also discuss our problems with colleagues or often time hold small classes.' The rooms should be lined with adequate built-in or free-standing bookshelves, have sufficient light but protected from glare and insulated from noise and the extremes of Canberra climate. Above all, the building had to avoid the 'horror of the interminable passage' so that soon after leaving 'his' office, the scholar should 'get some impression of the space, light and landscape, which perhaps has been a compelling reason for drawing him away from some big city to Canberra.'

Both Davidson and Hancock did not think an open competition for an architect was a good idea. An open-ended competition could conceivably throw up an inappropriate or unacceptable result which the university would be obliged to accept, especially if it was carried out under the aegis of the Royal Australian Institute of Architects. Far better for the Vice-Chancellor, Hancock thought, 'to make a careful study of half a dozen firms, make his choice among them, brief the chosen architect for the work and from that time onwards maintain continuous contact with him.'

Heeding their own advice, in 1958 both Hancock and Davidson recommended that the Melbourne firm of Grounds, Romberg and Boyd be commissioned to prepare a sketch for the building. Roy Grounds, the principal of the firm, was known to Davidson—he was the architect of the igloo-shaped Academy of Science building and designer of the building dubbed 'Academics Anonymous' in Forrest which had Davidson's own flat in it. A leading Australian architect, Grounds had promised to give the new building personal priority over other projects, rather than leaving it to his junior partners. Hancock and Davidson were full of praise for Roy Grounds whom they thought had everything they wanted: 'a consistent feeling about the treatment of space,' 'a sense of rightness of proportions, of the texture of surfaces, of the play of light, which lifts many of his works into a class where they can stand comparison with the best that has been done anywhere in his time.'

Strong words of endorsement, but the university decided in the end to hold a limited competition in accordance with the code of the Royal Australian Institute of Architects and asked that six firms be invited to submit proposals. Davidson and Hancock travelled to Sydney and Melbourne, inspected the work of the firms entering the competition, assessed their capability for successfully completing large scale projects, saw samples of their works and presented their report to the Site Development Committee. Three firms made the final shortlist: Yuncken, Freeman Bros, Griffith and Simpson; Grounds, Romberg and Boyd, and Mockridge, Stahle & Mitchell, but the final choice came down to the last two. The university appointed a Committee of Assessors to adjudicate. It consisted of Grenfell Ruddock (Associate Commissioner, National Capital Development Commission), Bruce A.J. Litchfield (University Architect) and Sir Keith Hancock. The Committee's criteria for selecting the successful bid included Utility, Economy and Delight.

Ground's overall vision was of a decentralised rather than a complex multi-story structure, intimate, private and with a 'sense of precinct.' The abundant area, gentle contours and fine trees on the site were, in his view, ideally suited to his vision. The Grounds plan, as the diagram shows, called for a series of separate pavilions and courts symmetrically arranged around a central water feature, a moat bordering an island with a 'Tea House of the August Moon': a kind of summer palace, as one observer remarked, with a distinctive tropical ambiance. Each pavilion would house a single or at most two departments.

The pavilion model appealed to many. For Robert Parker, the political science professor and a fine, almost concert-level pianist, the pavilions conveyed 'a sense of intimacy combined with quiet and isolation.' Oskar Spate liked the plan's 'island feature.' Yes, the pond and the island could be considered a bit fanciful, but 'isn't a touch of the fanciful just what Australia and especially Canberra needed?' Harold Brookfield, a geographer of the Pacific and of the developing world, thought the Grounds plan 'less pretentious and more of a whole than the polygonal courts [of the alternative], the symbolism being particularly well done.' Stephen Wurm, the Pacific linguist, thought the Grounds model gave the 'impression of having a pleasant air of tranquillity about it which I regard as an important factor when considering the type of work that is being carried out at this University.' Most assessments were in that vein, and Davidson grew in confidence.

There were some reservations though. John Barnes, the anthropology professor, thought that the concentration of seminar rooms in one building in the Grounds plan was not conducive to extended informal discussions, and the small number of windows in the enclosing walls might be a problem for lighting. John Passmore, the philosopher, preferred the Grounds plan but pointed out that the water feature in the internal quadrangle reduced intimacy and was 'unduly fancy,' and the pond could create a reflection problem already apparent in the Academy of Science building.

The thoroughly canvassed views were presented to Council. Davidson, with the backing of nearly all his colleagues in the School, won the first round for the Grounds plan. Hancock, who had supported Grounds as the preferred architect initially but who had changed his mind when he saw the actual plan, came to the meeting under-prepared and stared down the barrel of defeat. But the final decision was inexplicably deferred to another meeting. In the intervening period Hancock did his homework and, with the assistance of the formidable Ruddock, fought back at the deciding meeting, and won. He did this by using the oldest trick in the book, as Robin Gollan, the Australian Marxist historian of labour, recalled, by demolishing Davidson's case point by point before presenting his own preferred plan. After Hancock had spoken, there was nothing left for Davidson to say. Hancock, who 'oozed a permanent courteous but patronizing disdain' for Davidson, as Ron Crocombe recalled, could be a tough opponent. He 'pursued whatever his immediate objective was with ruthless determination,' according to Gollan. On institution building, his philosophy was 'start small and grow as the need arises, rather than starting with a grandiose plan.'

The Grounds plan was both grandiose and impractical, leaving too little room for future growth, and it was by far the more expensive of the two. It did not meet the criterion of economy— the moats and the island gardens would be expensive to construct and maintain. And the self-contained pavilion concept was static: what would happen if departments expanded or contracted? The summer palace idea was attractive—in summer; but would it remain attractive during Canberra's bleak winters? The Mockridge plan, on the other hand, met the three criteria set by the Committee of Assessors. The floor space was flexible and could be adjusted as departments expanded and contracted. Its hexagonal shape avoided the 'horror of the interminable passages'. It left room for further expansion. The use of three floors under one roof was economical. And its central gallery with views of the court yard and longer views of the open country beyond was aesthetically pleasing. Hancock won, and the Mockridge plan was adopted. As Stephen Foster and Margaret Varghese aptly put it, it was Hancock's building with Coombs' name.

Roy Grounds' 'Summer Palace' Plan

The Mockridge Plan, the competition winner

The battle over the design of the Coombs Building was bitterly fought, and for good reason: to get these things wrong has lasting repercussions. Take the edifice that houses the Cambridge University History Faculty, built in the late 1960s, less than a decade after the Coombs Building. After a huge fight, the contract went to James Stirling who designed a building that is, in the words of former Cambridge don David Cannadine, 'Part bunker, part factory, part greenhouse, all folly...' Visitors to Cambridge have their breath taken away by the stunning vista of King's College. It is forever etched in my memory. They go into oxygen debt, but in quite another way, when the Cambridge History Faculty building comes into view.

The Coombs Building was opened by the Chancellor Sir John Cockcroft on 11 September 1964. Built at the cost of £700,000 it contained some 365 rooms. Its external walls were built from tan coloured bricks from Ballarat, and its blue-green roof tiles were manufactured in Bendigo. It was a distinctive building architecturally, quite unlike any other in Australia. Vice-Chancellor Sir Leonard Huxley summed up how the new building had impressed different people. There were among 'those who work in it ...some who, for eponymous or structural reasons, note that it holds affinity with the abode of the early Christians in Rome. Others, who think in classical [biochemical] terms, recognise in its design the diphenyl structure. Still others, who have expansionist tendencies, welcome this design as being a basic hexagonal seed crystal upon which indefinite expansion and growth can take place in the future.'

The name? There was only one on everybody's mind: Herbert Cole Coombs. (Actually, there was a University policy to name buildings after the deceased, *a la* Canberra suburbs, but Coombs, although uncomfortable at the prospect, thought it would be churlish to decline the honour). At the opening, Perc Partridge, who had succeeded Hancock as Director of the Research School of Social Sciences in 1961, proclaimed the truth that Nugget Coombs, more than any other single individual, had been instrumental in getting the National University going, in 'forming the temper and spirit of the government of this University,' as he put it. Coomb's influence, he continued, 'has always been exercised on the side of liberality, generosity of conception, and boldness in planning' and his assistance 'invaluable in protecting the good relations which have prevailed between the university and successive governments.' Clifton Pugh's portrait of Coombs still hangs in the foyer between the offices of the directors of the two Schools as a permanent reminder of his immense contribution.

The essential structure of the building has remained unchanged over the years, even with the addition of the third hexagon, the lecture theatre and the lab wing in the late sixties and an extension wing in 2004. In the 1970s, a committee chaired by geographer Godfrey Linge spent nine months developing a directory located on vantage points throughout the building to give people proper direction, and they still manage to get lost! A Users' Committee identified maintenance problems in the building and brought them to the attention of the builder, and recommended policy about, among other things, parking, the criteria for allocating room to staff and students—Should professors have two rooms? Should married scholars with children have bigger rooms than, in that order, married scholars living at University House and unmarried scholars? Whose rooms should be carpeted and whose should only have felt tiles?—purchase of sculpture, murals and paintings, landscaping and air conditioning.

On the last point, Business Manager Peter Grimshaw—Mr G to some—was firm. Air conditioning would only be provided for areas like laboratories which required temperature and humidity to be kept at a certain level or where the structure of the building was such as to cause 'distress and discomfort' without air conditioning. And Peter held to the empirically dubious view that rapid movement between the artificial environment created by air conditioning and a natural environment was a health hazard. There the matter rested—except in one case which ended up launching a new investment policy for the university. Sir John Crawford wanted his office air conditioned because it got hot in summer. Peter advised Sir John (so he told me) to use funds provided by one of his many donors to buy and install the needed air conditioner. This Sir John did. Having got Sir John's ear, Peter suggested that the School might consider investing outside funds on the money market and feed off the interest. Sir John agreed, and from that day a new university investment policy was born. The remarkable thing is that a mere Business Manager was telling the University's Fiscal Advisor (who actually controlled the university's finances) how to go about his own specialisation. Within his domain, Peter was almost the master of all he surveyed, and many a legend has gathered around this big, essentially kindly man, partial to the Pacific since his days as the son of a police commissioner in the Territory of Papua and New Guinea.

There were other controversies. One which made it to the local newspaper was the complaint by some scholars about the absence of fly screens in the building. 'I would argue that fly screens are an absolute necessity in a building such as this,' wrote Bruce Miller to the Vice-Chancellor in February 1965. 'As I write, there are fourteen blow-flies in the room, either alive or dead.' Miller was not being melodramatic: the problem of flies in the Canberra summer was appalling in those days. The matter was raised at several high level committees, but in the end the university refused to provide the fly screens. Of course, individual scholars could install them at their own expense. 'All right,' several academics were heard to mutter within the earshot of a reporter: 'But if you sack me now, I will take my fly screens with me.' (Come to think of it, I could not imagine writing to *my* Vice-Chancellor about fly screens or matters of similar import. He would probably tell me curtly where to get off. The person I am likely to complain to would be my Divisional Administrator and expect *her* to sort it out!).

Brij Lal with now retired colleagues Hank Nelson and Jenny Terrell, long time executive editor of the *Journal of Pacific History*, housed in the Coombs

The other, more prolonged controversy concerned the colour of the metal screens located at the entrance to the building to act as a decorative foil to an assortment of toilets and office windows. Initially the screens were painted a bronze colour. Sensitive souls in the building considered this inappropriate because the colour did not match the white of the wooden screens. Meetings were held, opinion widely canvassed and it was decided, with the agreement of the sculptor, Matcham Skipper (who later denied that he had ever agreed) to paint them white. A few years ago, they were painted grey. 'Ah yes: overwrought iron,' Professor Dale Trendall, distinguished Greek scholar and Master of University House, is reported to have said of the screens.

The Coombs Building's architectural reputation has spread to all corners of the globe. While an unflappable solidity and a warm, welcoming embrace remain its hallmark, life within it now would probably be unrecognizable to the earlier generation. The pace of research in the early days belongs to an era long gone. 'Good scholarship is like making yoghurt,' an old timer told me recently. 'It can't be hurried.' His own lifetime's publications were completed as a Visiting Fellow, long after he had collected his superannuation and officially retired from the university. That kind of scholarly career is difficult to imagine now when production in 'refereed journals' and by 'prestige publishers' is closely monitored, rewarded by governments and demanded by departments. I cannot quite imagine a department head now tearing up a leave form for his secretary because he would not be dictated to by mere bureaucrats, insisting that it was his prerogative, after some obligatory consultation, to decide what the appropriate timing of the leave should be. Nor can I imagine senior academics refusing to scrutinize and approve acquittal forms for fieldwork expenses because such accounting was beneath their dignity and a complete waste of valuable research time.

'Publish or perish' is no longer an epithet reserved for American universities of a decidedly inferior order. Now a 'demonstrated ability to attract external grants' is often among the selection criteria for new appointments, as is the requirement to know about equal employment opportunity principles, and to alert women to possible employment opportunities in the university. Supervisors are required to take a compulsory course on how to supervise students (some of whom see themselves as clients and universities as service providers). Political correctness plays its part in regulating the tenor of social discourse. The tyranny of the email and the internet create their own havoc in an already harassed life, completely bewildering the remaining relics of the earlier days who even now do not know how to type, let alone use the computer, much less comprehend the mysteries of the cyberspace. Their puzzlement at being surrounded by new technology is somehow endearing, reminding us that we all become remnants in our own lifetime.

The Coombs population has grown exponentially over the last forty years or so as new projects, even disciplines, came on the scene. This has diversified the

Schools' research 'portfolio', to use a currently fashionable term, and enriched the general intellectual atmosphere. But it has also meant increasing pressure on resources—and on rooms, as Colin Filer reminds us. Yet, despite the pressures and demands that daily deluge our lives, the spirit of collegiality remains intact, even strengthened.

There are things about the Coombs life that will never leave you: the intellectual buzz, the tea room talk ranging from the previous weekend's footy results and Murali's *doosra* (serious stuff all this) to deep discussion of a current crisis, the unbreakable friendships that develop over time and across cultures, the loyalty we have to each other, the richness of the encounters with so many whose intellectual curiosity crosses cultural and national boundaries, the warm sense of a community dedicated to a common task, the quiet sense of pride and achievement in work well done. These things are difficult to measure, much less define, but they are real. They remain with you, even in retirement or after you have moved on. A house full of memories. And memorable stories.

NOTE ON SOURCES

A close documentation of all the sources used in preparing this essay would be inappropriate. Most of the material has come from the ANU Archives relating to the building of the Coombs Building, and from the J.W. Davidson papers. The secondary sources which I have used are W.K. Hancock's *Practising History* (Sydney: Sydney University Press, 1976); Stephen Foster and Margaret Varghese, *The Making of the Australian National University* (St Leonards, NSW: Allen and Unwin, 1996); Raymond Firth, 'The founding of the Research School of Pacific Studies,' *Journal of Pacific History*, 31:1 (1996), 3-7; Ann Moyal, *Breakfast with Beaverbrook: memoirs of an independent woman* (Sydney: Hale & Iremonger, 1995); L.T. Evans and J.D.B. Miller (eds), *Policy and Practice: Essays in honour of Sir John Crawford* (Canberra: ANU Press,1987); Heinz Arndt, *A Course Through Life: memoir of an Australian economist* (Canberra: National Centre for Development Studies, ANU, 1985); Dorothy Shineberg, 'The Early Years of Pacific History', *Journal of Pacific Studies*, 20 (1996), 1-16, and Doug Munro, 'J.W. Davidson and Western Samoa: university politics and the travails of a constitutional advisor,' *Journal of Pacific History*, 35: 2 (2000), 195-212; Francis West, *University House: portrait of an institution* (Canberra: ANU, 1980); David Cannadine, *G.M. Trevelyan: A life in history* (London: Fontana Collins edn, 1993). I am very grateful to Doug Munro for advice and additional useful information, and to Stephen Foster, Bill Clarke, Hank Nelson, Anthony Low, Ron Crocombe, and F.B. (Barry) Smith for their comments. The usual disclaimer applies.

PART II

A Room at the Top

CHAPTER 2

The Salad Days

Oskar Spate

> *... a horde of spendthrift scholars*
> *With more desires*
> *Than they have dollars*
>   Goethe, Faust.

Old Men Forget, the title of Duff Cooper's autobiography, is a plain blunt lie. It is the last thing they do. This paper is really oral history, a contribution to folklore, and suffers from the usual failing of that genre, notably a marked haziness as to dates and a propensity to heighten the role of the narrator, who is likely to appear as a bishop, or at least a rook, when in fact he was at best a knight, or perhaps more often a pawn. In the circumstances, it is futile to apologise for egoism. I will do my best to avoid a mere succession of anecdotes without sequence, but would like to begin with my own appointment, which now seems decidedly irregular. I was a Reader at the London School of Economics when Raymond Firth invited me to ask around to find if there was any geographer who could be induced to come to this new venture in the Antipodes; the early existence of geography in ANU is probably due to Raymond.

The brief for the Research School of Pacific Studies had an essentially geographical component but at that time in Australia the discipline, if such it was, was dominated by J. Macdonald Holmes, who held the only Chair in the country, at Sydney. Holmes was a man of great faith in his sometimes seemingly bright ideas, but of woolly mind. An interview in Canberra put him out of the running. The standing of academic geographers was very low indeed. Eminent figures in adjacent fields such as soil science were canvassed for the post, but Firth reasonably argued that if you wanted geography you had better have a geographer.

Hence my remit: I sat down at my battered old typewriter, which made a noise like a machine-gun, and had just got as far as 'Dear Raymond, I have made some enquiries and am sorry to say that …' when the penny dropped: this was Raymond's oblique way of finding out whether I was interested. The rest of the letter was a summary, restrained but not *too* restrained, of my career to date. It worked. I was appointed without interview or even further correspondence. This did not intimidate me from challenging other appointments when they came to the Board of Institute of Advanced Studies, BIAS. When I put up Joe Jennings for Reader, one of the best buys ANU ever made, the scientists were horrified by the slim publications list. I took a perverse pleasure in dividing the lists of their recommendations by the number of their joint authors, a species of reductionism which often produced startlingly effective results. I recommend it.

It is difficult to recapture the atmosphere of those days when physicists and historians, lawyers and geographers (one of each) were all packed into the little tearoom of Old Hospital Building, a collection of weatherboard and tin roofs surrounded by a rickety decking, with Law housed in what had been the Labour Ward and Joe Jennings in the operating theatre because it had a sink.

Canberra itself was a country town of about 27,000 people, big by Australian standards, but very raw indeed on the outskirts. Miller Street, for example, now a sedate tree-lined inner suburban avenue, was a ribbon of angular rocks, along which I had to bump for more than a mile to reach the nearest shop and phone. There was a degree of culture shock: bottled milk had been promised in 1938 for 1939 but did not arrive until 1954, so one had to put out the billy through cataracts and hurricane spouts. But it was still wartime austerity in England—bread rationing came in after the war, and so with:

> *Sherry at seven, whiskey 30 bob,*
> *Who would not sell his*
> *birthright, beg or rob*
> *That so, transported to New*
> *Holland's coast*
> *He rationless might carve his daily roast?*

The town was still small enough for everybody to know everybody else—or nearly—and it had an unsophisticated gaiety now long lost under the burden of Big Bureaucracy and the NCDC and commercialised entertainment—or is it only that I am a lot older? Canberra Rep was in its best days, and Trevor Swan put on a reading of Goethe's *Faust*, Part I, with Oliphant as God in Heaven, Siegfried Nadel as a suitably sinister Mephistopheles and myself, Faust, to a very agreeable Marguerite. In this atmosphere at once relaxed and bracing, and under the genial and dynamic leadership of Douglas Copland, we knew we were in on the ground floor of a good thing. Dear, dead days beyond recall! Perhaps the scale of things, Lilliputian compared with today, may best be illustrated by a memo from the Acting Registrar to the Professor of Geography in April 1951: 'Consideration has now been given to the allocation of rooms required in the permanent building (still 14 years away!)'.

Oskar Spate on the occasion of his D. Litt, May 1984

For Geography were proposed one Professor's room, two Readers' rooms, 10 feet square, three smaller rooms for fellows, one secretary's room, and one for research assistants with—obviously a great concession—a map room. 'May we proceed on the assumption that this will be your total requirements for about the next 30 years?' My reply was equally naïve. I asked for a closet or storeroom and 'it is, however, possible that when I get a Reader, who will be a physical geographer, he will need something in the nature of a laboratory or work-room, although I do not think his demand will be very elaborate'. In 1988, the successors to the old undivided department had about 72 rooms, including half a dozen labs and a garage.

I believe I wrote an Annual Report for 1951, which practically consisted of recording the assumption of duty by Professor O.H.K. Spate. The rest of the department consisted of a prismatic compass and one-sixth of a secretary. The first budget consisted of half a set of quarto, of which six lines were actual figures. When I ceased being Director, I was responsible for some $3 million, and I was never any good at figures. Of course Peter Grimshaw (Business Manager) was always in the background:

> *So pass the estimates around*
> *And juggle with your budget*

> *With an RF here and an RA there*
> *Old Peter he will fudge it.*

My first impressions were very favourable. Those were the days of ship travel; a lovely interlude if you didn't have small children, and we were met in Sydney and driven up by no less a person than the Registrar, Ross Hohnen. On arrival at the house allotted to us we were agreeably surprised to find the fridge well stocked. I thought this was wonderful Australian hospitality—the bill arrived some months later. But apart from the weather, which was vile even after London, the welcome was warm indeed. Friendships formed themselves at once and have lasted—and carried no bill: Geoff Sawer, for instance. I had read assiduously the BIAS (Board of Institute of Advanced Studies) minutes which had been sent to me in London, and one Sawer, the Professor of Law, seemed to be constantly raising petty legalistic points. I formed an impression of a humourless, lean and saturnine fellow, persistently narking. But very soon we formed the Triumvirate of The Acton School, with Alec Hope:

> *Let Hope with Sawer,*
> *Let Sawer with Spate,*
> *Let Spate with Hope confabulate.*

At the beginning the staff:student ratio was three to one, in favour of the staff. As Geoff put it, 'The professors here lecture to each other'. Considering our minimal size we seem to have spent an inordinate time in organising ourselves. The first Dean of Pacific Studies was W.R. Crocker. He was soon succeeded by Siegfried Nadel, a Viennese anthropologist of intellect and icy academic propriety, but rather too Teutonic. It was only in private that he showed any sense of humour. Still, we prospered. The first crisis occurred when he died very suddenly. I had been Acting Dean while Nadel was on leave, but thought that his successor should be Jim Davidson. Jim, however, was an *enfant terrible*, far too left and brash for conservative tastes. There was a legendary incident while he was Warden of Gungahlin House, then a sort of hostel—the idea of Jim as warden of anything seems rather quaint—and there was a party in which some student were alleged to have chopped down a flagpole, the Warden allegedly being present and not restraining. Jim denied this but there was no denying his general lack of reverence for authority.

Meanwhile, Copland had been succeeded as Vice-Chancellor by Sir Leslie Melville and the atmosphere changed—and the winds of change were chill. Copland was a wonderful operator; you would go to him full of enthusiasm for a new project and he would enter into your enthusiasm—'We might not have much chance to getting funds, but lets' have a crack at it.' One went away not at all sure of how far Douglas would go in support but feeling good. Melville was a complete contrast to Copland. He had the Treasury habit of mind, the response was, literally, 'You'd have to make a much stronger case than that before I could put it to Treasury.' He had a way of summing up a debate, publicly and at length, in a way which clearly suggested that he would act in one way and then, with little explanation, opt for an opposite course. Leicester Webb, who had known him closely for years, thought this was due to a curious scrupulosity, that he was so anxious to prove to himself that he was right, that he had to list all the objections to the course he was going to take to his hearers. Under Copland, we had come to think that the cornucopia would never dry up, and it was time we were reined in—but the manner was unfortunate for morale.

Returning to the narrative, Melville insisted that I become Dean. Quite soon, Melville felt himself unable to accede to what I still think was a reasonable request, that a permanent appointment due to my department should be brought forward when I took over extra admin, as indeed I believed I had been promised. In just three months I resigned. I was, of course, quite sore about this, and I shall never forget Mark Oliphant coming to my room to tell me I had done the right thing. In the upshot, Authority had to swallow hard and make Davidson Dean, and a very good job he made of it until Crawford took over as Director, not Dean, and a new era began. I think you will see why, after this Deanship fiasco, I actively wanted to succeed Crawford.

Before Crawford came there were many brave battles on BIAS. Perhaps the oddest—a walkover rather than a battle—was when we were called together rather suddenly and mysteriously and informed that the King of Thailand was visiting ANU and Prime Minister Menzies wanted to give him an honorary degree. We didn't like this and sat around glumly until Trevor Swan spoke up. His Department of Economic History was the smallest in the two Schools, reputedly because he wouldn't appoint anyone, staff or student, from whom he could not learn something, which naturally narrowed the field to microscopic proportions. Trevor didn't often turn up to BIAS, and seems to have regarded himself as an *eminence grise*. He certainly did the trick of getting a reluctant Pacific Studies to accept Crawford as our first Director. We had regarded this import from the Public Service as an intruder foisted upon us—there had been little consultation—but, after drinks at Trevor's house, we were eating out of Jack's hand. We sat not knowing what to say in face of this high-handed *diktat* from Menzies until Trevor spoke, very quietly but incisively. He argued that the monarch had no claim on an LLD or a D Litt. As a leading jazzman in South-East Asia, he might warrant an honorary degree in music, but then we didn't have a Faculty of Music.

So we turned the King down flat: 'So much the weight of one brave man can do.' Next day the King came to lunch at the University House and the scene in the foyer was engaging: Chancellor, Pro-Chancellor, Vice-Chancellor stiff in their gorgeous, gold-embroidered gowns, standing around and looking remarkably nervous. At the lunch, His Majesty regally ignored the slight and heaped coals of fire on our heads by endowing a scholarship.

Then there was the long saga of Lord Lindsay of Birker, son of A.D. Lindsay of Balliol. He had been on Mao's Long March and was, of course, an authority on Red China; somebody on the far Right once denounced ANU in print for wanting, out of pure vanity, to have on the staff 'a belted Earl' and so smuggling in a dangerous Red. As a matter of fact, Lindsay thought he could handle the Reds by sending the Chinese Central Committee long memoranda pointing out where they had departed from the principles of Marxism. When Lindsay was *not* appointed to the Chair of International Relations, he raised hell, going so far as to write to the Professor-elect saying that if he came to Canberra he, Lindsay, would make life impossible for him. Naturally, there was a row; at one point, International Relations was formally ceded to Social Sciences by an agreement with clauses given Roman numerals as in an international treaty. The department seemed to be creating its own raw material; there were any number of démarches, détente, démentis but never a satisfactory dénouement.

Lord Lindsay, seated centre, with International Relations colleagues

Much of the trouble was due to his wife, Sha Li, a shining example of the Bad Influence of the Good Woman. One would argue all afternoon with Michael Lindsay, in a hot little room thick with the vilest tobacco smoke I have ever come across, and at the end, reach a weary gentlemen's agreement to disagree. Next morning, one would receive a note: 'After your disgusting duplicity yesterday I can have nothing more to do with you.' So one would have to begin all over again, going round in endless vicious circles. One would get him to be halfways reasonable, then he'd go home and obviously Sha Li would say, 'You mustn't let them get away with it, Michael, you're so much better than they are.'

At one point I had a long talk with Sha Li herself. She took my breath away by asking: 'Oskar, you aren't doing this because of what his father did to you, are you?'—this because when A.D. Lindsay started the new University of Keele, I applied for the Chair of Geography and quite properly didn't get it—lucky for me in the long run for I came to ANU instead. It was extraordinary: all the old sayings about the Chinese which I'd thought vulgar, exaggerated Western stereotypes came alive and hit me in the face, questions of face and family loyalty overriding rational considerations. To be fair, she saw my shock and distress and realised that she had made as big a gaffe in my culture as I could have made in hers. We parted still friendly, but sadly.

The secession of International Relations was presumably made because it was thought that Hancock would be able to handle Michael better than I could, a view with which I was glad to agree. It didn't work; eventually Lindsay moved on to Georgetown University and sent us an *immense* typescript history of the affair, challenging that he would have it published. There wasn't anything to worry about, really it was so excessively detailed and dull that I don't think any publisher in his sense would have taken it, but it threw Social Sciences into a great flap.

Hancock appointed a committee to look into this dangerous document and see what could be done to counter it. My own solution would have been simpler: write to Lindsay saying that academic freedom was very important and that ANU would be willing to meet one-third of the costs of this case history, *provided* that this was acknowledged on the title page in a formula that was approved. I don't think my advice was taken but the publisher must have agreed with me for we heard no more about it.

Except for a footnote. About a year later I was in Washington DC and thought it would be only decent to contact Michael, though I was damn careful not to phone him until the last hour of my stay. I told him that Melville had retired as VC and he said he was very sorry indeed to hear it. My surprise must have come through over the wire, for he added that it meant that he could no longer press his charges of gross misconduct.

The most spectacular row on BIAS was the great Vietnam debate, in which I was involved, definitely as a pawn.[1] This began when J.W. Burton, a left winger who had been secretary for External Affairs under Evatt (or at any rate high up), and Jim Davidson concocted a letter to *The Canberra Times* denouncing imperialist intervention in Vietnam, and got dear old Bishop Burgmann, Patrick Fitzgerald and myself to sign it. We relied too much on Burton, I think, and while later events did much to validate the warning, the original letter contained many gross inaccuracies. That did not worry Burton and Davison too much and they stuck to their guns, and Fitzgerald signed their follow-up. But the Bishop discreetly retired and I was glad that I was in New Guinea and not available to sign.

The scientists in particular were outraged: the reputation of ANU was at stake and it was not fitting that academics should criticise the Government that paid them. John Eccles, Director of the John Curtin, rang me to say that on the morrow's BIAS he would move for a vote of censure on Davidson and Fitzgerald, and a ruling that nobody should write to the press except strictly on their own technicality. I begged him not to, pointing out that publicity and martyrdom were just what Jim would revel in, but he would not see the point. He did not know his Davidson; I did, but was not prepared for what followed, really the most brilliant display of tactics I have ever seen. The mood was tense, and as soon as the motions were open for discussion, Jim moved to the attack, beginning with a hint of censure to the Vice-Chancellor for allowing this assault on academic freedom to be aired. The original motions were lost to sight in a maze of rhetoric and dialectic, and a 'compromise' resolution was passed *nem con.*

This said, in effect, that academic freedom was precious but that people should be tactful in public pronouncements and should not use ANU's address except when writing technically on their own special discipline—which of course gives a large scope to, say, political scientist and human geographers. But that is why letters to the press are conventionally written simply from 'Acton', a subterfuge which deceives nobody. The amazing thing is that the final resolution was moved Davidson, seconded Fitzgerald, irony indeed!

I suppose that the great event of those years was the opening of University House by the Duke of Edinburgh and the Menzies Library by the Queen, who was not vastly impressed by the Hall. The great window at the dais end was occupied by glass faintly tinted in pastel shades to cut the glare. Her Majesty sniffed and remarked to the Duke, 'Seems churchy to me.' And indeed the design was weak and watery and reminded me of the vestry in the village church where I was once second boy in the choir.

The opening of University House was marked by a spontaneous party in the basement; it was graced, if that is the word, by the sudden apparition of the captain from the Royal entourage, resplendent in gold lace, who had scented it from afar. He was exaggeratedly upper-class Pommy, and Bob Gollan got up on a table and said all were welcome, but this was Australia, and all were expected to dob in. The gate-crasher vanished. Lord knows when the party ended; there was a hell of a lot of glass about, but we cleared up after a fashion.

Next morning, or rather later on the same morning, I was in my office, wan and shaken, when Gollan and Ron Hieser appeared, also very wan. Bill Stanner had complained of riotous conduct; as the senior participant/observer, would I stand up for them? I said yes, of course, or of course I said yes; after all, we had cleared up, more or less. Once again New Guinea was a convenient bolthole and by the time I got back it had blown over.

Those were brave days *'We have heard the chimes at midnight.'* But it is time to leave anecdotage and take a wider view. In general, those first few years were a success story, with one major failure, the development of the campus. The first concept, by Brian Lewis, was for one great building, a central block for Admin and two long wings, one for natural and one for social sciences, swept forward rather as if the wings of Versailles were brought forward at an obtuse angle. It left no room for changes with changing needs, but it was a splendid conception for a Baroque Prince who needed to stand no nonsense from Treasury or Trade Unions, and we had to cope with both. It has left not a wrack behind, except the rather substantial wrack of University House.

Each new site planner came with high hopes, but the clouds of glory have dissipated, the visionary gleam has faded. Piecemeal development and expediency has meant that there is no grand design for our beautiful site; perhaps we had too much space. Some sectors of the campus, some buildings have charm and dignity, but they hardly add up to a whole.

However, the aspirations of the Founding Fathers have been amply realised. As regards the first and fundamental objective, the recruitment of a first-class staff, there can be no question: returned expatriates, people attracted from within Australia and from overseas, our own graduates, all include names recognised as world leaders in their respective fields. And we have an alert and responsible student body; we came through that climactic year 1968 unscathed, in my opinion improved. There can be few issues on which the Australian Government and people have not received authoritative advice from Acton, solicited and unsolicited, some of it doubtless gratuitous in both senses of the word. Since 1951, there has been an amazing increase in intellectual and cultural sophistication in Australia, and to this we have made an honourable contribution.

Nor has this contribution been confined to Australia. At times, it seemed to me that half the staff of my School was overseas, field-working, consulting, advising, conferencing, even constitution-making, in glittering capitals and remote villages, mostly between New Delhi and Nuku'alofa, but with forays ever further afield. Demands on us have at times been embarrassing, but this is certainly an index of our standing.

On balance, the experience gained in such activities has resulted in a net gain of understanding, a two-way traffic benefiting both ourselves and our neighbours. The Research School of Pacific Studies may well have originated as a political ploy, with its stress on understanding our neighbours as a selling-point for the whole project; but it has contributed a great deal, not, of course, on its own but as an autonomous and weighty contingent in the Grand Alliance of Learning. I am sure that in their diverse fields, similar claims can be justly made for the other Schools and Faculties of the University. In this respect, I think ANU has indeed measured up to the vision of its founders. We have indeed come a long way from those quaint beginnings under the tin roofs of the Old Hospital Building. Like all big institutions, we have had our share of strains and stresses, feuds and factions, rigidities and anomalies, prima donnas and dead wood. The wonder is that we have not had more of all these.

We have achieved much, but there has been a price to pay, chiefly in the burgeoning of bureaucracy. This was first borne in upon me when I received a request for two copies of my signature, at a time when ANU already possessed some 15,000 such copies. Administration in the early days was singularly genial and relaxed; now it seems a nightmare. Of course, much of this is a function of growth, necessarily incidental to the bigness which Dawkins loves, but it carries the very grave risk of ossification. The imaginative concept of the Founders, backed by such men as Chifley and Menzies, which was one of the more lively and viable children of post-war reconstruction, is being smothered.

The machinery seems likely to negate its own ostensible objectives. Amalgamation generally means the creation of two-and-a-half bureaucracies where there were only two; Coordinating Committees for the Coordination of Coordinating Committees. Much of the rationale seems to spring from a crude anti-intellectualism. Certainly, the vision of humane culture, which should be one of the first things to be cherished in a great university, is likely to be the last thing to receive any attention; and *'where there is no vision, the people perish'*.

It may be only the tendency of old age to lament an idealised past, but I feel rather like Chatham coming to the House of Lords to spend his last breath protesting against the dismemberment of the first British Empire. But there was a Second Empire, and a greater one. I feel sure that in whatever form, under whatever difficulties, ANU will continue to render distinguished service to the nation, and indeed the whole world of learning.

And now it is fitting that I should end with an expression of deep gratitude for all ANU has done for me. It is no immodesty to say that I have no doubt that I would have carved out a decent career in British Academe; in 1950 a respectable Chair was not far away. But ANU gave me wider horizons, a new world and an ocean to explore. I hope I may have gained a little of that wisdom which Ulysses attained through knowing many cities and many men's manners and customs. Above all, ANU has a wonderful ambience for my sort of humanistic scholarship. In return *'I have done the State some service'* but this has been far outweighed not just by the material resources made available to me, but most of all by the stimulation and comradeship of so many colleagues and friends. To all, my most heartfelt thanks.

NOTE

Abridged version of essay 'Early Days at ANU; an anecdotage', first published in *ANU Reporter* 24 February and 10, 23 March 1989. Oskar Spate (1911–2000)

---

[1] The special meeting of BIAS was in 1955 (not 1954). Spate conflates details of the great Vietnam debate of 1954 with a different episode the following year that also involved criticism of government foreign policy by ANU academics.

CHAPTER 3

An OHB Beginner

Anthony Low

I belong to the OHB generation—those of us who go back to the Old Hospital Building where the Research School of Social Science (RSSS) and the Research School of Pacific Studies (RSPacS) as it then was, and the University Library all began. OHB's remnants have long since been taken over by the Research School of Earth Sciences, but its porticoed entrance still stands at right angles to Mills Road overlooking the patch of grass above the Vice-Chancellor's residence, and for its ageing denizens it remains *terra sacra*.

Its hub was a down-at-heel canteen fronting on an enclosed rectangle of grass. Here in those early years there was not only morning and afternoon tea and opportunity to meet practically every one of one's colleagues, visitors, and students from right across the two schools, but some of the best talk with people across a wide range of disciplines in which I have ever participated. There was also an uncomfortably elongated, somewhat dismal, seminar room, where among other things the first Director of RSSS, Sir Keith Hancock, held his three year long 'Wool' Seminars—perhaps the most notable of any ANU seminar programmes then or since. It was here too that 'Perc' [P.H.] Partridge, who had come to the ANU from Sydney to be Professor of Social Philosophy, chaired a year-long seminar programme on 'the sociology of power'. That I have always felt had more influence upon my generation of political scientists, historians and others than anything else that occurred there. Perc was to have written a great book on Liberty, but it never got done, and all we have is a relatively small clutch of articles. He had, however, read not only all the traditional British political science literature—Aristotle, Hobbes, Hume, Rousseau, Mill—but Max Weber and of course Marx, and much of the current American behavioral science literature as well (Talcott Parsons and his like). All of which was a rich brew for so many of us. Late in my time there (1959-64) Perc succeeded Hancock as Director RSSS, before becoming a key figure in the very active Australian Universities Commission. Between the two of them they gave RSSS its invaluable and memorable early cohesion and momentum.

When I first arrived in 1959 my impression was (and I was in Hancock's department in RSSS at the time) that RSPacS lacked both of these. By comparison this no doubt had a lot to do with the decision of the very distinguished New Zealand anthropologist, Raymond Firth, then at the London School of Economics, who had earlier been recruited as the Academic Adviser for the Pacific Studies school, not in the end to come to Canberra. The initial four departments—Pacific History, Anthropology, Geography, Far Eastern History—each had distinguished people at their head—Jim Davidson; following Nadel's death John Barnes (who went on to Cambridge); Oskar Spate; and Patrick Fitzgerald. Their interests, however, did not greatly relate to each other, and in the absence of a substantive Director they variously shared the quite temporary office of Dean of RSPacS. Thereby they kept the ship afloat, but inevitably could not give it very much strategic direction. Half way through my time, however, somewhat to many peoples' surprise, Hancock and others recruited the very distinguished public servant and Secretary of the Department of Trade, Sir John Crawford, to be Director of RSPacS; and from his corner study in the old nurses' quarters he soon filled the role with aplomb.

I would never have left the ANU but for the extraordinary invitation by present-day standards to be the founding Dean of a School of African and Asian Studies at the first of the new British Universities, the University of Sussex. Those were indeed halcyon days with the Vice-Chancellor telling me to recruit two professorial and fifteen other colleagues, and then see how things were going. We soon had prospective undergraduates shifting to us from other quarters—and ten years on a dozen of us with Sussex credentials sat down to dinner one night in Port Moresby to celebrate that birthday.

The one development which is relevant here lay in the decision of the new British Labour government following its 1964 election victory to proceed with its election commitment to create a 'special institution' devoted to sharpening Britain's aid and trade programme to developing countries. After a hard-fought Whitehall battle, that came to Sussex, to become the world-leading Institute of Development Studies.

After seven years as a Dean there I found myself at a far too young age being treated as if I was an elder statesman. So when I was approached to be a candidate for the Directorship of RSPacS I was ready to agree to fly with Belle, my wife, to Canberra. My own belief was, however, that there was already a notable senior scholar in the school who would surely be appointed. I found myself being fingered, however, instead.

But then a storm broke. As my research interests were neither in the Pacific, nor in Southeast or East Asia, but in South Asia, there was an understandable concern that I might not readily engage with the school's existing emphases, and might even divert resources in my own direction. And there was worse yet.

Vice Chancellor Anthony Low 1979 (Director RSPacS 1973–1975)

Although I had given three seminars in Seminar Room A before I returned to Britain, many in the school had not been told that I was under consideration for the directorship and were understandably vexed that they had not as a result had a chance to check me out. Things were made still worse by the crackles in the still uncertain international phone lines over which Crawford and I sought to resolve the issues. In the end, however, the assurances that I could very readily give were accepted, and by January 1973 we were back in Canberra.

The School had by then shaken down very well in the Coombs Building (which was, however, new to me). I join with others in thinking it has been a great success. There are no endless straight passages. The many steps and angles impart a well nigh domestic feeling to it, which is wonderfully accentuated by the internal courtyards with their trees and grass and quietness. Above all it is flexible; able to cope, with just a little forethought, and sometimes perhaps some gentle prodding, with the inevitable contractions and expansions in so many academic enterprises. Whilst the difficulty for the unknowing in finding their way around has always seemed to me a decided plus. People do not get casually disturbed. If people really want to see you they can readily be assured that, with any luck, they will eventually succeed in reaching you.

When the building was first projected a major effort went into designing the tea room, given its singular importance in OHB. The new one is by contrast very grand, and its balcony serves well enough, but somehow an old hand misses that enclosed rectangle of grass which provided such a wonderful, tea-cup-in-hand, standing platform for a miscellany of groupings immersed in earnest talk.

The one major failing in the new building is the seminar rooms. Even seminar room A is far too narrow for convenient interchange and a sizeable company, while the rest are aberrations—from which OHB's experience should have saved us. Close to the ideal is the Ross Hohnen room in the Chancery, seemingly here, however, unique of its kind.

Once installed in the Director's lavish suite there were three crucial sureties. One lay across the passage in the friendliness of close working relationships with two successive Directors of RSSS: Mick Borrie and Sandy Youngson. The second stemmed from the exemplary support of the Business Manager, Peter Grimshaw and his staff, Graham Hutchens, the School Secretary, and Margaret Carron and Mary Herbert in the Director's Office. The third came from the huge privilege which falls to a Director of being entitled to ask everyone in the school about their work. This seemed to work best when arrangements were made to do this in their rooms and hear about it from them there. It took some months to get around the whole school. It was, however, not only an exhilarating experience for one privileged to enjoy it, but provided an unequalled prospectus upon the activities of the school as a whole which for a new Director was quite invaluable.

Early on the Chairman of Faculty arranged that Belle and I should meet members of Faculty over an evening drink in University House. From that moment onwards, with only one exception, I received quite unfailing kindness. There was, however, the moment when I failed—or so I was told—to dress down a graduate student who had cast aspersions on the mental state of his supervisor, when I thought the important thing for me to do was to effect a separation between them and find another supervisor to see the student through to the completion of his thesis. Across twenty-five years I was never forgiven for the line which I took.

There are half a dozen larger matters from those years that perhaps warrant retelling (but without regard to chronology!). It is sometimes forgotten that the first intimations of budget cuts appeared as early as 1973—just as I became Director. My understanding had been that we were to have two new departments, of Political Science and of Sociology. Government provision for the universities was, however, ceasing to be on the previous scale, and it soon became apparent that there was finance for only one. We cogitated hard about this, and the upshot was the establishment of the Department of Political and Social Change, which soon became a great success. By the same token I had been told I could have one tenured and one non-tenured colleague in Indian history. In the event I had just the latter.

I had arrived in Canberra in the immediate aftermath of Whitlam's election victory. During the election campaign the Labor Party had pledged itself to establish an Institute of Development Studies, essentially on the Sussex model about which, as it happened, I was fully versed. Contact was soon made with Richard Butler (of Iraq and Tasmanian fame) then Whitlam's private secretary. Exploratory discussions ensued and papers then began to flow. Through no fault of Richard's, however, it eventually became clear that national budget considerations were moving against the idea, and once it dropped below the horizon we needed to contemplate what we might do instead. The outcome was the school's Development Studies Centre with its two Master's programmes—for which I think we did get some moneys. A decade on it grew into the National Centre of Development Studies, appropriately housed in the J.G. Crawford Building.

That was part of our outreach to Papua New Guinea. A considerable number of people in the school were already much engaged in working there, and we had a flourishing New Guinea Research Unit (NGRU) in its own building close by the campus of the University of Papua New Guinea. There was no gainsaying, moreover, the extent of our contributions to the urgent needs of a shortly to be independent Papua New Guinea. There nevertheless seemed to me to be something that was missing. Amid the onset of decolonisation we needed, I felt, to be decolonizing too. The NGRU staff took this very well, and after some persuading so did the immensely powerful Secretary of the University, Ross Hohnen. NGRU was accordingly handed over to the new Papua New Guinea government to become the PNG Institute of Social and Economic Research. Thereafter Peter Grimshaw held on to two or three houses across Papua New Guinea to house—and provide vehicles for—ANU researchers, and we soon drew on his and other people's expertise to create the North Australia Research Unit, essentially upon NGRU lines.

Visiting as many reaches of the school's activities as was possible was from the start of first importance to a new Director. Papua New Guinea had headed the list, but before long Fiji, Samoa and the Cook Islands figured too, the last upon the occasion of a Pacific Islands Forum attended by Whitlam and a full array of Pacific islands' leaders: Michael Somare, Albert Henry, Ratu Mara, for example. To that accredited visitors were given full access and so enjoyed an invaluable opportunity to make contact with so many of them. As I left it proved to be the one place in the world where having paid my hotel bill the receptionist lent over the counter and kissed me.

An initial task had followed upon Whitlam's immediate appointment of our colleague, Stephen Fitzgerald, to be Australia's inaugural Ambassador to China following the eventual recognition of its Communist regime. A three year secondment was a novelty for the university, but was soon arranged. In June 1973 a party under the auspices of our Contemporary China Centre then visited China. Thereafter a joint party from the School and the Faculty of Asian Studies was invited to go there in September–October 1973. In addition to Professors Wang Gungwu and Hedley Bull, and Drs. Pierre Ryckmans and Fred Teiwes, there were eight more of us. Leaving Hong Kong we entered upon an altogether new world. From Guangdong we were taken to Sian, Beijing, Shanghai, to a miscellany of places in between, and to a wonderful array of sights—the Great Wall and so on. Throughout we were very handsomely treated, housed in substantial Russian built hotels, generously fed, carefully transported, and assiduously shepherded by our always kindly English speaking guides. Many of us were greatly impressed by the very evident professionalism of some of the Commune officials whom we met, and as so often the children were an immense delight. Nevertheless a pall hung over the country. Mao was still active, his portrait hanging everywhere. Lin Biao, though dead for some time, was still being noisily denounced, whilst Zhou Enlai was being pilloried as a reincarnation of Confucius. Everywhere clothes were a drab blue or grey except for the tell-tale green of the ever present soldiery. The available cars were for the party privileged only (and for us!). Friendship stores were replete with empty shelves. Housing was as bad as the worst I had seen in India. And the silence sparked by an awkward question called for deftness in response.

There were no arrangements for us to see a university. Our reiterated requests to do so did, however, lead to our being taken to see several. Apart from some Science departments and some nominal batches of students many of them appeared largely eerily deserted. Worse: whenever we asked about what was being taught in any of the humanities and social science departments we invariably received the same answer: 'Marxism, Leninism, and Mao Tse-tung thought'. The visit nevertheless was a beginning, and it was important we should have made it.

Back in Canberra the most striking feature of the School was the change in its thrust since the early 1960s. Crawford and his successor Spate had worked wonders. There was now a full range of mostly founding Professors who together with their first colleagues were giving it cohesion and momentum on a scale which to my eyes at least had been missing earlier. There was Bruce Miller in International Relations; Heinz Arndt in Economics; Jim Davidson in Pacific History, and on his untimely death Gavan Daws; following Patrick Fitzgerald's retirement Wang Gungwu in Far Eastern History; Stephen Wurm in Linguistics; Jack Golson in Prehistory; in due course Jamie Mackie in Political and Social Change; and following the bifurcation of Spate's

Geography department Donald Walker in Biography and Geomorphology and Gerry Ward in Human Geography. One could not ask for a more stellar team.

It has always been my regret that following the resignation of the Vice-Chancellor, Bob Williams, and having said I would not do the job before I went away on three months in the archives in India, I was nevertheless summoned back and all too quickly found myself installed in the Vice-Chancellor's office. That meant giving up after less than two and a half years what I have persisted in calling, for the likes of us, the best job in the world. There are sometimes, however, occasions when to go on saying No can no longer be the right answer.

CHAPTER 4

People and the Coombs Effect

Wang Gungwu

Now that I have long gone from the Coombs (since 1986) and unlikely ever to work inside it again, I refuse to hear one word against its greatest claim to fame, and will not accept any doubts about the charms of finding one's way inside the magnificent building. Instead of that perennial subject, I shall talk about the people I found there, people I located in their various corner rooms only after I had been there seven years and only after I became Director of the Pacific Studies half of the building in 1975. My most important discovery as Director was to realise that I could call colleagues and students out of the depths of their rooms and they would actually come. I soon developed a taste for this because it became clear that most of the scholars were far more interesting than the titles of their books and theses suggested.

Let me put all this in a people context. My life changed in the building because Anthony Low was unexpectedly elevated to become ANU Vice-Chancellor and I was asked to come in from the periphery of Far Eastern History to the Coombs nerve centre. The very day I was appointed, there was a spectacular change. As I returned from my interview with 'Nugget' Coombs and his selection committee, Heinz Arndt rushed in to tell me that Gough Whitlam had just been sacked. Within weeks, we had lodged Gough in a room next to Jamie Mackie and, almost immediately, both the Coombs and the director were under close scrutiny by our 'Big Leader'. I had found an unofficial adviser about the politics of fine buildings whose suggestions about strategy and placements I took very seriously. His eye for inconsistencies and his endless curiosity forced the new Director to get to know the Coombs more rapidly than he expected. Gough brought a delightful edge to our world of scholarship, but I was soon to learn that his joining us was also a signal that tough funding days for the ANU were about to begin.

When money becomes tighter, people become even more important. Coombs was blessed with a great financial web-maker in Peter Grimshaw. Invaluable in the best of times, he was indispensable when times got harder. In the days before we had desk computers, faxes and e-mails, Peter's calculators and his spatial sense provided the hard data. From the perspective of my little department, I had thought he was a gem. As Director, I thought he knew every brick in the building and every view from the numerous angled windows. He was my walking Coombs encyclopaedia and the building's past, present and future seemed to have been framed behind his desk. He also made me realise that Coombs was not just a building. There was a Coombs effect that reached out to our scholars everywhere as our funds were distributed to units in Papua New Guinea and North Australia and to all the prehistoric sites of the continent. And as students and staff wander the South Pacific and our Asian Near North, it was Peter who knew at any given moment whether someone was hiding somewhere within the Coombs or spending Coombs money in the field. Peter monitored the Coombs footmarks on land and trimmed its sails on the high seas. The Director always tried to appear knowledgeable. Few knew how much Coombs intelligence depended on the phone line between him and Peter's office.

My counterpart who headed the Social Sciences half of Coombs was Sandy Youngson. We shared more than a common foyer. Every week, we would spend a little time on the landing plotting the Coombs strategy to make an impression on the hard heads of the laboratory-based Research Schools who always seemed to need the money that we could not spare. Knowing more economics than I did, he could made Peter's financial figures look even better. But his contribution to my education was broader than that. We shared a respect for the Scottish enlightenment and doubts about narrow Scottish nationalism. So his half of Coombs was a valuable corrective to our Asia-Pacific parameters.

This leads me to recall the critical importance of the Coombs tea room. When I was teaching in Singapore in the late 1950s, I met Eugene Kamenka who left a few years later to join the History of Ideas Unit in the Research School of Social Sciences. Thus, when I came to Coombs, he was my first bridge to its non-Pacific half. For me, he was the tea room and the great big Other that bound the two halves together. Whenever I wanted to uplift myself out of Asia, I turned to Eugene and his friends in the other School. Eugene not only ensured that I would not be left paddling in my own little pool but also helped me imagine an integrated Coombs. He identified the other parts of the world that I could locate at comparable levels and corners in their half of the building. This enlarged the Coombs for me in social and cultural ways. On the one hand, the Australian microcosms of humanity seemed more balanced in their corridors. On the other hand, Western ideas and institutions were made to converge with the reductions and adaptations of modern Pacific Asia. I could even imagine that the building was designed to underline some common pursuits and encourage discovery and self-discovery as we seek to find different ways to the common tea room.

Wang Gungwu 1989 (Director RSPacS 1975–1980)

In the end, our half was bound to different concepts of space and time. I can never forget Derek Freeman's concern for me when he heard that I was to be the new Director. He reminded me that 'Nugget' Coombs turned to aboriginal studies because, like Derek, he realised that large territories and populations might not give better answers about our human condition than small ones. He wanted me to know that how and what you studied, even in the smallest Pacific island, could tell you much more than all the generalisations you might draw from the lives of the billions on the Chinese and Indian sub-continents. I was struck by how our walls in Coombs protected both approaches. Eventually, when Derek 'the heretic' took on the Margaret Mead establishment, it symbolised what our building could contain. The perspectives Derek chose to differentiate also remind me of other spaces and other times that Coombs represents for me. They are captured best by two friends I dearly miss. The first is Oskar Spate's superb *Pacific since Magellan*, three volumes that clearly reflect the pioneering ideas that led to the foundation of the School of Pacific Studies. The second is Stephen Wurm's Linguistic Atlas series that started with all the known languages of Australia and Papua New Guinea, extended to those of the Pacific and the Americas, reached out to the historical complexities of the languages of China, and then to the endangered ones around the world. For me, these products, of Oskar's quiet reflections and Stephen's immense energy, make Coombs one of the finest memorials to Australian scholarship.

People may lose their way in the building, but the mysteries of Coombs have risen above brick and mortar. Embedded now in that name is a spirit that does justice to two hundred years of the Enlightenment heritage.

CHAPTER 5

In the Room at the Top

R. Gerard Ward

If you raise your eyes when walking towards the main entrance to the Coombs Building, perhaps to admire the wrought-iron frieze designed by Matcham Skipper, you will notice two white walls on the front of two outward extensions in the middle of the platform behind the frieze. It looks as if they have been designed as stages from whence to address a multitude—it seems ideal for a dictator, or two.

Fortunately, none of the Directors of either School has ever attempted to harangue their fellow Coombs residents from their respective stage. I doubt if any of them ever thought of themselves as dictators and, hopefully, their colleagues rarely saw them in that role. On the other hand the picture of two Directors trying, from these balconies, to calm a multitude of protesting Coombs residents is a fantasy with which to conjure.

In fact, the Directors' suites do not lie at the top of the building, but rather in the link between the original two hexagons—each suite set to the side of the School that is supposedly directed from it. I say 'supposedly' because of a personal belief that in the world of academe, and particularly in a multidisciplinary research organisation, a flat, relatively non-hierarchical administrative structure is likely to be the most productive of innovative research. Thus academic administration should largely be diffused out to the centres of research activity where the leading researchers make individual and joint decisions about research initiatives themselves. It seems that the ANU's leaders in earlier decades held a similar view. The 'conditions of appointment' which I signed in 1970, before coming to ANU as Professor of Human Geography in late 1971, stated that 'a Professor shall devote the whole of his time to the duties of his office.' No mention of recreational leave or statutory holidays—clearly a 'full time', 365-day a year job. A professor was 'expected to cooperate with the Director or Dean and with his colleagues in the research work of the School as a whole, but consistently with this principle, a Professor will not be subject to direction by the Director or Dean in respect of the research work which he himself or his department or group will carry out.' In terms of research the Director could not 'direct'. So 'facilitating' might be a better description of what should go on in the 'Room at the Top' rather than 'directing'.

The slightly eccentric location of the Director's office could be a disadvantage, placing the Director outside the main circulation routes through the building. Life in and movement around the Coombs building circles around the various levels of hexagonal corridors, and of course this can lead strangers to feel somewhat disoriented and lost. But for an inhabitant of the 'Room at the Top' there can be an advantage. Because there are usually several almost equidistant routes between any entrance to, or starting point within, the building and one's internal destination, taking a different route each day can produce many different chance encounters. Such encounters, and the resulting informal two-way exchanges, can help keep a Director in touch with a lot of what is happening in the School at all levels.

Although the building shape may seem to be awkward for newcomers walking through it, it does have the advantage of giving virtually every office an outside window and a view to trees. Residents have often exploited this to attract sulphur-crested cockatoos, crimson rosellas and other birds to rest and feed on window ledges. Occasionally of course, administrators have felt it necessary to mildly caution residents against over-liberal use of birdseed because of the risk of attracting rats into the courtyards below!

Few residents of Coombs will not have had the experience of being asked to help a stranger locate a specific office or seminar room, frequently while the enquirer stands trying to decipher one of the standard directional diagrams in the building designed by the Coombs Navigation Committee. Perhaps someone had this in mind when, in June 1993, copies of M.C. Escher's graphic work *Relativity* were posted alongside several of the directional signs with the caption, 'Alternative Directional Plan to Coombs'.

One morning Oskar Spate's likeness was at the centre of another notable graphic jest. The Clifton Pugh portrait of 'Nugget' Coombs, which normally hangs on the mezzanine floor between the two 'Rooms at the Top', was missing. In its place hung an extraordinary painting in oils—garish greens, yellows and blues. Consternation was followed by amusement as it became clear it was all a jape. It emerged that Noel Butlin, Professor of Economic History in the Research School of Social Sciences and a close friend of Oskar, had created the 'work', and effected the swap. Coombs was safe and the replacement, although vaguely recognizable as Oskar, was scarcely worthy of prolonged hanging.

R. Gerard Ward 1994, a year after retiring as Director of RSPacS

Orientation Week for new students, at the start of the academic year, rarely impinges on the Research Schools regardless of the extraordinary events that sometimes take place elsewhere on campus. One year, however, a very tall pink rabbit knocked at my door, and asked if there was a job which she could do to earn a little money for that year's Orientation Day appeal. Mary Herbert was away for a few hours so I suggested that the rabbit sit at her desk and answer the phone. In the next hour or so people would come through the secretary's office en route to mine, get half way through my door and suddenly stop and look back, startled by what they only partly saw in passing. Both my daughter (then President of the Students' Union) and I greatly enjoyed their surprise and wry discomfits.

One of my strongest impressions of life in the Coombs building, is the spirit of collegiality within the Research School. Collegiality was not always evident elsewhere in the University. As I left my first meeting of BIAS, the (possibly appropriate) acronym for the Board of the Institute of Advanced Studies, Professor Wang Gungwu asked me what I thought of proceedings. Having been struck by the evident power, authority and confidence of long standing Directors like Titterton, Catcheside, Fenner, Craig, Borrie, and Spate as they jousted with the Vice-Chancellor, Sir John Crawford, I replied, 'it reminds me of the barons and King John at Runnymede'. At that time it was clear that each Research School had a great degree of independence within the Institute of Advanced Studies. During the fortunate decades of the 1970s and 1980s our own Research School was remarkably free of inter-disciplinary or inter-departmental tensions. As a Director, one has a window into the internal workings of other parts of the university through attendance at Heads of Schools meetings and other university forums and committees. The impression I gained during the 1980s was that Pacific Studies had few of the internal tensions that periodically disturbed life in some other Schools. My own theory was that because of a common regional interest in the Pacific Islands or Asia, scholars in one discipline would often find the work of colleagues in other disciplines of interest and relevance for their own work on the region. There was thus a tendency to value those different disciplinary approaches, and respect the distinctive contributions of the others. This reduced the risk of great rivalry between departments. It was also probably important that in these decades the financial climate was relatively benign. By 1980 the initial period of School growth and establishment of new fields was largely complete. Most departments were of a viable size and groups were not fighting competitively for resources. If there were proposals for new initiatives, budgets could usually be adjusted without too much impact on existing programmes.

One striking example of this collegial academic climate could be seen in the operation of the main governing group of the School, the Faculty Board. This Board, the principal advisory group for the Director, was then composed of the Head of each Department and Centre in the School, another academic member of each department, and three elected student members. Some organisational theory would say that this was too large a body for making decisions in contested situations. Yet the Faculty Board worked remarkably harmoniously. Twice a year each department or unit would nominate candidates for the dozen or so postgraduate PhD research scholarships awarded every six months. Here was a context for possible bitter argument over the relative merits of nominees from different departments. Yet this rarely occurred. The merits of each candidate would be outlined by the head of the nominating department. There would be questions on specific nominees and general comment. At this stage it was not uncommon for a department to withdraw its candidate in favour of a nominee from another department as acknowledgement of a superior case. It was this ability and willingness of departmental heads (and others) to take a broad school, rather than a narrow disciplinary or departmental view which made the system work. I cannot recall a single occasion during over 12 years of chairing Faculty Board 'scholarship rounds' when it was not possible to come to an agreed list of nominees without acrimony or undue waste of time.

The relatively benign financial context did begin to suffer during the 1980s. The process had started earlier, in the 1970s, as funding from the Commonwealth Government did not keep pace fully with inflation. Through the 1980s the block grants to Schools gradually began to become inadequate to maintain the existing levels of academic and support staff and scholarship students, and the levels of field research which are so essential to an area studies institution. Once again, in finding ways to adjust to the changing financial situation in the late 1980s and early 1990s, the School managed to work with considerable collegiality. By the mid-1980s, it became clear that if the School were to be able to develop new research initiatives in this financial context it needed new collegial structures to advise the Director on resource allocation, and especially on staffing priorities. Intensive discussions resulted in the School being the first in the University to draw up its own strategic plan (1988–92), which established agreed mechanisms for setting priorities, and a program under which staff numbers, academic or 'non-academic', would be reduced as posts became vacant. A Strategy Committee was established and its composition of three tenured and three non-tenured academic staff, one student, and the Director as Chair (rather than, for example, a meeting of Heads of Departments) reflected something of the School's ability to think as a School, rather than as a collection of separate principalities. This group oversaw a reduction in the number of academic positions on an agreed schedule which did not threaten the viability of any of the departments or disciplines, and maintained reasonable levels of funding for fieldwork and other crucial research support needs. As posts became vacant through retirement, a 'strategic fund' was established specifically to provide seed money for new research initiatives. New projects were proposed and positions allocated on a competitive basis. As a result, despite shrinking resources, the School was able to establish a number of new projects, often of an inter-disciplinary type. Again it was a good demonstration of the School's collegial style.

Inevitably, from 'The Room at the Top' one also became aware of research enterprises that had not achieved their full potential, or simply needed a boost to reach completion. Lack of sufficient time, human resources, energy, or funding could all be causes. The strategic fund made it possible to address some of these problems and part was used to provide 'harvest money' from which specific allocations were made to restore momentum in a number of cases. Thus, for a time at least, and through its own collegiality, the School, was able to counter the shrinking of core funding at a time when it, along with other Schools in the Institute of Advanced Studies, was not permitted to seek funds from the country's main source of research grants, the Australian Research Grants Committee.

As Departments became a little smaller through the strategic planning process, as computers made more and more researchers less dependent on typing services, and as outside pressures increased administrative demands on departmental heads, it seemed desirable to modify the structural arrangements within the School. It was decided that departments should be grouped into a set of 'divisions' and that a number of administrative roles should be transferred from departments to divisions, thus freeing heads of departments from the increasing load of routine administration. It also had the goal of increasing cross-departmental and cross-disciplinary links.

How successful this was is for others to say, but my own impression is that, with considerable goodwill in the School, the changes worked well. In a sense it was a part of the much wider social changes taking place in universities, including the gradual fading of the dominating role of the founding 'god professors', each of whom had been appointed as Head of Department until retirement age, and the emergence of something more akin to rotating headships. By the early 1990s the School was different in many ways from that of the late 1970s, yet it retained most of its internal coherence and remained a congenial place in which to work.

Somewhat to my surprise, I had been appointed Director of the School in 1980, after about nine years as head of the Department of Human Geography—a very congenial and satisfying role. The change in scale and range of responsibility was very significant and no specific or formal training, preparation or advice was provided. The closest one came to training was on occasions when Directors were away, perhaps trying to maintain their research interests in the specific country or countries of their expertise, and one was asked to be Acting Director. But then, if difficult issues arose, Acting Directors could usually stall on difficult decisions until the Director returned! When a student came to see me, as Acting Director, because of concern about his supervisor whom he felt was a paranoid schizophrenic, he described all the symptoms. It was clearly a case to hold over for the Director, scheduled to return next week. This decision seemed even more sensible the next day when the supervisor came to see me, concerned about the student, whom he felt was a paranoid schizophrenic. He too listed all the symptoms.

One might also learn other skills, such as the art of delegation. Once, when Acting Director, I received a phone call at about 10 o'clock at night from the University's security office. The police had rung them to advise that 'Professor Wang's house had burned down'. I jumped into the car and drove to the next suburb where the house was, trying to list the things which would need attention—insurance—risk of looting—contacting Wang—locating his family to ensure they were safe. I turned into the surprisingly quiet street to find the house was there, with lights on, and no sign of fire. A knock brought a family member to the door—we looked around and agreed there was no fire. But whose house was burnt? A call to Security revealed further and better information. It was another Dr Wang's house; it had been a small fire in the garage; the tenants had put it out; there was no immediate danger. Dr Wang's house was a fair distance away, so I called the head of the relevant department and suggested he had a problem with which to deal—after all I was sure that, as a former ambassador, he was used to handling crises.

In being Acting Director, and as a new Director, the help of the Director's Secretary, the Business Manager and the School Secretary was invaluable. I was particularly fortunate that Mary Herbert had been secretary for my two predecessors, and probably knew more than anyone else about the way the Room at the Top did, and should function. And Peter Grimshaw and Edward Helgeby, Business Manager and School Secretary respectively in 1980, were great supports. They could solve many difficult problems. For example, another mid-evening call from Security advised that two Russian scholars, en route to the School, were marooned in the transit lounge at Singapore airport, without onward tickets to Canberra. We had not been given advanced details of their arrival date. I phoned the airport number provided. It was true. They had been put on an Aeroflot flight to Singapore, but without a booking or tickets for the next leg to Sydney. The Soviet Embassy did not want to know about them. If they were not out of the transit area within 24 hours they would be expelled back to Moscow. I told them to stand by the telephone in 12 hours time. A late call to Peter Grimshaw, and by 10 a.m. next morning he had organised seats for them to Sydney and on to Canberra; tickets for them to collect at a specific desk in the terminal; someone to meet them at Canberra airport and their accommodation in University House. It later turned out that the Soviet Academy's travel organizer may have creamed too much off the top of their travel allocation with the result that funds did not stretch to more than the Moscow-Singapore ticket!

Soon after becoming Director, I instituted a regular meeting at 9.15 each Monday morning with the School Secretary and the Business Manager to share information about events of the previous week and issues for the coming week. This proved a very useful custom and kept each of us informed. Equally, an 'open door' policy meant that members of the School generally felt free to come to the Director's office to raise questions, or impart information, on a relatively free and informal basis, or to do the same when we met by chance while traversing the corridors.

Good colleagues made my years of occupation of the 'Room at the Top' a remarkably pleasant and interesting time for me. Where else would one find such a remarkable collection of scholars with whom to work—coming from such a broad range of disciplines, but all with some common interest in the region? Recently, I attended a conference of the European Society of Oceanists and was surprised, and very pleased, to find how many of them, from several disciplines, had done their graduate work in the School, and now looked back on their times in Coombs with great affection. It is an affection I share, along with a strong appreciation of the major contributions of many colleagues. No list of these intellectual achievements would be complete. But all such lists would include the role in establishing much of the known prehistory of Australia; work in several disciplines which made the School the world's leading centre for Indonesian and Papua New Guinea studies; elucidation of Pacific languages leading to the landmark linguistic atlases of the region; helping build the intellectual context which led to much of Asia's economic cooperation through organisations such as APEC; work in international relations and strategic studies across the range from theoretical analyses to contributions to current policy; programs leading to new fundamental understanding of past and present environmental change in our region; and of course the very many projects of individuals which led to the resulting books being described by reviewers in terms such as 'the most intellectually sophisticated study ...', 'the level of synthesis, judgement, and insight are so high as to entirely reconstruct our understanding ...', or 'by far the best book available on ...'. The Coombs building is a great place in which to work—one of my predecessors said that being Director was 'the best job in the world'. Certainly, for me, colleagues made 'the room at the top' the most interesting place in which to work.

In the last week of my directorship I chaired an appointment committee for a senior position. Somehow one of those involved, a friend and former colleague, discovered that it was my birthday. He visited the Australian Geographic shop in Civic and, late in the afternoon presented me with a gift. Perhaps it was appropriate that, on almost my last day as Director, I was to be seen roaming through the corridors towards my car with an inflated stegosaurus dinosaur under my arm.

CHAPTER 6

Coombs Reflections

Merle Ricklefs

I look back on my time as Director of the School (1993–98) as the culmination of my career in Australian academic life. The position brought me many things, of which the most notable were probably: opportunities to come to know and to support some of the finest scholars of Asia and the Pacific in the world; chances to visit places where my own research would never have taken me, notably Papua New Guinea and other Pacific nations, China and Korea; the heavy responsibility of maintaining the excellence of the Research School of Pacific and Asian Studies (RSPAS) in challenging—and at times hostile— circumstances; the challenge of positioning the whole of the School more effectively within the political and diplomatic world of Canberra; and new insights into the conduct of my fellow human beings.

I imagine that many of my colleagues will recall my request that they consider their priorities for research positions. I challenged them to say what research-only academic positions they would wish to have if they had, say, 50 per cent, 75 per cent, 100 per cent or 125 per cent of their present staffing. I couldn't see that RSPAS had any choice but to set its priorities in a transparent and formal fashion. Already in 1993 money was tight and there seemed to me no way forward on the basis of short-term politicking and back-room deals, the standard practice in most Australian faculties. The ANU research schools were unique because the absence of undergraduate students meant that they were free of student-demand issues in deciding academic appointments. They could establish priorities on the basis of what research most needed to be done. So I asked the School's divisions to set their priorities publicly: academic appointments would then follow those priorities.

No division of the school found this task easy, but one or two found it challenging in the extreme. For some divisions, the idea that they should establish priorities for the future and be held responsible for implementing them—rather than playing short-term politics each time an appointment was possible—was a novel idea. Should I name names? Probably not. I did tell one distinguished professor, accustomed more to genuflection than challenge from interlocutors, that I couldn't understand why he seemed to find this task so difficult. I was never sure whether he took that as constructive criticism. In the end, every division had priorities established and publicly announced. Each year they could revisit and revise these priorities, but anyone in the School could see what past priorities had been.

It was fine for a division to shift priorities in a new direction in its annual reconsideration, but then staff positions filled under old priorities would disappear when they fell vacant. Two divisions—I observe standard rules of discretion here and won't name them—saw opportunities to maintain older ways of doing things. One took the view that whenever a position fell vacant it necessarily became the top priority post—so that it might be advertised on a longer-term basis as a chair. The division's conduct was so transparently unacceptable that the School's Strategy Committee (I think that's the correct name—how memory fails in only a few years!) agreed with me to remove that division's right to establish its own priorities and imposed priorities upon the division that it was obliged to live with. Embarrassing for all concerned. The other division saw its academic staffing increase in numbers and thought the new system was great, until some of those posts established under older priorities fell vacant and the post actually did fall away. That division had not, I think, actually thought that it would be held accountable for its decisions about priorities. This happened in the wake of the financial crisis that hit all Australian universities from 1996 and produced a major crisis for the School—of which more later.

Among the problems I perceived when I became director was an excessive amount of the budget committed to administration. The Business Manager was Peter Grimshaw, who was already noted for many things, among them the observation that Directors come and go but the Business Manager goes on forever. In Peter's case that was almost so. I was at times reminded of the quip about Henry Kissinger and the presidents who served under him. I liked and admired Peter, found his confidential insights into the School's staff invaluable (had they not been confidential, many would have been actionable) and enjoyed working with him. He fully supported the effort to reduce administrative overheads and over my five years as Director helped me to cut back very substantially the proportion of the School budget going to the Business Manager's office. His summer appearance in shorts and walk socks gave a boy-scoutish style to the School that was endearing. But he could never accommodate himself to the rule against smoking in the Coombs building. So who's perfect? Peter was a distinguished servant of the School and its purposes and I felt fortunate to be able to work with him.

Merle Ricklefs, 1994 (Director RSPAS 1993–1998)

In 1995 the ANU research schools were collectively the target of an attempt by the Australian Research Council (ARC) to get its hands on the block grant funding that supported them and gave them independence in their research activity. The ARC's preferred means of attack was a high-level international review that would, many ARC partisans believed, prove that the schools were not as distinguished as they claimed. This would justify relieving them of control over a part or all of their funding. It was even being put about that one or more of the schools might be closed. It has always been the case that the research schools are judged in Australia by the performance of their weakest staff, whereas internationally (where no one has heard of those poor performers) the schools are judged by their best performances. So the generally negative and jealous view of other Australian academics and the ARC would now be put to the test with high-level reviews of each school and an overall review of the entire Institute of Advanced Studies.

On the ANU side, we were served by Professor Sue Serjeantson as Director of the Institute of Advanced Studies (IAS) and heads of other research schools who were, in my opinion, among the most distinguished academics I have ever had the opportunity to work with. The review produced results that were disappointing for the ARC. The schools were confirmed as distinguished contributors at international level and an important part of the Australian national research effort. RSPAS was judged to be:

> The leading world centre for historical and social science research on Indonesia and the Southwest Pacific Islands, on Australia's relations with the region, on Australia-Sunda Quaternary research,

on Austronesian linguistics, Asia-Pacific economies and economic cooperation, and Asia-Pacific security.

The school was also described as

> the leading national resource for historical and social science research on Southeast Asia, China, Japan and other East Asian countries and the Pacific islands, cognate research topics such as international peace and conflict issues, Asia-Pacific international relations and global issues, including implications for the Australian region.

Not much ammunition for the ARC there. Eventually, after my time, the ARC decided it had to adopt more direct but less transparent means to gain control of part of the IAS's block funding.

There remained, as always, the question of what to do with under-performing staff on coveted research-only appointments. I encouraged a few to seek more appropriate opportunities elsewhere by helping them to understand more fully the performance review regime then in place at ANU. There were also some crooks—two if memory serves. They held full-time research-only posts and did a conspicuous amount of research overseas. They each held another full-time post in violation of their RSPAS contracts; I'm not sure how they explained to those employers their occasional trips to Australia. When they were found out, both decided that the overseas employer offered a more supportive environment for their future than in the School.

Among the most satisfying things for me at RSPAS was to achieve some success in ameliorating the lamentable proportion of women amongst its academic staff. Attempts to encourage more female applicants for positions at first had limited success. So we went for the novel approach of advertising women-only positions. From 1993 through 1995, out of a total of 50 academic appointments, 20 (40 per cent) went to women. Some fine academics were thereby recruited to the School. Thereafter, the rate of female applications declined again for reasons which were never clear to me.

I was also pleased at the degree to which academic expertise from across the School—not only from the more instrumentalist end of the institution—began to be seen outside academic circles as a valuable intellectual resource. Multiple diplomats took an active interest in events at the school. I was delighted on the occasion of a diplomatic reception for a new ambassador in Canberra to hear the new-comer being advised by a more seasoned European diplomat that, while his relations with the Australian government were important, those with the ANU would be of greater significance.

The year 1996 saw the launch of one of my favourite—albeit eventually unsuccessful—projects, *The Asia-Pacific Magazine*. This was intended to present the fruits of the best research on Asia and the Pacific in a more popular format, with photographs, without footnotes, and written in an accessible style. In this endeavour I was lucky to have Elizabeth Kingdon as editor—a person of great creativity, imagination and energy who was later to die tragically early of cancer. My assistant Jan Bretherton also supported this effort—as she did others—with much good sense and Scots energy. While articles were accepted from writers anywhere, much of the content showcased the outstanding expertise of RSPAS scholars. The first issue of the magazine appeared in April 1996 and was launched by Australia's new Prime Minister John Howard. No one at that stage guessed how little Howard would do to support Australia's relations with Asia and Pacific in his first years, a situation thankfully ameliorated later in his prime ministership. But *The Asia-Pacific Magazine* was never financially viable. In the end it had to be closed. The last issue appeared in December 1998.

Things got tougher in 1996 when the newly elected Howard government adopted policies towards universities that, had Labor held power, would have been adopted by a Labor government. It is nice to be able to be bipartisan on at least one issue: the devastation of Australian universities by Australian federal governments of both persuasions. Intellectual engagement was, however, certainly more productive with the Labor government. The Howard government came in with a palpable animosity towards academic establishments in Australia that they regarded as partisans for Labor. A particular target at the start of the Howard government was the School's Peace Research Centre (PRC), an initiative of the preceding Labor Foreign Minister Gareth Evans. The Howard government simply tossed out the previous government's commitment and the PRC sadly came to an end.

In some respects Pacific and Asian Studies was better placed than other Research Schools to deal with the post-1996 financial crisis because by that time the divisions of the School had considerable experience in setting priorities. In principle, responding to the financial crisis meant mainly dropping off the lowest-priority academic posts as they fell vacant. But logic does not always prevail, nor integrity, in such crises.

One division immediately decided to try to do a deal behind closed doors at university level, avoiding normal consultative processes both within the school and at IAS level, to escape the cuts—some of which were not the result of the immediate crisis but rather simply the expiry of posts it had said publicly some time before were no longer a priority. Fortunately documents kept falling off the back of university-level trucks onto my desk, so that I was not kept in the dark. I assembled a small group of the wisest heads in the school and together we worked to manage what was, in my view, a secret attempt to secede from the School. The low point for me was when I asked one professor who was engaged in this exercise whether any written documents existed to set out what the plans were. He said there had been some general ideas discussed but no documents prepared; by that time I had on my desk a substantial, detailed plan signed by him among others. At the time, I saw this secretive exercise as an abandonment of ethical conduct on the part of several people inside and outside the School. An open discussion and debate, that either did or did not end in secession, would have been the right way to go.

Another division got colleagues around the world to write letters of protest and mobilised access to a major national radio program to denounce the loss of the post that it had itself identified as the lowest priority in the division. I asked the head of that division if I could see what he had said in describing the situation in his contacts with people elsewhere. He said that he would give me that and was confident that I would not find his account too egregiously dishonest. But I never got that material.

Nevertheless the school weathered the crisis. When I left in 1998 its financial position was sound.

I was pleased that the Directorship allowed me some time for my own research. Over 1993–8 I published four books and a dozen articles. I had to leave in 1998 because of family health concerns that were no longer manageable from a Canberra base. Perhaps, in the midst of the crisis, there was a small part of me that was relieved to be departing from Coombs. Nevertheless, I much regretted the necessity for this move. I went to the University of Melbourne, where the Vice-Chancellor was determined to build Asian Studies after years of hostility and neglect by the Arts Faculty. I did not guess how much unethical gutter politics I would witness at that bastion of parochialism and cronyism. It made me feel still more warmly about those many colleagues at ANU with whom my time had been too short, and even about those very few with whom my time had been too long.

CHAPTER 7

Turn Right at the Buddha

James J. Fox

For newcomers to the Coombs Building, I have often offered the advice to 'turn right at the Buddha' if they are looking for the Director's office. Poised at the top of the flight of stairs leading up from the entrance, the large wooded statute of the Buddha is a defining feature of the Coombs vestibule. This statue, 'Meditating Buddha sheltered by the Naga King' is the joint creation of a visiting Cambodian artist, Nath Chun Pok, and an Australian student, Matthew Harding. It was purchased from a fund established by the Research School's long serving Business Manager, Peter Grimshaw, and is one of a host of distinctive works of art that define the building and give it a personal history.

Turning right at the Buddha and mounting a second set of stairs leads to the open area between the two Directors' offices where a large portrait of 'Nugget' Coombs by Clifton Pugh lends a brooding presence to gatherings—usually either inductions or farewells—that are occasionally held there. 'Nugget' Coombs had little to do with the building named in his honour. After his retirement, he did, however, locate himself for part of every year at the North Australia Research Unit in Darwin—the School's research facility, which he helped establish. Having confronted his portrait on numerous occasions, I finally met the man when he offered me a beer beside the pool at NARU one late afternoon in Darwin and I came to realize that Pugh's portrait captured only one aspect of our building's namesake.

As with everyone else in the Coombs Building, Directors have the opportunity to furnish their office as they wish. They have usually selected artwork from the University's collection. Since Gerry Ward's time, a painting by Margaret Ollie of a 'Native Stall in Kokie Market'—acquired by the University in 1969—has been a feature of the Director's office.

When I began as Director, I brought to the office various furnishing: textiles from Timor, some Chinese tables, including a handsome altar table and a corner chest and a number of Indonesian pieces: on one wall, a print by the Javanese artist, Lugiyono of Arjuna, in the form of a meditating *wayang* figure and on the other wall, a painting entitled, *Dalang* ('Puppeteer'), by the Achenese artist, Bahri. With a large wooden Semar and *kletek* puppet of Panji, there is a clear message in this decorative theme.

The Buddha at the main entrance

Jim Fox with His Holiness The Dalai Lama

One of the first students at the ANU whom I supervised, Raharjo Suwandi, involved me personally in his research among a community of East Javanese who regard the *wayang* as the representation of life. He invited me to join him in Blitar at a critical moment in the community's celebration, and I arrived to fulfil a prophesy that the Dutch would return in support of the poor. Instead of 'professor', I became, by Javanese wordplay, the 'pro–asor', someone who favours the lowly. With Raharjo and Patsy Asch, I have made two films of the community, *In the Play of Life* and *Conversations with Mbah Wali*. The role of professor and puppeteer are curiously merged in the position of the School's Director.

In contrast to Director's inner office, the outer office where Pam Wesley-Smith presides features three colourful prints by the Aboriginal artists Jimmy Nerrimah and Hughie Bent, from Western Australia, an Indian folk painting of Ganesha, given to me by Kuntala Lahiri-Dutt and a work of art by Pixie Borlase, 'Vocabulary from the Series Scrolls' that the Research School acquired as part of its continuing support as a Patron of the ANU School of Art.

Each year the School awards a prize to a graduating student from the School of Art for a work, in any media, with an Asia-Pacific theme. The School has made a succession of outright awards but has also acquired a number of prize-winning works: a set of ceramic shields with design motifs from Bougainville; ceramic pieces with Pali script; textiles and interesting transparency that combines motifs of the Australian bush with Korean images.

The School has regularly acquired art to decorate the corridors of the Coombs building and its art and artefacts reflected the School's history from its foundation. Sir Raymond Firth can be regarded as the founder of the School; he was involved in School's planning and was offered the position of its first Director. In 1952, the ANU financed Firth's second field trip to Tikopia, where he had done his initial fieldwork in 1928–1929. There he and James Spillius made a collection of traditional Tikopian artefacts. These were originally stored in the old Anatomy Building, which has now been transformed into the National Film and Sound Archive. In 1986, many of these objects were transferred to the School. A number of them are handsome works of art: a tumeric mixing bowl, a chief's head rest, carved canoe ornament and an impressive bark cloth beater—all of which are displayed in various cabinets in the Anthropology Department.

Through its involvement in the Pacific, the School has acquired a great variety of barkcloths. From Jim Davidson, the School has a 'coronation tapa' from the Coronation of the king of Tonga, Taufa'ahau Tupou IV, as well as an '*i'e toga*' that was presented to Davidson by Samoa's Self-Government Committee in

1950 for his contribution in framing the constitution. Rusiate Nayacakalou presented Oskar Spate with a fine patterned Fijian *masi kesa* in 1972. And John Waiko, who did his PhD in Pacific History and went on to become Minister of Education in Papua New Guinea, presented Hank Nelson with a striking tapa cloth from Tabara village in Oro Province. Peter Rimmer and Godfrey Linge also donated a Tongan tapa cloth.

On the ground floor of the Coombs Building, there is a large drawing by a Papua New Guinean artist by the name of Barabas India. This is a donation from Sir John Crawford. In the University's records, the drawing is described as an ink and gold paper—probably cigarette wrapper—collage. In 1975, Sir John bought the drawing at an exhibition of Papua New Guinean art that was held in the A.D. Hope Building. As I recall, it was Anthony Forge, the Foundation Professor of Anthropology, who organized the exhibition through his friend, Uli Beier. (I bought a textile collage—a good example of sewing machine art—at the same exhibition and for a long time had it hanging in my office in the Anthropology Department.)

Clearly, among the most valuable artwork in the Coombs Building are several works of Aboriginal art. The first is a painting by the artist Pandak of figures with Murimbata ceremonial designs; the second, a painting of 'Bandicoot Dreaming' by the artist Charles Tarawa Tjuparai, a member of the Papunya Tula artist group; the third is a drawing of the Walpiri/Pintupi story of Rainbow and Cave by Long Jack Phillipus Tjakamarra. The first of these comes from William Stanner; the second was purchased and donated by Derek Freeman; but records do not make clear how the third made its way to Anthropology. All three were hung along the Department corridor until Wally Caruana, on his way to a seminar, stopped and had a good look. He immediately recognized their historical importance and advised us to keep them safe, pointing out that they could easily be removed by anyone passing through the building. This led us to put them within secure frames. Kathy Robinson moved 'Bandicoot Dreaming' into her office.

The Anthropology corridors are particularly revealing if one knows how to interpret them. Besides the Aboriginal paintings and some Firth objects and masks from Papua New Guinea that the Department purchased from John Ondawame, I have provided the Department with a Balinese painting of a Naga and Garuda locked in struggle. For a Department that pursues research on local systems of dualism, the painting can be regarded as symbolic. In addition to these objects, there are also photographs. In the 1980s, Tim Asch gathered photographs from members of the Department and had these blown-up and mounted on the walls. If you can recognize the image, you can identify whose fieldwork they relate to.

Opposite my old office there were two photographs from Savu and one from Rote. The Rotinese photograph is of a group of chanters performing at a ceremonial in honour of my chief informant during my fieldwork in 1965, a man known as Old Meno—someone whom I can consider one of my life's gurus. Tim also created for me a photo-montage of another of my close informants, Mias Kiuk—the man who adopted me into his clan, Ingu-Beuk in Termanu. Tim took a number of photographs of Mias along the beach in Sosa-Dale and put them together as group. I then provided him with some lines from a Rotinese poem to complete his collage.

> *Cut and slice a branch of the Bau tree*
> *Slice and take a limb of the Tui tree*
> *To plant at the Lake Hela*
> *And to sow at the River Kosi*
> *That its roots may creep forth*
> *And its tendrils may twine*
> *For shrimp to cling to*
> *And crabs to circle round,*
> *Not for shrimp to cling to*
> *But for orphans to cling to*
> *And not for crabs to circle round*
> *But for widows to circle round.*

Most of the photographs in Anthropology have now begun to fade. They are of historical interest but they no longer relate to contemporary work in the Department, so one would expect that most of these photographs will be replaced. What are unlikely to be replaced are the fine photographic portraits taken by Roger Keesing that now line the downstairs corridor of the Coombs. Although one of the series has disappeared, they remain a handsome set and a testimony to Roger Keesing's skill as a photographer.

Another object, an Iban *papan turai* or 'writing board', given to me by Derek Freeman, has yet to find a place within the School. For the moment, I keep it in the Director's office. Its story has yet to be completed. In 1949, in Rumah Nyala on Sungai Sut in Sarawak, Derek arranged to get the oral poet, Igoh anak Impin to recite a long *timang gawai amat*. This was the time before tape recorders so the whole recitation had to be described as it was recited. The recitation took days. In addition to the recitation, Derek persuaded Igoh anak Impin to carve a replica of the *papan turai* that he used to remember the narrative. Each *papan turai* is a personal mnemonic—a succession of images carved on both sides of the board. The poet could carry this mnemonic board as he walked the longhouse reciting his epic. Eventually Derek found an Iban student, James Masing, who worked with Derek on a translation and produced this as a thesis, which was published in two volumes as the *Coming of the Gods*.

Although this translation has been done, no one has yet keyed the Iban text to the recitation, a task that I kept pressing Derek to complete. I even had Bob Cooper photograph each of the tiny carved images to facilitate the task. When Derek realized that he would not be able to get to this work, he turned over to me the *papan turai*, his text of the recitation and the photographs. There they rest in the Director's office awaiting the work that needs to be done to link them. When this is done, Derek's *papan turai*, carved in 1949, can take its place among the cherished research artefacts of the Coombs building.

The Coombs Building in its way is a kind of *papan turai*—a House of Memories. The images and artefacts on its corridors are redolent of memories of the research and researchers who have inhabited its corridors. Every corridor in the building reveals its past.

PART III

The Coombs Journeys

CHAPTER 8

Hexagonal Reflections on Pacific History

Niel Gunson

When the Coombs Building was first occupied in 1964, the two Schools and their member Departments already had a life of their own and those who moved into the new rooms brought their group memories and personal histories with them. To appreciate both the continuity and the new developments it is necessary to begin the story before the union of the Institute of Advanced Studies with the old Canberra University College, now The Faculties, in 1962.

In May 1955 I arrived in Canberra as one of Jim Davidson's 'lambs'. Dale Trendall, Master of University House, welcomed me to that august institution by asking Davidson if I was one of his lambs. Having been hurtled from the railway station through the brisk morning air in an open sports car at over 80 miles an hour I felt more like a freshly shorn sheep. Thus began my apprenticeship at the Australian National University. In those days our intellectual life centred on University House and the Old Hospital Buildings (OHB) where historians might rub shoulders with nuclear physicists at tea or where a student might sit next to Sir Mark Oliphant at dinner. On alternate months the History Society or Club, hosted by Jim Davidson and Oskar Spate in the University House bar, took us off campus to Manning Clark's house. The New Guinea Society, on the other hand, with membership in government departments and the CSIRO, always met in University House under strict Chatham House rules.

Having come from Melbourne where students still wore jackets and ties it took me some time to adjust to the informality and outback verandah style of the OHB and the Oxbridge formality of University House, which was largely confined to High Table. Jim Davidson once told me that one only wore a tie if one's neck was cold so it rather surprised me to see him hastily putting on a tie in the washroom when we were summoned to afternoon tea with Sir Keith Hancock in his office. As Jim wore a suit to my first dinner party it was clear that, whatever his own views, he respected those of others. Otherwise his dress was extremely casual, leading Harry Maude to describe him affectionately as a 'sartorial disgrace'.

Research Scholars in Pacific History with Jim Davidson. *From left to right back row:* Dick Gilson, Ken Gillion, Niel Gunson, Colin Newbury. *Front row:* Rae Matthews, J.W. Davidson, Trudy Newbury, 1955

Everything was done to facilitate research in the 1950s and early 60s, the librarians regularly called on staff and students to discuss their requirements and the library came to reflect the individual research interests of the Schools. All staff and students had keys to the library so that they had access to the books at all times. My staff colleague, the late R.P. (Dick) Gilson kept strange office hours, 4 p.m. to 4 a.m., so that I would often call on him after an evening out and then—usually after midnight—proceed to the library to find a book we might have been discussing. Once the lights were on, an armed security guard in uniform with a German Shepherd in tow would call to see if everything was as it should be. Later 'rationalisation' of the library destroyed the personal nature of the research collection and as Oskar Spate reflected, it took him three times as long to do the research for the last two volumes of his Spanish trilogy as it took him for the first.

Academic life in the OHB and the early Coombs was far more democratic than it has become. Despite the hierarchical ordering of office furniture and the other 'class distinctions' of a bureaucratic Canberra, the University demonstrated a collegiality and congeniality uncommon or absent in other universities at the time. As Davidson was never tired of saying, we were 'a community of scholars'. A student had the opportunity to meet visiting international luminaries such as Sir Arnold Toynbee and Sir Steven Runciman. I well remember the visit of the celebrated (but then in decline) prehistorian Gordon Childe as Jim Davidson included me in the visit itinerary. On the occasion of Childe's evening lecture in the Old Drill Hall, Davidson, with affectionate malice, began by saying he would not do what his distinguished guest did when introducing a speaker at Cambridge—he forgot the speaker's name. 'No one could forget the name of Gordon Childe'. This triggered a chortling response on the part of a professor's wife who had drunk too much at dinner. As Childe placed his handwritten pile of tissue-like notes on the rostrum a sudden gust of wind came through the open door sending the notes wafting over the audience to the accompaniment of uncontrollable drunken laughter, a truly Wagnerian introduction to a lecture on the amber trade.

I saw quite a bit of Bob and Hazel Hawke when they arrived, as we had mutual friends and contacts, and I introduced them to my colleagues in the Department of Pacific History as it then was. Bob formed a close friendship with Emily Sadka, another student like myself who became a staff member specialising in Malaysian history. I was sorry Blanche d'Alpuget described Emily in unflattering terms in her biography of Bob Hawke, but I suppose it was to suggest that the friendship was intellectual and not romantic. Emily was 'a beautiful person', as Arthur Burns described her. It was while I was on fieldwork in the Gilbert and Ellice Islands that one of my friends sent me a colourful first-hand account of the much vaunted episode involving the future prime minister's nocturnal adventures in the University House fishpond and related incidents for which he was sent down. I rather suspect ASIO has relieved me of that document as I have not been able to find it.

I would not be surprised if ASIO took an interest in all members of our Department. Shortly after I arrived I was told by a student's wife that I should be careful as my professor was 'pink'. Having been history tutor at Women's College in Melbourne in the Macarthy years when Myra Roper, the principal, was on the League of Rights hit list, I was not unduly fazed. Certainly Jim Davidson and his friends Dr John Burton junior and Bishop Burgmann formed an influential lobby group that frequently embarrassed government.

Jim Davidson had expected and trained his first batch of students to return after some teaching experience and take over the key areas of specialisation. My student contemporaries Colin Newbury (French Polynesia) and Ken Gillion

(Fiji Indians) both chose careers elsewhere, Newbury in Africa and Oxford and Gillion in Western Australia. Those who returned when the appropriate opportunity arose, such as Emily and myself, were christened 'boomerang boys (and girls)' by Trendall's secretary at University House. Deryck Scarr was the next student who joined the staff to take over the Western Pacific and Fijian specialisation. His many books are a testimony to his industry and dedication. Like Davidson, he spent much time in the islands and was held in high regard, particularly by some of the Fijian leaders. He is currently writing the authorised biography of the late Ratu Sir Kamisese Mara.

But Davidson also encouraged another type of student (and staff member), those who had chosen another form of career but who then developed an interest in Pacific history or some important facet of Island life and culture. Another of my contemporaries was Bernard Smith, the art historian, whose *European Vision and the South Pacific* has been of seminal importance. I well remember his evocative lecture on Coleridge's 'Ancient Mariner'. Harry Maude, the distinguished British colonial administrator, who had become passionately interested in the history of the Gilbertese people and who had a lifelong interest in Pacific literature, was welcomed to the staff while I was still a student. One of my earliest memories of life in the Coombs was the long line of Pacific acolytes (members of other departments, visitors, students) waiting outside the door of Room 5101 resembling more the exterior of a surgery rather than that of a scholarly retreat. Harry, with the support of others such as Greg Dening and myself, introduced the concepts of ethnohistory to the Coombs. Together with Jim Davidson, Harry played a major role in establishing the *Journal of Pacific History* and the Pacific Manuscripts Bureau.

Ron Crocombe, a former district officer in the Cook Islands, was 'the new boy' in my last year as a student and when I joined the staff in 1962 he had already left and was running the New Guinea Research Unit. Other students with wider experience included David Stone, also a former district officer and Peter France, a British official from Fiji, afterwards a well known television broadcaster. The navigator David Lewis, whose adventures in Pacific and Antarctic waters made world headlines, was a Research Fellow of similar mould. David's small daughters accompanied their father on weekends in the ACT and NSW bush learning how to survive by eating Aboriginal 'tucker', including bogong moths winnowed over a camp fire. Before he died Jim Davidson asked me to take an interest in the Reverend Geoff Cummins, a missionary in Tonga, who had compiled a source book of Tongan history and reprinted various Tongan historical texts. Geoff completed two degrees before returning to the Church.

Of the Pacific history scholars supervised in the Coombs many have had interesting careers. Peter Corris, well known for his work on the labour trade, is also a distinguished writer of detective fiction. Professor Hugh Laracy of Auckland, recently honoured by the Solomons government and by the Alliance Française, gets some small satisfaction from being identified as a character in a Corris novel. Nicholas Thomas came to us with the reputation that he had already changed the course of Australian prehistory as a student and he had obtained his first chair before the age of 30. Two other professors, Barrie Macdonald (now a Pro Vice-Chancellor) and Kerry Howe, head the list of other ex-Coombs academics serving in New Zealand. Graham Hassall is Professor of Governance at the University of the South Pacific. Diane Langmore heads the *Australian Dictionary of Biography* project. Of the numerous Pacific Islanders Sione Lātūkefu was an associate professor and a pioneering influence in the new University of Papua New Guinea. Ahmed Ali had a similar role at the University of the South Pacific, and was a member of the Fijian government. Kilifoti Eteuati, who now holds the title Leiataua, is the High Commissioner for Samoa in Australia while Fele Nokise is Principal of the Pacific Theological College. Most of the other former students have held or are holding senior academic posts. All have contributed significantly to the intellectual life of Australia and the Pacific.

When I joined the staff in 1962 I recall Francis West, a professorial fellow in the Department, saying to me how our situation was like being paid to live the life of an 18th century gentleman scholar like Sir Joseph Banks. But I was always aware of an inbuilt discipline. Despite the great freedom of action there were disciplinary pressures. Students in anthropology under Nadel (and staff by implication) were obliged to attend all School seminars. Davidson expected all staff and students to attend all Pacific seminars and belong to the New Guinea Society. Seminar papers had to be articles or chapters that would be published and they were usually circulated one week before the seminars. Attendance at tea in the Coombs tea room was almost obligatory as a way of keeping check on progress. The work ethic was greatly respected in the Coombs Building, and it was not unusual to see many of the Coombs Building office lights burning through the night as various scholars made up for time lost to meetings, consultations and other daily pressures.

Davidson was scrupulously aware that we had to account for the use of public money, checked regularly that students were working in their offices and exercised a kind of public parsimony, turning out lights and even refusing to make allowances for the Melbourne Cup. Many a seminar was held while the race was run. When I was lecturing in Queensland in the early 1960s the comparative 'unproductiveness' of the ANU was a constant theme. I always read the situation to be that we had wonderful opportunities at ANU to engage in pure research, visit libraries all over the world, go on extensive field trips and build up large collections of source material that would probably last us for life. Certainly an untenured staff member would take advantage of the situation knowing that he or she might soon be teaching at a state university where research opportunities were then greatly restricted.

Jim Davidson took a great interest in the structural formation of the Coombs, fought hard against double professorial suites and disapproved of departmental tea alcoves and mini kitchens arguing that everyone should use the tea room. On the matter of flyscreens he argued that flies would always fly out of open windows. I paid for my fly screens and also had my office windows treated to counter ultraviolet light. As a result of his interest in the 'plan' the Department of Pacific History was destined to move as the building expanded. Our first home was downstairs, we then moved upstairs when the next wing was built and our eventual home was to be in the third hexagon which has never been built. The original plan did not make provision for PhD student rooms as students were supposed to use the carrels in the Menzies Library. Inevitably Departments began to place students in the empty rooms in the Departmental corridors partly to 'claim' the territory and partly for the convenience of supervision. As a result students soon assumed a right to room space in the Coombs.

The Faculty Board of the Research School of Pacific Studies was the chosen guardian of the School's democratic character and issues about which academics felt strongly were always raised there by sub-professorial staff. I recall many meetings when Faculty Board members such as Joe Jennings used the Board to campaign against such issues as the admission of church-sponsored residential colleges. Departmental staff had a full say in the selection and appointment of students and staff. Gradually, however, the democratic structure was eroded by the increasing powers of the Directors and the growing influence of (unofficial) Heads of Departments meetings which tended to reduce the Faculty Board to an assembly which acted as a rubber-stamp to professorial decisions. At least up until Sir John Crawford's time, the democratic nature of the Faculty Board was recognised. It was not unusual to hear Sir John say things to this effect—'We have heard your views before Professor Stanner. I would like to know the views of the sub-professorial staff. Gunson, what do you think?' Not a moment I necessarily cherished, but I regret its passing.

Perhaps because of its monastic, beehive structure, even the Coombs took on some of the least desirable features of a closed community and at times a measure of Byzantine intrigue affected university and departmental politics. There were cliques, the most notable being the Cambridge push, the Melbourne push and later the New Guinea push. Jim Davidson, a Cambridge man, preferred to play an independent game and Pacific historians were regarded as mavericks. As a Melbourne man I was not regarded as a player or pawn until the appointment of Gavan Daws and by then the Melbourne push was in decline. On one occasion when internal tensions threatened to lead to litigation and I was asked to give evidence against a staff member spreading calumnies, I offered to take the matter to the Vice-Chancellor direct. It was summer time, red dust was blowing everywhere and rain was in the offing. As I left the Coombs for the Chancelry big globules of rain containing red dust began to fall. Manning Clark was heading for the Coombs. 'It's Armageddon, it's Armageddon', he said. I rather thought it was.

During the Davidson years the Department was very much 'in the Pacific' which then included the islands and peninsulas of Southeast Asia. Jim was in the forefront of the decolonisation process serving as a constitution maker in Samoa, the Cook Islands, Nauru, Micronesia and Papua New Guinea. Regional leaders such as Lee Kuan Yew, prime minister of Singapore, and many Pacific Island politicians visited the Department, a tradition that has been carried through to the present. The Department's name was changed to include Southeast Asia after Davidson's death mainly to satisfy students working in the Southeast Asian area. In recent years Brij Lal, himself a Coombs graduate who had my colleague Ken Gillion as one of his mentors, has been honoured for his work as a constitution maker in his homeland Fiji.

Under Davidson's successors Gavan Daws and Donald Denoon there was a change of emphasis. Daws, an environmentalist with a flair for popularising history, introduced us to psychohistory and, together with Hank Nelson, promoted the use of other historical media such as film. Denoon took a postmodernist approach as exemplified in his *Cambridge History of the Pacific Islanders* in which contributors were permitted to express contradictory viewpoints and, like Daws, he has promoted the advantages to scholarship of computer technology. The last 30 years have also seen advances in theory and historiography and, at School level, a greater concentration on the problems of contemporary Melanesia.

Of all the distinct 'characters' in the Coombs the one I knew best was Derek Freeman. He had been very kind to me in my student days inviting me home to dessert, introducing me to Nadel and arranging for me to give a seminar in Anthropology. His decennial enthusiasms—kinship, Freudian analysis, ethnology and finally Buddhism were at times almost pathological. When planning the festschrift for Harry Maude, I asked Derek to contribute a chapter. He flatly refused saying that he was no longer interested in Samoa and that he was working exclusively on primates. Over a period of weeks I worked on him arguing that it was a great pity and even unethical not to do anything with the enormous amount of material he had gathered on Samoan society. I had almost given up when he came to me and said he had reconsidered and found just the topic to develop for the festschrift. He reread his Samoan material including an earlier lecture on Margaret Mead and from then on there was no stopping him. Some years later when he found satisfaction in atheistic Buddhism he burst into my room wearing a Sherpa outfit and announced he was off to the Himalayas. He evidently did not go as the next time I saw him he had found the Boas-Mead correspondence and said he was going to be a historian. Although he had a deeper understanding of Samoan values than Mead I believe he was equally mistaken in his analysis. But a wise man would not question his 'truths' to avoid his most withering response, 'Only a fool would think otherwise'.

When I look back at my own time in the Coombs, I am probably proudest of having initiated *Aboriginal History*. This was quite a long struggle and Crawford thought I was a 'sucker' for getting involved in Aboriginal affairs. In the period before the 'freedom riders' even those most sympathetic to Aboriginal issues such as Paul Hasluck, Bill Stanner and 'Nugget' Coombs appeared to be committed to the policy of assimilation. Bill Stanner argued strongly against a journal believing that it would somehow create a backlash against the Aboriginal people and much later Hasluck wrote me a long letter condemning the idea. Diane Barwick was at first the only social scientist I knew prepared to support the idea and she made it plain that it would have to be a success or the Aboriginal people would be let down yet again. In that era, although there were some Aboriginal activists, the general atmosphere was apathetic and pessimistic. Whetu Tirikatene, a scholar in the Department who afterwards became a Minister in the New Zealand government, told me she was frustrated because she could not get Aboriginal women to take the initiative in demanding reforms.

Plans for a journal were first discussed with Peter Corris and later with another student in the Department, Bob Reece (now Professor of History at Murdoch University). By the time Bob joined the Department I had been encouraged by Charles Perkins 'to do something about Aboriginal history'. The climate changed radically after Perkins and his 'freedom riders' began a new wave of Aboriginal activism. Bob and I became the self-appointed editors of a new journal and wrote to historians and anthropologists likely to be interested. Apart from Hasluck the response was either lukewarm or positive. Stanner, though not approached, was to contribute an article to the first issue. As Peter

Corris was in Sydney we decided to invite Diane to join us and also to make the journal interdisciplinary. A meeting was called to form an editorial board. Through Peter Grimshaw's influence School funds were found to finance the operation. Wang Gungwu, then Director, made it plain that although the School would help us in other ways we were in no way to consider ourselves part of the School structure. He was afraid there might be a radical takeover of the journal, something that had happened to a journal he was connected with in Singapore.

For nearly 20 years *Aboriginal History* editorial business not handled by the editors directly was conducted from my office in the Coombs. In more recent years it was transferred to the History Department in the Faculties and now it has come full circle back to the Coombs as it has its own office under the umbrella of the History Program, Research School of Social Sciences.

Although the Coombs has lost much of the intimacy of the early years it still serves as a crossroads for Australian and Pacific intellectual life. As new faces and new ideas occupy the hexagonal corridors, I am perhaps more familiar with some of the ghosts.

CHAPTER 9

Seriously, but not solemnly

Bryant Allen

I have absolutely no recollection of my first entry into the Coombs Building, despite retaining a reasonably clear memory of what happened after I had entered. Pavlov's dogs are said to have lost their memories after the Moscow River flooded their accommodation and left them swimming with their heads bumping against the roofs of their cages. My situation was not as dire as theirs. I was merely trying not to appear stupid in front of what I assumed were some of the best minds in the business. But it seems to have had a similar effect on me as the flood had on the famous salivating dogs.

I had applied for a PhD scholarship from New Zealand where I had heard Oskar Spate, then the Director of the Research School of Pacific Studies, give a talk on the work of the School and the scholarships that enabled people to work in Papua New Guinea. I had been fortunate enough spend six months in the Cook Islands on fieldwork for a masters degree, had read a lot of the New Guinea literature published out of the School and desperately wanted to go there. With a considerable amount of temerity, I had applied for a scholarship from a very provincial New Zealand university, hoping to study rural development under Harold Brookfield. However Harold had left for the United States in 1969 and my application letter was answered by acting head Godfrey Linge, who said the department could not supervise me at present and would be in touch later. I assumed this was a polite way saying 'don't call us, we'll call you' and applied for a tutor's job at Flinders. From Adelaide I informed ANU of my new address and received an invitation and an airline ticket to travel to Canberra for an interview. Those were clearly the days before the 'Block Grant' had been whittled away to its present inadequacy by inflation, unfunded salary rises and a shaky Australian dollar.

Somehow or another I got into the Coombs and was led by the six foot plus, unsmiling and looming Godfrey Linge to a seminar room. It must have been Seminar Room C, but I have no memory of the windows along the side, or of Fred Nadel looking down his nose on the proceedings from the back wall. Hank Nelson once told me that after arriving at Coombs, he waited for years, like the doomed man, for 'them', that is all the other scholars in the place, to find out how stupid he was. I was assuming that my stupidity was going to be revealed fairly swiftly by this interview.

Bryant Allen circa 1975

I sat at one end of a long table, Oskar Spate sat at the other end and Godfrey Linge and Peter Rimmer sat at either side, near to Oskar. I had no idea then that Godfrey and Peter disliked each other so much that if one of them made a statement, the other one opposed it on principle. So I was puzzled at the way the interview went, with every question asked by Godfrey being contradicted by Peter before I could answer, to be followed by a different question from Peter, which was challenged by Godfrey. As this was going on, I mentioned that I had spent six months on a rather small island in the middle of the Pacific. At this Oskar launched into a long story of his own fieldwork on Fiji where he had been presented with a side of pork by some chiefs and had put it in the boot of his car, where it had lain forgotten in the tropical heat for some days. Godfrey and Peter listened politely and I had my first insights into the God-like nature of Directors in Coombs. At the end of his story Oskar announced, to the annoyance of Peter and Godfrey who obviously still had plenty of curly questions about Pacific transport or industrialization left to ask and about which I knew very little, that I seemed like an ideal candidate and could have a scholarship, beginning next January. Oskar later retired from the Directorship to write his brilliant histories of the Pacific, an outstanding example to those of us approaching the same watershed of what can be achieved after retirement.

So it was that I became a resident of Coombs in January 1971. The Department of Geography was in the process of splitting into Human Geography and Biogeography and Geomorphology. The three eminent international geographers who reviewed the department in 1977 all thought the split had been a mistake. In 1971, the reasons for the separation were not made clear to new students, and I was left to guess that perhaps the exuberant and jovial Joe Jennings wished to put some distance between himself and the dour Rimmer and Linge.

Until 1971, the work of the 'human' side of the department had been dominated by Harold Brookfield, and his postgraduate students: Isireli Lasaqa, David Lea, Dianna Howlett, Alastair Couper, Roger Frazer, Eric Waddell, Peter Krinks, Rosemary Barnard, Dick Bedford and Ian Hughes. Their work is exemplified by Harold Brookfield and Doreen Hart's book, *Melanesia: a Geographical Interpretation of an Island World*, published in 1971. Doreen was Harold's research assistant. Two years later these students with Bill Clarke, and with Harold editing, published *The Pacific in Transition: Geographical Perspectives and Adaptation and Change*. Godfrey Linge was working on Australian manufacturing and a number of students were also working within Australia. Peter Rimmer was working on transport in Australia, Papua New Guinea and the Pacific.

The 'physical' geography side was being led by Donald Walker, who became professor and Joe Jennings, the specialist in karst landscapes and renowned caver. Walker led the new department deep into the paleontological past and although this research was to result in a revolutionary understanding of the time depth of Papua New Guinea agriculture, it meant the department had little time for contemporary problems of vegetation change, erosion and land degradation or agricultural intensification in PNG. The long term result was that Biogeography and Geomorphology eventually disappeared as a department, into the Department of Archaeology and Natural History.

In early 1971, the students of both departments still shared rooms. My contemporaries included David Walmsley (now at University of Queensland) and Bob Robertson, a Canadian. Both were working on Australian topics, David on Australian farming innovations and Bob on the impact of recreational housing on the NSW south coast. John Baker from Hull in the UK was studying Pacific shipping. John was later Australian High Commissioner to Tanazania and a senior public servant. Bob Fagan (now Professor at Macquarie University) who was a couple of years ahead of us was working on Australian mining. Geography was in the early throes of what became known as the quantitative revolution, led by the advent of computing and advanced statistical techniques. The computer we were given access to was set up in the basement of the Menzies Library, known as the Elephant Stalls, and was fed, on site, with punched cards. Students who had completed fieldwork sat for hours in the area now occupied by the Coombs Computing Unit and punched their data into huge clanking IBM card punches. What is now called 'IT assistance' was provided by people who when you asked for help, hunched over a terminal, barely visible in a cloud of cigarette smoke, would snarl, 'Whadda you want?' without looking up. My confidence in dealing with computers was not restored until ten years later, when I purchased an early model micro-computer and taught myself to program in BASIC in the privacy of my own home.

In 1971, the geography students were still sharing rooms, but were administered separately. I was supervised by the diminutive, in stature, but not in intellect, Bobby Ho, whose feet did not touch the floor when he was sitting in his overly large office chair. Bobby was a Malaysian Chinese and had been professor at the University of Malaya. It was Godfrey's turn to be Head of Department and in my first week Bobby warned me to keep out of Godfrey's way and let him deal with matters administrative. And so he did, with great panache. He not only negotiated a fieldwork budget for me in the face of Godfrey's insistence that the department was broke, but he also phoned the Department of Territories to ask why my entry permit was taking so long. He sat bolt upright in his large chair, feet on his rubbish tin and interrogated them in rapid fire BBC-accented English. The tirade stopped and he spun his chair around to gaze at me. 'Are you an Indian?' he barked. 'No', I said, 'I'm a New Zealander'. He spun away from me. 'He's not an Indian. So let's have no more hold ups?'. After putting down the phone he spun around to face me again. I felt as though I should apologize on behalf of the white races for the racist slur implicit in the question. 'Quite right to keep those bastards out', he said, and waved me out of his room.

I began what seemed to be an interminable process of writing draft research proposals, which Bobby tore to pieces with his extremely sharp mind, and returned to me for a rewrite. The result was a proposal backed by such a depth of reading and argument that in the middle of a dark night in an isolated village in Papua New Guinea, when I woke in a sweat with no idea what I was doing there, I could get out of bed, read it again by torch light, and go back to sleep, reassured. Sadly Bobby died suddenly while I was on fieldwork.

Shortly before I was due to leave for the field, Dick Bedford (recently retired from the Chair of Geography at Waikato) who was in the department finishing a frighteningly good thesis on circular migration in the Pacific, invited me to his house to meet Harold Brookfield, who was visiting Canberra. 'Well', said Harold, after dinner, sucking on his pipe, 'What are you proposing to study in New Guinea?' I briefly described my proposed research. 'Ah', said one of the world's leading geographers, 'Never mind. I'm sure you'll find something interesting to work on when you get there'. He was right, I did.

After 15 months away in Papua New Guinea, I returned to the Coombs to write a thesis. I didn't have much idea of what it was going to be like. I was struggling to get out from underneath the details. I kept that to myself and was privately reassured by stories of David Lea in Geography (by now a Professor at UPNG) and Nick Modjeska in Anthropology, who, it was rumoured, did not 'have a thesis' when they got back from the field. I was pretty sure I 'had a thesis', if only I could find it amongst the mass of material in my patrol boxes. I procrastinated by doing a beautiful index of all my notes and photographs, while grieving for the simplicity of the village and the people whose lives had become my daily bread.

During my absence, Gerard Ward had been appointed Professor of Human Geography. I had met with him at the University of Papua New Guinea where he was Professor, and he had visited me in the village, where his hammock almost caused my house to collapse. Fortunately he came to rest on the floor before the walls were pulled far enough away from the vertical for the roof to fall in. Gerry proved to be a great supervisor, an even better editor of my fractured prose and a good friend. Coombs was heaven for a New Guineaist then. In the Department of Human Geography alone were Gerry, Diana Howlett (to become Professor in The Faculties) and William Clarke (to become Professor at UPNG and USP). With Gerry they proposed 'maket raun', a radical change in Papua New Guinea service delivery, in which the services came to the people at market places. It was admired, but never adopted, being too different for the entrenched Papua New Guinea public service to contemplate seriously. Ian Hughes, the wise old man of the students, was finishing a thesis on trade based on long patrols across New Guinea. Andrew Strathern was in Anthroplogy, Ric Shand, another of my supervisors, in Economics and Jack Golson in Prehistory. Peter Grimshaw, the Business Manager, had been a colonial policeman in Papua New Guinea and admired the 'dirty-boots' approach of the field-based disciplines.

I left Coombs in 1974 to return to Papua New Guinea, with my thesis only half written, and became a lecturer at UPNG. I managed to finish the thesis in Port Moresby and flew into Canberra for an oral in Coombs, with examiners Harold Brookfield and Alaric Maude, one of Harold's former students in Coombs in the 1960s, in the same Seminar Room C where I had listened to Oskar Spate's Fijian stories some years earlier. Harold very decently told me I had passed before saying that he thought the final chapter of the thesis was missing, but what came before it was enough to pass it. I had never managed to get on top of the detail and Harold's great skill is to make sense of the detail, even to the extent of ignoring the odd bit of it that doesn't seem to fit.

Six years later Gerry appeared at the door of my Port Moresby house to tell me the Department was advertising a Research Fellowship and he thought I might like to apply. I did, was successful and returned again to Coombs in 1982. Gerry had become Director of the School and Harold Brookfield had become Head of Department. Harold was writing a book every 12 to 18 months and immediately started putting on pressure to resurrect a proposed book on frost and drought in Papua New Guinea. It was published as a special issue of *Mountain Research and Development*. When drought again gripped Papua New Guinea in 1997, we had to photocopy large chunks of it to convince gung-ho military men and aid donating bureaucrats that we knew something about this phenomenon in Papua New Guinea.

Harold worked Saturdays and most Sundays and his first remark at morning coffee on Mondays was, 'I didn't see you in over the weekend'. Writing co-authored papers with Harold was similarly fraught. He would often do a major rewrite and reinterpretation over a weekend, while I was racing to keep up with his last lot of comments on an earlier draft. But out of this collaboration grew the Land Management Group and the mapping of Papua New Guinea agricultural systems, a major achievement (Harold was frustrated because we stopped at the Indonesian border and did not carry on through West Papua to Java and Sumatra) and the innovative Resource Management in Asia-Pacific Project. As Harold approached his retirement he seemed to speed up, such that I thought he would disintegrate when he had to stop working. However he did not stop, but moved off to Anthropology to establish and lead, the UN-funded People, Land Management and Environmental Change (PLEC) project, covering six research 'clusters' in different parts of the world. He proceeded, with unbelievable energy, to offer intellectual leadership to the project, to visit all his 'clusters' and to organize conferences in exotic places like Kunming, Belem and Kabale. With PLEC assistance I was able to return to Tumam, 'my village' in Papua New Guinea and do what I had always wanted to do, understand the shifting cultivation system properly.

I managed to slow Harold down only once. One night Harold, I and Ken Lockwood, our technician, later tragically killed in a car accident, were working late in the Coombs. Ken came into my room to show me how it was possible to send messages to other computer terminals connected to the Coombs server (no PCs then). We could hear Harold banging away at a great rate on his terminal a few doors down the corridor. Harold was largely computer-illiterate and made little effort to understand how computers worked. He just used them. Ken knew the address of his terminal. We sent him a message that appeared to come from the server: 'Please type slower, you are causing the Coombs computer a problem'. A muttered profanity emerged from Harold's room, but the typing slowed down noticeably. We send another message, 'Not that slow. Speed up a bit'. An even louder exclamation erupted from the room, but he enjoyed the joke and told it against himself many times.

Although Human Geography had its very own neurotics, none compared to Anthropology's Derek Freeman. Then as now, aspirants for chairs in Coombs visited and gave a seminar. Possibly the most outstanding memory I will take from Coombs is of a seminar given by Kenelm Burridge, who had applied for the Chair in Anthropology. During the seminar in Seminar Room C, Derek took exception to Ken Burridge's use of the word 'redemption', which Derek said was a religious term that should have no place in anthropology. What followed was the most exciting debate I have ever witnessed. Burridge was a conservative Catholic English scholar with an ANU PhD, deeply concerned with why Papua New Guineans became involved in 'cargo cults'. I had found Burridge's book *New Heaven, New Earth* particularly insightful and sympathetic in my own struggle to understand millenarianism, so I was not a disinterested observer. Freeman was a brilliantly crazed New Zealander with a Cambridge PhD, convinced that the primitive structures of the human brain explained much human behaviour. Burridge ignored Freeman's piercing *ab hominem* jibes and calmly debated him point by point. For sheer intellectual brilliance and adrenalin-producing tension, it will take a lot of beating.

Shutting my eyes and thinking back over 30 years in Coombs, I see a kaleidoscope of faces that I can no longer put names to: cleaners who almost always spoke the language of the latest Australian migrants; nightwatchmen, one of whom had been in New Guinea during the war, but when asked where he been, looked distraught and said he didn't know but it was awful; a student, now the head of a US geography department, who when her pedantic supervisor had changed her draft chapter back to what she had written originally for the third time, opened the window of his room and screamed into the courtyard until help came running; the students in a department, males and females, who exchanged spouses in a spectacular display of marital rearrangements; the cartographers, from those who worked with drawing paper, pens and ink, to those who work today in a completely pen-less office; the research assistants, often cleverer than the academics, always female, and always under-acknowledged; the technicians who had to move from dark rooms and developer, to Ethernet cables and mother boards; and the School administrators who had to put up with arrogance and rudeness from some academics and had to wage a fight that continues into the present with an inefficient and bloated central administration.

Coombs, with its maze of endless corridors that bring you back to where you started makes you wonder why we took it all so seriously at the time. As Oskar Spate used to say, 'You don't have to be solemn to be serious'.

Some of the staff of Human Geography in 1980 at a farewell for David Drakakis-Smith. Their later careers demonstrate how time in the School was often the prelude to significant careers elsewhere.

Back row left to right:
David Drakakis-Smith, later Professor of Geography, Keele University, UK and Research Professor of Geography, University of Liverpool.
Peter Rimmer, later Professor, RSPAS; Professor of Global Logistics, Inha University, Korea.
Nigel Thrift, later Professor of Geography, University of Bristol; Professor of Geography and Head of the Life Sciences and Environment Division, University of Oxford; Vice Chancellor, University of Warwick.
Gerard Ward, later Director RSPacS.
Middle row left to right:
Michael Taylor, later Professor of Geography, Universities of Western Australia, Portsmouth, UK, and Birmingham.
Christopher Kissling, later Professor of Geography, Lincoln University, NZ.
Dean Forbes, later Professor of Geography, Adelaide University.
Front:
Richard Peet, later Professor of Geography, Syracuse University, USA.

CHAPTER 10

A Wurm Turned in Coombs

Darrell Tryon

When I entered the portals of the Coombs Building for the first time on 1 February 1965 as a research scholar in linguistics, I was mightily impressed by the newness and style of the double hexagon with its stylized Melanesian art facade.

I was more impressed, however, when I entered the office of Professor Stephen Wurm, who was soon to become the foundation professor of linguistics. For at that time linguistics and prehistory were still part of the Department of Anthropology and Sociology, headed by Professor John Barnes. [Linguistics and Prehistory became separate departments only in 1967].

Stephen Wurm's office, which I was later to inherit, was a veritable Alladin's cave. One entered when a small light flashed, signaling that Stephen was in, since the door had been sound-proofed. Not only that, the window of his office was completely covered over. In fact it was many years before I realized that there even was a window in his office. One entered a darkened room, lit only by a desk lamp. Through the partial obscurity one could make out a number of filing cabinets in the middle of the room, and ceiling to floor books lining all available wall space. There was just room for a single chair for visitors, all other spaces being occupied by either filing cabinets or a very large reel to reel tape recorder.

Stephen Wurm was a tall, handsome Austrian who had come to the then Research School of Pacific Studies from the University of Sydney in 1957. In Sydney he had worked with the Rev Dr Arthur Capell, the founder of Australian linguistics. However, Stephen's main goal was to survey, map and classify the languages of greater New Guinea, at that time almost totally unknown. He had the ear of the Director, Sir John Crawford, and funding for research was abundant.

So it was that the first research scholars Don Laycock, and Alan and Phyllis Healey, as well as Stephen himself, devoted themselves to surveying the unknown Papuan languages of the New Guinea highlands, followed shortly afterwards by Tom Dutton and Karl Franklin. When I arrived I was assigned to the Melanesian languages of the southwest Pacific, the languages of the Loyalty

Islands, a dependency of New Caledonia, in the first instance.

Don Laycock circa 1970s

Don Laycock was the first appointment to the Department, followed by the Dutchman Bert Voorhoeve, whose area of expertise was the Asmat people of West Irian. I was appointed in 1967, with a brief to survey the languages of the then New Hebrides, today Vanuatu, and later the Solomon Islands. Tom Dutton, whose area of specialization was the languages of the Papuan coast and hinterland, completed the quartet of young linguists who were to make up Stephen Wurm's initial team.

This team of field linguists had one thing in common, apart from their linguistic abilities: they were all six feet tall and of strong build. Perhaps this was no accident, for their physical strengths were constantly required as the famous publication series *Pacific Linguistics* gained momentum. Why, one might ask. The printing of *Pacific Linguistics* was carried out at the University Printery over near today's Law School. For some reason the paper for the printing of *Pacific Linguistics* had to be physically carried from the Coombs Building to the Printery. This was an arduous task, involving many many reams of paper. Our ingenious leader, Stephen Wurm, had a coffin-like trunk constructed, in which the reams of paper were placed, and then carried with some muttering on the part of the 'pall-bearers', through the front doors of the Coombs and down the road to the Printery, much to the amusement of onlookers.

Darrell Tryon with PNG High Commissioner Vincent Eri, Sir John Crawford and Stephen Wurm

Those were the days of the golf-ball electric type-writer, the pre-computer age, when carbon-copies and correction tape were *de rigueur*. The drafting and editing of manuscripts was a very different and sometimes hazardous operation compared to today. On one occasion my late friend and colleague, Jack Prentice, had almost completed laboriously typing the manuscript of his thesis on the Murut languages of Borneo. Before retiring to Lennox House for the night, he inadvertently left the final draft resting on top of the waste-paper basket in his office. When he returned the next morning, the waste-paper basket had been emptied and the final thesis draft nowhere to be seen. Panic ensued, with frantic phone calls to the cleaning staff supervisor, who confirmed that anything left in or on the waste-paper basket would have been removed and had in all likelihood already been dispatched to the dump for incineration. Jack and I leapt into a vehicle and raced to the dump, where there were men busy consigning waste paper to the flames. As Jack sprinted towards the incinerator, he saw that one of the men had his draft thesis in his hand and was just about to fling it into the fire. Jack's screams stayed the hand of the incinerator attendant and the thesis was restored to its distraught owner.

The 1960s and early 1970s saw a huge surge in research into the Papuan and Austronesian languages of New Guinea and the southwest Pacific, as the number of research students steadily increased in the Department. By 1975, Stephen Wurm and his team of intrepid field linguists were ready to attempt a first synthesis of the languages of New Guinea, resulting in the publication of a massive four-volume set of books published by Pacific Linguistics, one of the proud moments in the life of the Department.

This was to lead to the compilation and publication of the first of a series of linguistic atlases, the *Atlas of Languages of the Pacific* (editors Stephen Wurm and Shirô Hattori), in two parts, sponsored by the Australian Academy of the Humanities and the Japan Academy (1981, 1983). This atlas became the standard reference work for over two decades and is only now undergoing a thorough updating and revision. Since the first atlas there have appeared several more from the Wurm stables, a Language Atlas of China, another on the Languages of Korea, one on the Languages of Intercultural Communication and two on Endangered Languages of the World.

Stephen Wurm retired in 1988, to be succeeded by Andrew Pawley, although Stephen continued his linguistic peregrinations around the world almost right up until his final illness. Stephen's winter absences from Canberra, usually from May until September, were often the subject of much humour, especially upon Stephen's return. For he never failed to return without hair-raising tales of his narrow escape from death at the hands of bandits or pirates. Of course, many of these tales had a linguistic spin, since Stephen was one of the most remarkable polyglots ever to grace these shores. He claimed to be able to speak fifty languages, and his colleagues in the Linguistics Department were convinced that he had a mastery of at least thirty, including Hungarian, German, French, Spanish, Turkish, Chinese, Arabic and Russian, to say nothing of Papua New Guinean languages such as Kiwai, and Australian Aboriginal languages from northern New South Wales and Queensland.

One of Stephen's Russian friends, Vladimir Bjelikov, tells the story of Stephen's linguistic ability foiling the KGB in St Petersburg back in the Soviet days. Stephen was on his way from his hotel to the university to visit a well-known Russian professor when he dropped his city map on the bridge across the Neva River. As he picked it up he was greeted by a policeman who informed him in Russian that the distinguished Soviet professor was waiting for him in his office at the university. Stephen was evidently quite impressed by the efficiency of the KGB, so decided to play a trick on them, a dangerous undertaking at the best of times.

Once Stephen had completed his visit to the university, he walked back to his hotel, which he knew very well would be bugged. So he went into his bathroom and said in Russian the equivalent of 'All right, boys, this is what the real story is'. He then proceeded to speak excitedly in Kiwai, a language of Papua New Guinea, completely outside the competence of the KGB. Stephen chuckled to himself, left St Petersburg the next day, and thought no more about it.

Not so his friends at the KGB. Having exhausted their linguistic resources without success, they contacted the language experts at the Russian Academy of Science in Moscow in an endeavour to decipher the secret recording of Stephen's baffling message. To no avail, however, as none of the Academicians had the slightest inkling of which language Stephen had been speaking. It was not until the post-Soviet era that Bjelikov asked Stephen about the matter, and with much merriment was treated to a re-run of the Kiwai speech which stumped the KGB!

As noted above, Stephen's winter migrations were the subject of much comment and humour around the School, although sometimes the humour was a little strained, as was the case with a well-known Dutch Jesuit linguist and theologian, John Verhaar. John had visited the Linguistics Department in the Coombs on a number of occasions. On one particular visit, frustrated at having missed Stephen yet again he asked the linguists over morning tea:

Q: 'What is the difference between God and Stephen Wurm?'

A: 'God is everywhere. Stephen Wurm is everywhere except in Canberra'.

One of Stephen's greatest triumphs was his founding of *Pacific Linguistics* in 1963, begun with a small grant from the Director of the School in the sixties and seventies, Sir John Crawford. *Pacific Linguistics* has today produced well over five hundred titles and is by far the major international publisher on the languages and linguistics of the Asia-Pacific region. In the 1960s, 70s and early 80s. The *Pacific Linguistics* operation employed an increasing number of typists, varitypists and editorial assistants. In the early years these devoted and skilled production staff included Hilda Leach, Sally Sinisoff, Nora Mason, Sue Tys, and Jeanette Coombes (still faithful to her post thirty years later), and later Christine Billerwell, Miriam Curnow, Mary Craft, Judy Gilman, Mira Kwasik, Judy Wise, Elaine Sommer, Diane Stacey, Evelyn Winburn, and Ling Matsay, as well as Basil Wilson and Joan Burnie. The cartography was ably produced in the early days by Hans Gunther and his staff in the cartographic unit of the School, especially Keith Mitchell, Leo Pancino and Ian Heyward. However, the cartographer upon whom the major atlas production work fell was the very talented Swiss, Theo Baumann. Theo was to draw all of the maps for at least six major language atlases over a twenty-year period, on the Pacific, China, Korea, the Languages of Intercultural Communication, and two on Endangered Languages, commissioned by UNESCO. The research assistant who worked tirelessly on the Language Atlas of China was Mei Wah Lee (later known as Mei Smith).

Mira Kwasik first joined the Pacific Linguistics staff as a newly-arrived Polish migrant. Her job was to receive and record manuscripts and communicate with authors. While in later years her command of English was excellent, there were a few infelicities in the beginning. In fact a couple of authors were prompted by her letters to enquire whether Mira might be Japanese. Not so of course. One of her better efforts, which resulted in a prompt response from a number of authors was a form letter to contributors informing them that 'the deathline for the receipt of manuscripts is…'.

One of the great characters in the Department of Linguistics was the indomitable Lois Carrington, an eagle-eyed research assistant, copy editor, author and mother/maternal aunt to staff and students alike. Lois joined the department as a research assistant after Pauline Chant and Basil Wilson, sometime in the late 1970s, and rendered great service right up until her retirement in the late 1990s. Just after World War II she was employed as an English teacher on migrant ships coming from Europe to Australia. Later she and her Polish migrant husband George were to spend some time working in Papua New Guinea, returning to Canberra after PNG independence in 1975. She was a well-known and respected figure in the Coombs building. Her bibliography of Papua New Guinea linguistics is still widely consulted today.

One cannot conclude these reminiscences of the Department of Linguistics without mentioning Annegret Schemberg, who succeeded Hilda Leach as Stephen Wurm's amanuensis. Annegret, who has been a member of the Coombs staff for more than thirty years, hails from Germany.

Perhaps it is the international and multicultural staff and students who have worked and studied in the Department of Linguistics since its inception which have made it such a vibrant and successful department. For apart from the Australians (such as Don Laycock and Tom Dutton), there have been Dutch (Bert Voorhoeve), Vietnamese (Nguyen Dang Liem and Tran Huong Mai), New Zealanders (Darrell Tryon, John Bowden and Andrew Pawley [born in Tasmania, but migrated to New Zealand aged two]), Estonians (Sally Sinisoff), Indonesians (Ling Matsay, Han Kartawinata), Chinese (Mei Wah Lee), French (Jacques Guy), Poles (Mira Kwasik), Japanese (Ritsuko Kikusawa), Americans (Charles Grimes, Jeff Marck), English (Hilda Leach, Jack Prentice, David Birk, Malcolm Ross), Irish (Basil Wilson, Joan Burnie), Papua New Guineans (Otto

Nekitel), and a constant stream of visiting scholars from all over the Asia-Pacific region.

It is this superb mix of Australian and international staff and students which has characterized not only the Department of Linguistics, but the whole Research School of Pacific and Asian Studies right from its beginnings more than fifty years ago.

CHAPTER 11

Northern Exposure: The New Guinea Research Unit

R.J. May

Some time in late 1971, after a frustrating day at the Reserve Bank (where I was then senior economist in the Papua New Guinea Department), I came across an advertisement for the position of field director with the ANU's New Guinea Research Unit (NGRU) in Port Moresby, and decided to apply. I wrote to my former Nuffield College supervisor in Oxford, Sir Norman Chester, asking if he would act as a referee. He promptly wrote back asking why on earth someone with a promising career in the Reserve Bank would think of giving it up to go to Papua New Guinea! From a career point of view he might have been right, but by that stage I had been seduced by Papua New Guinea, and in any case the Reserve Bank was no longer what it had been when 'Nugget' Coombs was governor. So, auspiciously, on 1 April 1972 I joined NGRU.

At the time the Research School of Pacific Studies was established—in the aftermath of World War Two in the Pacific and with the beginning of awareness that Australia's colony to the north was about to begin the transition to independence—Papua New Guinea was a significant element of the School's agenda. In 1953, three ANU academics—Oskar Spate, Cyril Belshaw and Trevor Swan—were invited by the government 'to investigate the economic structure of the Territory with a view to suggesting gaps in knowledge which it is most essential to fill and lines of advance which hold most prospect of producing positive results'. Although research was not a particular concern of the group, it did note in passing that 'knowledge and informed discussion [were] probably lacking' in relation to the formulation of social objectives of policy in Papua New Guinea, and called for 'careful research and thoughtful thinking (*sic*)' as a foundation for 'intelligent social and economic policy'. Eight years later, in 1961—five years before the establishment of the University of Papua New Guinea (UPNG)—the School, then under the directorship of Sir John Crawford, created the New Guinea Research Unit (NGRU). Its mandate was 'to carry out work on problems of an inter-disciplinary nature which have both practical importance and scientific interest'.

The Unit had an executive officer (David Bettison) initially based in Canberra and a research fellow (Nigel Oram) looking after operations in Papua New

Guinea. Operations in Papua New Guinea included assistance to ANU and other visiting foreign researchers. Bettison and Oram were joined by a young Ron Crocombe. The NGRU was 'controlled' (the word used in contemporary ANU documents) by a committee comprising Sir John Crawford, John Barnes, Jim Davidson, Harold Brookfield and David Bettison. Bettison headed NGRU until 1965 when Crocombe replaced him as field director.

The Unit's early research focus was on internal migration and urbanization (subjects which remained central to the Unit's work throughout its existence), and land use and productivity, and emphasis was placed on 'the interdisciplinary and applied character of the Unit's work'. Some of those engaged in the current debate about land in Papua New Guinea would do well to revisit the well informed field-based research of this period, contributors to which included, as well as Oram and Crocombe, Dawn Ryan, Nancy Bowers, L.L. Langness, Diana Howlett, Anton Ploeg and Sachiko Hatanaka. Following receipt of a 'generous grant' from the Rural Credits Development Fund of the Reserve Bank of Australia, research was extended to include subsistence agriculture and cash cropping. Early studies in these areas were carried out by Peter Krinks, Ian Teo Fairbairn, Bob Kent Wilson, Ben and Ruth Finney and Eric Waddell, who brought a range of disciplinary backgrounds to the field, and this tradition was subsequently maintained by T.K. Moulik, Don and Jill Nash Mitchell and Jocelyn Powell.

Administrative Staff of the New Guinea Research Unit 1966. *From left to right:* Sylvia Saevaru, Shirley Matthew, J.B. Toner and Helen Gray

In 1964 NGRU coordinated a major study of the elections for the first Legislative Assembly (which replaced a mostly appointed Legislative Council). This was the first of an unbroken series of studies of Papua New Guinea's national elections, in which ANU scholars have been continuously involved. Crocombe and others from the ANU and the Reserve Bank of Australia also initiated a lively debate about economic development strategies, following a World Bank report in 1965, generally endorsed by the Australian administration, which was widely seen as favouring expatriate-led development over indigenous participation in the cash economy.

Dissemination of research by Unit staff and others was seen as an important function of NGRU, and in 1963 the first of a series of some 46 *New Guinea Research Bulletins* was published, on *The Erap Mechanical Farming Project*, by Crocombe and G.R. Hogbin. Later, a series of summaries of selected monographs, in simple English, Tokpisin and Hiri Motu, was added, and in 1975 a discussion paper series.

In 1967 the NGRU, UPNG, and Administrative College collaborated in organizing the first of the celebrated Waigani Seminars, which came to provide a focus for debate on a range of issues in the lead-up to independence in the Melanesian island states. A selection of papers from the first Waigani Seminar, which was on 'New Guinea in Transition; indigenous participation in business, industry, politics and society', was published as *New Guinea Research Bulletin No.20*. The full papers from later seminars were edited by the NGRU and published jointly by UPNG and ANU. Three years later these same institutions met to discuss ongoing and prospective future social science research.

The NGRU's original premises were in the Port Moresby suburb of Badili, where the colonial administration had maintained a staff mess. In 1968 it moved to a new building at Waigani, across from the newly established UPNG. At the opening of the new building a breadfruit tree was planted below the main entrance, to mark the occasion. Among those attending the ceremony was Tongan historian the late Sione Latukefu, then a lecturer at UPNG. As Latukefu saw it, the breadfruit tree was planted without the ritual necessary for its healthy growth, and I am told he came back later that evening, dug up the tree, whose roots were still encased in plastic, and replanted it, after he had removed the plastic bag which had been left on at the official planting and performed the appropriate Tongan ceremony.

Following Crocombe's departure for the University of the South Pacific, the NGRU directorship was taken over in 1970 by Marion Ward, whose husband R.G. Ward, then Professor of Geography at UPNG, subsequently became director of the School. Two years later I became the Unit's fourth, and last, field director. By then, the NGRU establishment had peaked at eight research fellows, one research officer, and three research assistants. In 1974 the Unit appointed its first Papua New Guinean academic, Boio Bess Daro, who produced a discussion paper on Josephine Abaijah and the Papua Besena movement.

There was a small general staff, mostly Papua New Guinean, led by a field manager, the enigmatic Jim Toner. Toner later became the first field manager of the ANU's North Australia Research Unit, which was largely modeled on the NGRU. On his retirement in 1993 he listed among his memories of NGRU 'being asked to accompany a Senior Fellow in Anthropology as Minder at an evening meeting with [a particular Minister] whom she was convinced had arranged it for no other reason than to Carry Leg at the Gateway Hotel'.

One of the general staff was Oruga, the gardener. Oruga, an Eastern Highlander, periodically borrowed (and mostly repaid) small amounts of money from me, and dropped in regularly to check on the balance of our transactions—more a social call than a business appointment. On one occasion he came by while I was briefing a visiting World Bank mission. I tried to gesture to him, by a movement of the head, that I was busy and he should come back later; he got the message but gestured back that it was OK, he could wait. The World Bank team found this a little disconcerting, and I eventually had to interrupt the meeting to deal with Oruga: '*E, apinun.* [nodding to the World Bank officials] *Dinau, em i haumas nau?*' '*Mi no save gut; tu kina samting?*' '*Em nau. Orait, mi bekim long Trinde*' translated as, 'G'day. How much is my loan, now?' 'I'm not sure. About two kina?' 'OK. I'll pay you back on Wednesday'. This was, I think, one of the World Bank's first encounters with micro finance in Papua New Guinea.

The 1970s were an exciting time in Papua New Guinea. Following the 1972 elections, Michael Somare became chief minister of the first fully elected government of Papua New Guinea. Self government followed in 1973 and independence in 1975. The new government lacked experience but had enthusiasm and vision. In seeking to draft and carry out an ambitious agenda of reform and democratic consolidation, the Somare government sought expert advice from a variety of sources, including NGRU researchers: David Stone became a permanent consultant to the pre-independence Constitutional Planning Commission (CPC); Ross Garnaut (the first new appointment while I was field director, although Marion Ward had appointed him as a temporary research assistant earlier) was a member of the Bougainville Renegotiation Team and the Tariff Advisory Committee before being seconded to the Department of Finance in 1975; Marilyn (now Dame Marilyn) Strathern assisted in the preparation of village courts legislation and some aspects of law reform; Diana Conyers was attached to the Central Planning Office to help organize district planning in Morobe and subsequently helped establish the provincial government in Bougainville and the Village Development Task Force; I served on the board of the Bank of Papua New Guinea and provided some assistance to the CPC; and the Unit was part of a government-led Joint Programme of Studies in the Transport Process, which Marion Ward had helped initiate.

The NGRU (through Garnaut, myself and Michael Wright) also collaborated with UPNG in a major nationwide study of internal migration and urbanization, which had significant policy implications. Indeed it was a salutary experience, in talking with Papua New Guinean politicians—some of them at that time barely literate—and people in villages, to have to answer questions about what use our research was to them. One research fellow appointed in the latter days of NGRU applied to do work on 'infant precosity', but was persuaded to modify his research focus and ended up producing one of the first field-based studies of the village court system.

UPNG itself was a hive of nationalist rhetoric and activity, drawing committed scholars from around the world. The Waigani Seminars attracted prominent international speakers, emerging Melanesian political leaders, and large crowds of students and interested locals. The 1972 seminar (the organization of which I inherited from Marion Ward) had as keynote speakers Ivan Illich, René Dumont and Lloyd Best, and included on the program many of the emerging nationalist leaders of the region.

In 1973 the then Director, Anthony Low, wrote of the NGRU: 'There has been no more successful socio-economic research institute in a third world country during its period of terminal colonialism'. But with independence approaching, and UPNG well established, it was decided within RSPacS that it was no longer appropriate to maintain NGRU in Papua New Guinea, and initiatives were taken to hand the Unit over to the Papua New Guinea government. (During this process—which included a brief review of disputed land titles—I was surprised to find that plans drawn up for NGRU in 1967 provided for tennis courts and a swimming pool.) During 1974–75 discussions were held with relevant parties in Papua New Guinea and I took part in the drafting of legislation for a Papua New Guinea Institute of Applied Social and Economic Research (IASER). The transition was accomplished in 1975 and IASER was formally launched on 1 January 1976; I was invited to stay on as foundation director of the new Institute. IASER was subsequently expanded to include the Institute of Papua New Guinea Studies initiated by Ulli Beier, and UPNG's Education Research

Centre, and was renamed National Research Institute (NRI). The ANU has retained close links with IASER/NRI; several ANU scholars—including Anthony Regan, Sinclair Dinnen and Colin Filer—are 'graduates' of IASER/NRI, and in 2005 I returned to NRI for three months as an AusAID-funded adviser. Sad to say, the breadfruit tree died after my departure in 1978, but in its place a handsome flowering tree is flourishing.

CHAPTER 12

On the Wrong Side of Coombs?

John Ravenhill

My introduction to the International Relations department in the Research School of Pacific and Asian Studies came on my very first day at work in Australia. I had just arrived from the United States to take up a lectureship at the University of Sydney and was sitting in a grimy empty office overlooking Redfern station (a long way removed from the pictures of the harbour in the University's publicity). Having been interviewed over the phone for the Sydney post and not having set foot in the country previously, my only other exposure to university life in Australia had come courtesy of the Monty Python sketch on the Philosophy Department of the 'University of Woolamaloo'. There a new appointee from the United Kingdom, like me arriving to take up a position in political science, was disconcerted to find that all professors at Woolamaloo went by the name of Bruce. It was consequently with a mixture of amusement and great expectation that I received the news that Professor Bruce (J.D.B.) Miller from the ANU's Department of International Relations was visiting Sydney that day and was on his way to see me. In responding to the knock on my door, however, cognitive dissonance set in. For, instead of the Monty Python caricature of Australian academics all wearing outback hats complete with corks, a tall, distinguished-looking gentleman in a dark suit and a bow tie stood in the doorway.

Eight years were to pass before I had any further significant contact with the International Relations Department in Coombs, this coming initially from an invitation to interview for one of several posts the Department had advertised. I stayed overnight at University House and had left my room in what I anticipated would be plenty of time to make the interview appointment—before the Coombs curse struck. Several circumnavigations of the building later, I still could not locate the seminar room in which the interview was to take place. Fortunately, a friendly face at the front desk pointed me in the right direction: 'Wrong side of Coombs, mate!' I eventually found the seminar room, although by this time I was thoroughly rattled. Knowing that the other short-listed candidate was an internal applicant and presumably able to locate the room (an assumption I later learned that was not necessarily warranted), paranoia set in. Was this a conspiracy? It was a relief to find that under Gerry Ward's directorship, the competition for advertised posts was real, and I was delighted to accept an offer of a Fellowship at ANU.

John Ravenhill, 1994

International Relations was in a rebuilding phase in 1990 when I took up my appointment. Bruce Miller had retired and the Department had been weakened by a series of developments in the previous 15 years. Its other Professor, Hedley Bull, the country's pre-eminent theorist of international relations, had left ANU in 1977 to take up a Chair at Oxford University. The establishment of the Strategic and Defence Studies Centre in 1974 (see Des Ball's chapter in this volume) had drawn key personnel away from International Relations. While Jim Richardson, a leading scholar of international crises, had been lured away from his Chair in the Faculties to a professorial fellowship in the Department, he had not been overjoyed to find that retirements from the Department had left him with primary responsibility for the Department's administration. These retirements, however, together with the Department's success in being awarded the initial contract to run a new Diploma for the Department of Foreign Affairs and Trade for its graduate trainees, afforded an opportunity to make several new appointments simultaneously.

Richard Leaver and Richard Higgott joined the Department at the same time as me. We shared interests in international political economy and in Australian foreign policy, and set about re-building the Department's international standing. One of our first successes was to win the inaugural competition held by the Australian Fulbright Commission for funding to stage an international conference. The papers from this conference were published as *Pacific Economic Relations*, the first of several volumes the Department produced in the 1990s that were to become standard references for work on international relations in the Asia-Pacific region.

The next step in rebuilding was filling the Chair that Bruce Miller had vacated. This was offered to Andy Mack, then Head of the School's Peace Research Centre. Andy is one of the great characters in the international relations profession, not just within Australia but internationally. He had enjoyed a colourful past before joining the academic world, with experience as a fighter pilot, as a radio journalist for the BBC, as a meteorologist in Antarctica, and as a diamond prospector in Sierra Leone, and is an accomplished yachtsman (with staff and graduate students benefiting from invitations to spend time on his boat). While at the Peace Research Centre, he had been more successful than any other member of the School in raising research funding from international foundations.

It would be difficult to imagine two more dissimilar characters than the two professors of international relations in the first half of the 1990s: the flamboyant Andy Mack and the taciturn Jim Richardson. But they worked together very well as a team. Both were not only tolerant of but encouraging of diversity in approaches to the study of international relations. They created an extremely happy working environment for staff and students alike, despite the difficult period that the School was experiencing at the time.

The Department also worked closely with the Northeast Asian Programme, a small unit headed by Stuart Harris, with three other researchers, James Cotton, Greg Austin and Garry Klintworth (the former a specialist on Korea; the latter two on China). Stuart had returned to ANU after a stint as permanent secretary of the Department of Foreign Affairs and Trade, and brought a wealth of expertise to the Department—especially on Australian foreign policies, on political and economic integration in the region (Stuart having been a long-time participant in the Pacific Economic Cooperation Council), and on China. And like Andy and Jim, Stuart encouraged independent thinking and has always been very generous in the time he gives to postgraduate students. With the ending of funding for the Northeast Asia programme, Stuart joined the Department as a Visiting Fellow.

As with most other areas of the School, the funding difficulties of the mid-1990s took their toll on the Department. In fact, the Department was more severely affected than most in RSPAS, unluckily having posts fall vacant because of retirements and resignations (including those of Richard Leaver and Richard Higgott, who left for Flinders and Manchester respectively) during the various hiring freezes of this period. The Department was reduced to one half of the size it had been in the 1980s. Despite the good relations that existed within the Department, morale suffered. This was exacerbated by the then Director's unwillingness to accept the logic of the compromise that had enabled a department of International Relations to exist within a regionally focused School from that School's foundation—that such a department inevitably must combine work on the global with that on the national and the regional if it is to make sense of developments within the region and to sustain an international reputation for its work.

Why a Department of International Relations would be located within the School of Pacific and Asian Studies rather than in the Research School of Social Sciences is one of those ANU mysteries that in the absence of any rational explanation is typically described as an historical accident. ANU lore has it that the founding professor of political science and his counterpart in international relations had quarrelled, with International Relations consequently being located on the other (wrong?) side of Coombs. The individuals themselves and the cause of the dispute have long since been forgotten. But at a time when whole areas of the School were being cut—most notably our friends in Archaeology and Prehistory at the end of our corridor—and all departments were scrambling to safeguard their own interests, International Relations with its lack of country-specific focus was particularly vulnerable. At one point discussions were held about transferring International Relations to Social Sciences in exchange for Demography—but the School eventually realized that, given International R's track record of generating external income, it would suffer a significant financial loss should such a transfer take place.

The Department attracted substantial international support in its struggle for survival. For despite the financial problems and distracting School politics, it was enormously productive in the 1990s. A series of international conferences produced publications that set the agenda for debates on the international relations of the Asia-Pacific. Following the *Pacific Economic Relations* volume (Higgott, Leaver, and Ravenhill) were *Pacific Cooperation* (Mack and Ravenhill), *Asia-Pacific Security* (Harris and Mack), and *The Asian Financial Crises and the Global Financial Architecture* (Noble and Ravenhill). Henry Bienen, a political science professor at Princeton who went on to become President of Northwestern University, commented on visiting Canberra how many names in the Coombs corridor (Mack, Ravenhill, and Richardson in International Relations, and Harold Crouch in Political and Social Change) he had recognized from *World Politics*, the journal published by Princeton

University Press that is frequently ranked internationally as the top journal in political science. International Relations was the only department in the School to have its own book series with a commercial publisher—Allen and Unwin. Several of these volumes (including Greg Fry's *Australia's Regional Security*) made significant contributions to the debate on the redirection of Australia's foreign policies in the 1980s and 1990s. The Department also hosted the Cambridge University Press book series, *Cambridge Asia-Pacific Studies*, and at various times the *Australian Journal of International Affairs*. In 1999, the Department staged a lecture series, which brought a number of distinguished international speakers to Canberra, to celebrate its 50th anniversary, a landmark that other areas of Coombs curiously failed to commemorate.

The Department also made excellent use of those few positions that became available in this period. In appointing Peter Dauvergne, it pioneered the study of the international politics of the environment in the Asia-Pacific region (sustaining this initiative with the appointment of Lorraine Elliott when Dauvergne left, first for Sydney and then for a Canada Council Research Chair at the University of British Columbia). The Department also acquired an international reputation for its expertise on regional political economy during these years, with the appointments of Natasha Hamilton-Hart (a Southeast Asia specialist from Cornell) and Greg Noble (a Japan/China/Taiwan specialist from Berkeley). And Stephanie Lawson made important contributions on the new agenda in international relations on democratization, with special reference to the South Pacific and Southeast Asia.

The instability within the School hampered recruitment at the senior level, however. When Andy Mack finally tired of the apparently never-ending bureaucratic battles within the School in these years, and left to take up the position of Director of Strategic Planning in the Executive Office of the UN Secretary-General, the School twice failed to fill the vacant Chair. In the end, a post was advertised at a more junior level; we were delighted to recruit Chris Reus-Smit, whose Princeton book of his Cornell PhD thesis had established his international reputation as one of the leading exponents of constructivist approaches to international relations.

A Vibrant Corridor

Besides the difficulties of navigating the hexagons of Coombs, the comment most frequently made by visitors about the building is that it often seems deserted. With many academics on fieldwork, researching in libraries, or writing at home, and the number of support staff having shrunk significantly in the last decade, visitors frequently find that the corridors of Coombs have a *Marie Celeste*-like atmosphere. Not so that occupied by International Relations.

With large numbers of postgraduate students, the International Relations corridor has always been full of life.

For many years, International Relations was the only department in Coombs to run a Masters coursework programme. This had been established under the direction of Geoff Jukes with funding from the Ford Foundation to provide training for aspiring diplomats from the region. Greg Fry, Australia's leading specialist on the international relations of the South Pacific, has headed the programme, now renamed 'Graduate Studies in International Affairs' (GSIA), since the late 1980s. Under his enthusiastic direction, the programme has enjoyed enormous success, growing from an intake of around a dozen students a year to the current figure of over 80. Graduates from the programme have gone on to PhDs in many of the world's leading universities while others have taken up senior positions in departments of foreign affairs and trade in Australia and the region.

The GSIA programme has been the major source of growth in Department staffing in the last five years. Two of the Department's former PhD students, Cindy O'Hagan and Paul Keal, have returned to the Department in posts funded by the GSIA, joining Heather Rae who came to the Department from Deakin University. Kathy Morton, another ANU PhD, also rejoined the Department in a School-funded position as a China specialist. Len Seabrooke, an extraordinarily productive student of international political economy, came to the Department on a postdoctoral fellowship, and enjoyed immediate success in winning the only ARC Postdoctoral Fellowship awarded in the social sciences in 2004. With the arrival of Bill Tow, a leading international scholar on Asia-Pacific security, at the start of 2005 the Department had a full quota of staff for the first time in nearly twenty years. This, combined with record student numbers in the GSIA, and continuing strong enrolments in the PhD program found the International Relations corridor in Coombs to be bursting at the seams, with Department activities spilling over into the new Coombs extension.

The International Relations corridor in Coombs has also housed support staff, some of whom have been in the Department for much longer than most of its academics. Of particular note here are Robin Ward, who retired as the Department's Research Officer a couple of years ago after nearly three decades of service; Lynne Payne, who now works exclusively on IT issues but who had for many years the principal responsibility for preparation of the Department's publications and more recently its web pages; and Amy Chen, the Department's administrator since the mid-1990s. The Department has also been well served by a succession of administrators in the GSIA programme: Nora Barrow, Jan Preston-Stanley, and currently Farnaz Salehzadeh and Barbara Bryan.

The Department was delighted when the Review Committee that examined research and teaching at ANU in 2004 recognised its achievements. The report of the Committee commented that International Relations in RSPAS is an 'excellent department' and noted that the 'Department demonstrates a strong showing in international theory...[and] strength in both international security and international political economy, the two leading sub-fields in International Relations'. The Department has every reason to believe that, having survived the upheavals of the 1990s, it can look forward to maintaining its leading role in the vibrant intellectual life of Coombs in the future.

CHAPTER 13

Prehistory: a Late Arrival

Jack Golson

In the wings

At the end of the 1950s and the beginning of the 1960s archaeology, or prehistory as it was officially called, was one of a number of new disciplines to make a modest appearance in RSPacS, others being linguistics and biogeography. They were established as single appointments in existing departments, linguistics and prehistory in the Department of Anthropology and Sociology, biogeography in the Department of Geography, where there was already a physical geographer in the redoubtable person of Joe Jennings. They all found a supportive environment, to the extent that by the end of the 1960s they had become large enough to stand on their own feet and were encouraged to do so.

I took up the archaeological appointment in May 1961, with a general responsibility for devising a programme of research in the archaeologically underdeveloped fields of Australian and Southwest Pacific prehistory and with a particular commitment to Papua New Guinea, where the first serious archaeological work had taken place only two years previously. It was an endeavour that, if justice was to be done to it, needed the cooperation of a range of disciplines and I found a wealth of relevant talent and experience in Canberra on which to call. In the Research School there was a concentration of effort on the ethnography and human geography of the Papua New Guinea highlands, which had been discovered by the outside world barely a generation before, a situation that, as has been said of similar situations elsewhere, allowed prehistory to be virtually caught alive. In other areas of the region there was a longer history of contact and historians in the Department of Pacific History were ready with help and advice about European sources on contact situations. In the Department of Geography there were physical and biogeographers working, particularly in the PNG highlands, on the reconstruction of the past landscapes and environments in which the prehistoric subjects of interest to the archaeologist had lived and with which they had interacted. There were scientists in CSIRO active in field research in Papua New Guinea and tropical Australia on climate, landscapes and land systems, soils, botany, ethnobotany and wildlife. The then Bureau of Mineral Resources, Geology and Geophysics was also active in Papua New Guinea as well as Australia in geological mapping and in regional tectonics and volcanism.

In the mid-1960s I held seminars in the RSPacS hexagon drawing on people from within this range under the working title of 'Materials for a prehistory of New Guinea'. A few years later a more systematic exercise of similar type focused on the Australian field, organised by John Mulvaney, the second academic appointment in archaeology at ANU, and myself. Its proceedings were published in early 1971 by ANU Press under the title of *Aboriginal man and environment in Australia*. This now ranks as a landmark book, which its editors find gratifying but unexpected.

Jack Golson delivering a lecture in 1985

Meanwhile a number of specialist appointments were made to support the work of the academic staff and research scholars recruited to carry out our archaeological brief. The first was that of Wal Ambrose, who was to establish a laboratory for the preparation and conservation of finds from the field and a photographic studio and darkroom. The second appointment was that of Ron Lampert as field officer, responsible for field survey, especially in the archaeological unknown that was Papua New Guinea, in order to assess the potential of areas that seemed archaeologically promising on the basis of information we collected from a range of sources. Later, towards the end of 1966, came the appointment of Win Mumford to set up a studio for archaeological draughting and illustration.

A significant development was the establishment of a radiocarbon dating laboratory on campus to meet the need of the new disciplines of archaeology and biogeography for dates at the younger end of the geological timescale. This was a cooperative venture between RSPacS and people in the then Research School of Physical Sciences who would shortly form the Research School of Earth Sciences. Henry Polach from the New Zealand Radiocarbon Laboratory arrived in 1965 to set the operation up. He and subsequent staff were members of RSPacS but housed in RSES.

John Mulvaney joined us from Melbourne in 1965 to lead work in Australian archaeology, while at the end of the decade Rhys Jones was recruited from Sydney for Australia and hunter-gatherer studies and Les Groube from Auckland for the Pacific and small island colonisation. In between we advertised a post in the field of environmental archaeology broadly defined, an earnest of the intent to establish a science-based archaeology, providing in-house facilities where it was impossible to make cooperative arrangements with other departments or institutions. We appointed Con Key, a geologist who had done work with the Israeli Antiquities Service, and he came to specialise in the compositional analysis of pottery and the chemical fingerprinting of volcanic glass from New Guinea archaeological sites to provide evidence for trade and contact.

Rhys Jones circa 1990s

There was a strong Cambridge flavour to the archaeological unit that was being built, as there was to archaeological developments at other Australian universities at the time. This was understandable in the absence of any established department of regional archaeology in the country and the commitment of the Cambridge department to the study of world prehistory, but there can be little doubt that it represented a late manifestation of the imperial connection. The Cambridge links extended to both staff—Golson, Mulvaney and Jones—and graduate students. One of these, Peter White, was an Australian who, like Mulvaney before him, had gone to Cambridge for archaeological training, returning to do doctoral research at ANU and subsequently to pursue an influential archaeological career, mainly at the University of Sydney. Another Cambridge student of the early years, the Englishman, Jim Specht, returned to Australia after graduation at ANU to play a similarly important long-term role to White in a position at the Australian Museum. Students, of course, came from other parts of the world and a few of them chose to pursue their careers in Australia, like the American Brian Egloff who has worked and taught in the field of cultural heritage studies. There were also the first homegrown Australian students: Jim Allen from Sydney and Campbell Macknight, a student of Mulvaney at Melbourne. Both of them had topics at the interface of prehistory and history in Arnhem Land, the former looking at the British presence at Port Essington, the latter at the sites of Macassan trepangers along the Arnhem Land coast.

Most students were in the prehistoric field, working in the New Guinea highlands, lowlands and islands, New Caledonia and Tonga, as well as Arnhem Land. The hugely experienced field anthropologist Bill Stanner called all fieldwork in New Guinea 'meadowwork' in comparison with that in outback Australia and he no doubt would have described fieldwork in New Caledonia and Tonga the same way. Wherever they worked, however, students contributed equally with members of staff to advances in knowledge. Thus student work was soon to confirm and extend Mulvaney's very recent demonstration of the late Pleistocene antiquity of human settlement in the Australasian region, 20,000 years and rising, in different circumstances of climate and environment from those of the present. By the end of the decade Mulvaney himself was in Sulawesi working with Indonesian colleagues on a project exploring some of the background to Australian prehistory and a student of his, Ian Glover, was in Portuguese Timor partly with the same purpose.

Others of us were in active cooperation with Donald Walker and his students in biogeography, who were reconstructing vegetation and climatic histories through pollen analysis in the New Guinea highlands. In 1966 Ambrose and myself joined Lampert and Jocelyn Wheeler (now Powell), one of Walker's students, in investigations at a swamp in the Wahgi Valley being developed as a tea plantation. The excavations produced evidence of swamp drainage for agriculture at the then surprisingly early date of 2000 years ago, associated with well-preserved wooden artefacts and plant remains such as do not normally survive on dryland archaeological sites. The discoveries led to a departmental commitment for the next 30 years, focused on a swamp at Kuk Agricultural Research Station, to the study of the origins and development of highlands agriculture. They also led Wal Ambrose into the application of freeze-drying to the preservation of waterlogged archaeological timbers, in which he was to make a wide reputation.

Another important research linkage of these early years came when Jim Bowler from Melbourne joined Joe Jennings as the second geomorphologist in the Department of Geography. He was interested in the landforms of the Willandra Lakes area of western New South Wales for their evidence of past climates and environments and was soon reporting to his archaeological colleagues the abundance of the associated archaeological evidence, including human skeletal material of late Pleistocene antiquity at Lake Mungo.

All this activity took place after the two hexagons of the original Coombs complex had been planned and, together with parallel developments in bio- and physical geography, it presented the School with the need for space for laboratories and other facilities which the Coombs then being built was unable to meet. As departments of RSPacS and RSSS moved during the mid-60s from the Old Hospital Buildings to their new quarters, the archaeologists stayed behind and took over a free-standing building, the Old Nurses' Quarters, for their purposes. I remember Bob Horan, one of the School adminstrators, coming to see me after a high-level meeting in the Coombs Building had raised the question as to how the archaeological unit that for a couple of years seemed to have been been managing with a couple of rooms was now putting in a request for 22. The success of the case that was made in reply provided the opportunity to plan for an extension of the Coombs which the authorities now realised was necessary. Known as the laboratory wing, this extension was a finger pointing south from the southernmost angle of the RSPacS hexagon and built in the same style.

The ground floor of the laboratory wing was allocated to the archaeologists, who, as the Department of Prehistory, were also to occupy some of the adjacent hexagon's bottom floor to the left and right of the laboratory extension. In part of the hexagon's southwest leg facilities were provided for the reception, washing, drying, sorting and, when necessary, quarantining of excavated material brought in from the field, as well as for the housing of surveying and excavation gear. In the other direction the department came to occupy the whole of the hexagon's southeast and eastern legs, where most of the staff and all the scholars were to have their offices. This was a time when the entitlement of students to office space was under discussion and we were successful in arguing for separate offices for archaeology students, given the nature of their research materials.

The top two floors of the laboratory wing were to house bio- and physical geography, both the staff and the laboratories, as the Department of Biogeography and Geomorphology. The Radiocarbon Laboratory stayed physically with the earth scientists, though its personnel belonged to the Department of Prehistory.

On stage

The Department of Prehistory took up residence in the Coombs in late 1970 and settled down to 20 years or so of stability and solid work. There was a small core of tenured staff, a shifting complement of non-tenured staff and students and a number of technical and keyboard staff giving specialist and administrative support. Now that archaeology was firmly established at universities in Australia and New Zealand, non-tenured staff and students were as likely to be recruited regionally as from Britain or the United States. John Mulvaney moved on early to set up archaeology in the Faculty of Arts. Jim Allen, a former student who had gone on to teach prehistory at the new University of Papua New Guinea, and Alan Thorne from the University of Sydney joined Rhys Jones and myself on the tenured academic staff.

Research was organised round a few major lines of investigation, for which non-tenured staff and students were sought as posts became available. Allen developed projects in coastal and island New Guinea, culminating in the multi-institutional Lapita Homeland Project which had teams at work in targeted areas through the Bismarck Archipelago in 1985, with results that revolutionised not only knowledge but understanding of the region. Jones and his Australianist colleagues and students were associated with a varied range of projects from conventional archaeology to studies of hunter-gatherer subsistence and settlement in Arnhem Land and central Australia, with, in the early 1980s, a large archaeological project in Kakadu National Park for the Australian National Parks and Wildlife Service. Doug Yen, a leading student of Pacific food plants and the systems of their exploitation, joined the staff in the 1980s to lend his expertise to departmental projects in New Guinea and consider the implications of Aboriginal systems of plant use where the same genera and species were sometimes in use.

Alan Thorne and his students worked on different aspects of the physical anthropology of the ancient inhabitants of the Australasian region. His own particular study concerned early skeletal remains from Kow Swamp and Lake Mungo in the Riverina until these were transferred to Aboriginal custodianship in the 1990s.

Wal Ambrose took over Key's work on the chemical analysis of New Guinea obsidians. In collaboration with scientists of the Australian Atomic Energy Commission Research Establishment at Lucas Heights, he developed it as a powerful tool for the identification of the sources of the obsidians widely distributed by trade and exchange at archaeological sites in the western Pacific.

Departmental work in progress was a frequent topic at the weekly seminars, open to all, which were held jointly with Mulvaney's department in the Faculty of Arts. These were also occasions for presentations by visitors. They took place at 3 pm on Friday afternoon and continued in the University Staff Centre after 5 pm. They were known for their frank and critical exchanges. Students gave three presentations during their course: thesis defence, progress and completion. These were restricted to departmental members, except that students were entitled to invite appropriate outsiders. Because of the importance of student contributions to the fulfilment of the departmental brief, we launched a monograph series, Terra Australia, in the early 1970s primarily for the publication of the results of their doctoral projects.

The nature of the Research School itself was conducive to a sense of identity among its members. Cross-departmental connections were strong because people were often working in related fields of research in the same geographical areas. The governance of the School was another integrating factor. A Faculty Board with two representatives from each department and a number of student representatives met monthly with the Director to discuss and make decisions about School and University matters and report back. Particularly when academic appointments came up for approval or at the twice yearly meetings where scholarship applications were competitively reviewed, one learnt a great deal about the research aims and programmes of other departments and came to deal in a collegial way with their interests.

The sense of collective endeavour at School and departmental levels carried over into other activities, notably in departmental cricket matches. These started as an annual fixture against Sydney University Anthropology Department, held in alternate years at grounds around Sydney and in the Canberra district. In between there were social matches against other departments of School or University. For a short period Prehistory could field a strong enough team to get challenges from beyond the University, including one from a Foreign Affairs XI who shamed us by actually turning up at the ground to play in whites. We continued in less exalted fashion until the final match against Sydney in the early 1990s. This took place at the Bradman Oval in Bowral, where Richard Mulvaney, John's son, a prehistory graduate himself, was, as he still is, Director of the Bradman Museum. The day concluded with dinner and dancing in the genteel setting of the Bundanoon Hotel. The entire experience seemed to epitomise the changing times.

Scene shifting

Jim Allen's departure in 1985 to take the chair of archaeology at La Trobe University and his replacement the following year by Matthew Spriggs, a graduate student of his and mine of less than 10 years previously, marked the beginning of gradual generational shift in the Department of Prehistory. This was itself overtaken by more rapid structural, organisational and financial changes in the middle 1990s that influenced every level of Research School activity. In the complex course of these the Department of Prehistory and the biogeographical half of the Department of Biogeography and Geomorphology came together to form the Department of Archaeology and Natural History, with reduced staff numbers but changed arrangements for funding that allowed a wider research agenda. The new Department occupies the laboratory wing, for whose existence the early success of the two disciplines now combined there was responsible.

Acknowledgments

I have talked with Wal Ambrose, John Burton and Jean Kennedy, members of the former Department of Prehistory, about this contribution and appreciate their thoughts.

John Barnes, who was Head of the Department of Anthropology and Sociology when I joined it in 1961, lent unstinting support and effort to the development of archaeology in the 1960s. Jim Davidson, Patrick Fitzgerald and Oskar Spate, other Heads of Department in RSPacS, gave their backing. Heads of School from John Crawford to Gerard Ward were equally supportive of the discipline and the department in which it became institutionalised.

My personal thanks go to all its members for 30 years of collegiality.

CHAPTER 14

We, the Ethnographers*

Kathy Robinson

The corridors of the Department of Anthropology in the Coombs Building are hung with large black and white photographs that celebrate well-loved anthropological images: Rotinese chanters in their dramatic hats, Trobriand Kula canoes with decorated prows; pigs awaiting slaughter in the New Guinea Highlands. For me, these images are a bit like family photos: mementos of a happily remembered past and a group of anthropologists senior to me with whom I share a collective identity and from whom I learned about the extended fieldwork that is the 'craft' of anthropology. Today's students don't have such a fond relationship to these photos, or the odd collection of ethnographic objects.

Every few years the students collectively protest about the images which for them represent an 'old-fashioned' anthropology from which that they want to distance themselves. However, the department retains its commitment to ethnographic field research in the nations of Asia and the Pacific as the core of our scholarly practice, although the time available to students (and staff) has shrunk as research funding becomes scarce and the government puts pressure on completion times for PhDs: the 22 months I spent in my doctoral fieldwork is no longer an option. The files of correspondence with department members in the '60s and '70s reveal a world that was in many ways more leisured—departmental secretaries (as they were then known) like Ann Buller (now Administrator, Division of Society and Environment) kept up a newsy correspondence, but also dealt with publications and administrative matters on behalf of academics on fieldwork, who sent long handwritten letters with correspondence to be typed and publications to be progressed.

The flavour of these halcyon days came back to me when a spray of dried bougainvillea popped out of a letter that Michael Young wrote from Papua New Guinea, the flower reciprocating the spray of wattle Ann had sent him, to remind him of the Canberra spring. The letters also reveal that fieldwork had more privations than we face now: Marie Reay details her intimate relationship

---

* A play on *We, the Tikopia: A Sociological Study of Kinship in Primitive Polynesia,* by Raymond Firth (one of the four Advisors to the establishment of the ANU).

with her cranky carburettor at Borroloola, Roger Keesing writes of his impending running-out of stationery. Ann Buller kept us supplied with necessities of life like toothpaste, vegemite and jam which were then unavailable in the remote regions of our fieldwork. Letters were written on ANU aerogrammes and much of the correspondence reveals the intermittent communication with Canberra.

Anthropology was one of the first departments established in what was then the Research School of Pacific Studies, and the early vision for what was then the Department of Anthropology and Sociology was laid out by the first professor S.F. Nadel in 1951. Recommended by Firth, Nadel had been a member of Malinowksi's famous seminar at the London School of Economics. Nadel's vision captures the flavour of the post-war period and the high expectations of academic research delivering a better world, exemplified in the professional H.C. Coombs himself. Nadel envisaged a research program focusing on social change in the Pacific (including notably the New Guinea Highlands) and Indonesia, as well as the 'assimilation' of the wave of post-war European immigrants. Indeed the first PhD graduate (in 1954) was Jean Craig (Jean Martin) who studied European immigrants in Goulburn and who later pioneered research on Vietnamese migration in the 1970s.

Kathryn Robinson on fieldwork with Indonesian colleagues circa 1980

After his untimely death Nadel was succeeded by John Barnes and Barnes saw the expansion of a research programme in Papua New Guinea, including significant work by linguists such as Stephen Wurm and archaeologists like Jack Golson who at that time were members of the Department. (The strong links with linguistics are best represented in 2005 in the research in linguistic anthropology conducted by Alan Rumsey in Papua New Guinea). Barnes was an innovative theorist of social structure and kinship, in the mode of British anthropology, and this theoretical approach stamped the work of the department in those early years. W.E.H. Stanner was appointed as a second Chair in 1964. He oversaw the development of an innovative research programme in aboriginal Australia. In the spirit of work by distinguished graduates of the Department like Marie Reay and Jeremy Beckett who pioneered studies of 'fringe dwellers' in the small towns of western NSW, Stanner's 1969 Boyer lectures *After the Dreaming* struck a blow against the policy position that had dominated anthropological advocacy, that of Sydney University Professor A.P. Elkin who saw the role of government to 'smooth the dying pillow' of the shattered remnants of aboriginal society. Stanner saw the fringe dwellers not as the detritus of history, but as its heroes who had reached out to engage with and accommodate white settlement. Stanner's lectures were presented as the freshest perspective to undergraduate students like myself, at the University of Sydney in the early 1970s. Many of my distinguished and beloved teachers: Jeremy Beckett, Michael Allen and Les Hiatt and Peter Lawrence were graduates of this department, putting the RSPacS stamp on the intellectual tradition at Sydney, which in the 1960s and 1970s was teaching the premier undergraduate anthropology course in Australian universities.

Jim Fox with his close friends from Termanu on the Island of Rote

An Indonesian anthropologist once leaned across a dinner table to say to me: 'Anthropology—it's a man's world Kathy', and this has certainly been true of the RSPAS Department. Marie Reay recorded her distaste for the actions of male 'god professors' in the 1992 book *Ethnographic Presents*, edited by Terence Hays. Indeed, in contrast to the scenes from the field adorning the corridors, the seminar room in the Coombs building named for Nadel has a stern portrait of the paterfamilias described by Michael Young and Judith Wilson as having 'dictatorial tendencies'. However, in the 1980s, the department hosted the formation of the Gender Relations Project, headed by Margaret Jolly, which has now become a Centre. The current group of students (about two-thirds female) comment on the unfavorable gender balance in the Department's academic staff (three women to six men) but change is evident to me when I remember that I was the only female of about ten students in the late 1970s.

Anthropology has produced a distinguished crowd of graduates, many of whom have gone on to make their own special mark on the field. I remember the *kretek* cigarette smoke that wafted through the corridors of the veteran Indonesian anthropologist, Koentjaraningrat, who was a visitor in 1979. Another distinguished Indonesian scholar, the late Masri Singarimbun, graduated from the department in 1965. Masri was awarded an honorary D Litt. in 1996 during the ANU's 50th anniversary year, in recognition of his significant scholarly career and contribution to policy debates in Indonesia. At the same ceremony, Judith Wilson, who joined the department as Stanner's research assistant, was awarded an honorary Masters for her contribution to the discipline. She can take credit for the high quality production standards of the journal *Canberra Anthropology*. Another distinguished graduate is the Tongan scholar and writer Epeli Hau'ofa who conducted doctoral research among the Mekeo of Papua New Guinea. (Another well-known scholar of the Mekeo, Mark Mosko, is the current Professor). Other notable graduates include Donald Tuzin (now professor at UC San Diego), Nancy Munn (University of Chicago), the late Peter Worsley and J.P. Singh Uberoi.

The Department of Anthropology has always attracted first rate and innovative scholars. When I was a PhD student, the Professor and Head was the late Roger Keesing, a second generation anthropologist who died very young (aged 57 soon after leaving the Department, at the same age as his anthropologist father Felix Keesing), but whom I always think of as having lived his life on fast forward. I remember visiting Roger's home while he sat writing his text book— still a standard text in introductory courses—in longhand on a pad balanced on his lap, while following my conversation with his wife Shelly Shreiner and also watching the football on TV. The handwritten drafts, legend has it, were typed up and barely corrected before being published. Roger was well known around campus as an enthusiastic and competitive tennis player—he wrote back from the Solomons in 1977 that he had won the Guadacanal tennis championships.

The late Derek Freeman was a fixture in the Department for many years; known to all students of my generation as the author of the concept of the kindred, a fundamental shift in the way the discipline thought about kinship (which my first year tutor had called the 'life blood' of anthropology). By the time I was a student, Derek had begun his flirtation with biological bases of behaviour, contesting the interest in culture that was central to the anthropology of American scholars like Keesing. In his view anthropology 'had its ladder up against the wrong wall' in seeking for cultural explanations of human behaviour, the answer obviously lying in our unique biology. His intellectual battle with cultural anthropology, personified in Margaret Mead, was the subject of David Williamsons' 1996 play *Heretic*, which characterized Derek as an iconoclast facing up to a unified wall of orthodoxy presided over by an all-powerful Margaret Mead, who was his nemesis in regard to authorized versions of Samoan social organization. He joined us in the tea corner one morning wearing black goggles that looked like half tennis balls with holes punched in them—his 'dragon fly glasses'. I am still not sure if he was 'taking the mickey' when he assured us these were the perfect fieldwork tool, in particular in situations where the research subjects did not like to be observed. Derek's idiosyncratic approach to scholarship and life and his resolute commitment to his own path mark a special feature of the Department: its intellectual breadth and the failure of a 'single school' to emerge in the significant theoretical work its scholars produced. Indeed, it would be difficult to find a single figure with the authority to regularize knowledge, as Derek portrayed Mead.

This intellectual diversity is personified in James J. (Jim) Fox who has been in the School since 1975. Derek was unstintingly committed to develop the Southeast Asian program of the Department, and he and Roger recruited Jim as a significant 'rising star' in Indonesian ethnography to this end. Their recruit certainly realized this goal. Jim became Head of Department in 1990, and Director in 1998. His major intellectual pursuits range from his classic ecological anthropological study, *Harvest of the Palm* (continued in his current interest in Indonesian fisheries), through his pathbreaking work on origin and precedence in the analysis of eastern Indonesian societies. He has produced a body of his own work, and supervised a large crop of PhD theses which have redefined the parameters of thinking about social organisation in Eastern Indonesia. In the late 1980s, Jim brought together a group of eminent anthropologists who worked with linguists, and archaeologists in a program of comparative research on the Austronesian speaking peoples. This has given rise to a series of books that are the definitive texts of the history, culture and social organization of Austronesian peoples. A third major strand of his work in the 1980s and 1990s was on Islam and pilgrimage in Java, and with another group of PhD scholars, he has redefined the parameters our understanding of the verities of Islamic practices in Java. Indonesia now represents about one third of the thesis topics of current research students, and Jim's legacy is continued through my own work and that of Andrew McWilliam (both graduates of the Department) on projects concerning (inter alia) eastern Indonesia, resource management and Islam.

The Department reflects an engagement with the diverse traditions of anthropology on a global scale, in both staff and students. This inclusive nature, represented in the embrace of a broad range of intellectual work, accounts for its ability to serve as a hub for the scholars who have passed through, as students and research fellows. There is a constant flow of students returning for some time to write, former members dropping in on their way to and from the field. When I came back to take up an appointment in 1995, one of my senior colleagues was discussing an incident with me which I couldn't remember: 'That's right—you've been away—only twenty years!' Coombs is like that—it draws people back.

Anthropology postgraduates still routinely undertake around 12 months fieldwork in a location in the Asia-Pacific region, and while some continue the tradition of documenting the lives of others in remote parts of the world, many now undertake studies in urban areas, and any field research is necessarily inflected by concerns for the impact of the global economy and associated 'global cultural flows'. We are still able to generously fund their fieldwork (relative to other Australian universities) even in these days when university finances are a constant anxiety. However, the maxim that 'there is nothing new under the sun' is evidenced by some hot correspondence concerning the failure of our much loved late Business Manager, Peter Grimshaw, to approve the use of University funds for the purchase of a departmental bicycle.

About half of our current enrolment of 40 postgraduate students originate from the region. Indonesian scholars have predominated but the sounds of Bahasa Indonesia are now being challenged by Chinese as the second language of our section of the Coombs. Andrew Kipnis and Nicholas Tapp have developed a significant China program, with students from the People's Republic of China and Taiwan, as well as Hong Kong and Singapore. We have had some of the finest young anthropologists from Papua New Guinea in recent years, and there is an increasing flow of scholars from Thailand. The department has developed a culture that encompasses both the varying anthropological traditions and cultural traditions that have formed the postgraduate scholars. That is, the commitment to honoring the life worlds of others extends to the intellectual approaches employed in writing anthropology. One of our students was writing on the belief system of his own Southeast Asian culture and had added footnotes explaining how anthropologists would have analysed or explained certain phenomena. Jim Fox was about to say to the student that he had written it back to front when he questioned himself, why should that be so? As anthropologists, we must be sensitive to the relativity and historical specificity of our own interpretative stances, and the folly of trying to enforce a single interpretive stance.

The centrality of fieldwork to Anthropology in RSPAS is perhaps no better signified than in the grand project of Michael Young (who retired in 1998): the first volume of his biography of Malinowski (often acknowledged as the 'father' of ethnographic research) published in 2003 won universal praise. He has also published a book of the beautiful fieldwork photos of F.E. Williams. Michael has set a high bench mark for ethnographic writing and he brought this focus to the role of editor of the department's journal *Canberra Anthropology* from 1977–1996. I now struggle to follow in his footsteps editing the journal, now renamed *The Asia Pacific Journal of Anthropology*.

In spite of the contemporary student criticism of the message indicated by the paintings on the wall, fieldwork is still the hallmark of an anthropology PhD, although current students are perhaps more likely to be conducting fieldwork in urban locations, or other 'sites of modernity.' The experience of being an anthropology student is enhanced by the 'multi-cultural' character of the Department and the chance to make links in the everyday working world with scholars who represent the cultures we study. In turn, those scholars who come from the poor countries of our region, where full-time research and writing is a luxury, benefit from the rich intellectual life of the Department, the School and the university. Many of these scholars have strengthened the culture of scholarship in their own countries and institutions, and, true to the original vision of the Research School of Pacific Studies, make significant contributions to social policy debates in their own countries.

CHAPTER 15

Real Australians in Economics

Ross Garnaut

Genesis

Tuesday afternoon, 1966, Seminar Room B in the Coombs Building was a welcoming place for a third year undergraduate with interests in development. I would slip in now and again to hear Max Corden discussing the new idea of 'effective protection'; Heinz Arndt on the Indonesian economy spinning out of control and now having a chance to spin back, and David Penny on whether this mattered in a Javanese village; Fred Fisk on primitive affluence in the Pacific; Scarlett Epstein on the village economy in New Britain; or, once, Bruce MacFarlane on the economics of the Yugoslav experiment in 'workers' control' of business.

David Bensusan-Butt may have been slightly published, but, we told each other with respect, Keynes had acknowledged his assistance in the forward of the General Theory. David only gave a couple of seminar papers in the Economics Department's 'Work in Progress' series, but both have lodged in my mind—a retention ratio that exceeds that of the papers from many scholars whose work continues to be read and known. One of these papers was not 'Work in Progress', David insisted, but 'Work Stuck'. It tried to come to grips with the implications of replacing the assumption of 'rational' economic man by various more realistic characterisations of human motivation. The second paper had calculated the number of articles and books a good reader could absorb in a lifetime, leading to the melancholy revelation that even a purposeful twenty year old could aspire to direct absorption of only a tiny fraction of the published wisdom of the economics profession.

Development economics was young in the world and in Australia, and many of the thoughts that mattered found their way through the Coombs Building. Charles Kindleberger challenged the economic nationalism of a young Australian with a presentation on direct foreign investment from his new book on international economics. And Arthur Smithies in the twilight of a professional life at Harvard—the Tasmanian who had journeyed to America for graduate studies and, unlike his clever fellow-islander Roland Wilson, had come to think Australia too far away. I recall the disbelief of we students at

Smithies' exposition of the easy development that lay just around the corner for South Vietnam, alongside the establishment of democracy. The recollection of the Smithies presentation sent a shiver down my spine when the same sentiments were uttered by some influential Americans of another generation as the drums began to beat for war in Iraq a couple of years ago.

The small international development economics profession, and Australia's distance from the established centres of learning, meant that few early appointments were of people whose capacities included both considerable strength in economics and historical and institutional comprehension of individual Asia Pacific economies. Academic personnel tended to be general economists, or scholars with small pretensions in economics but a lot of 'muddy boots' experience of one or other developing country in Asia or the Pacific.

Conditions for applied economic research were difficult. Audrey Donnithorne's work in a dedicated China economy Chair in the Cultural Revolution years, supported by a full time 'research officer', was spent in carefully cultivating fields of barren data. The early work on Indonesia was built on sparse and unreliable statistical information. A large body of research on Papua New Guinea and the South Pacific required scholars to build the data as they went along. All of these factors, and lower expectations of scholarly output, meant that the volume of publications and numbers of students per staff member were tiny compared with what became the norm in the 1990s.

Audrey Donnithorne, Department of Economics, 1977–1986

I liked the name of the Coombs Building. Nugget Coombs had spent part of his childhood a couple of streets away from my father in the working class Perth suburb of Maylands. His signature had been on the currency notes of Australia from my earliest memory. My Grandad told me that Nugget's father had been the stationmaster at Maylands. Coombs' name came to be linked in my mind to that of John Crawford—another clever lad, whose own Dad had been stationmaster in the tiny town of Grenfell on the Southwest Slopes of New South Wales.

Coombs and Crawford—Secretary and Director of Research in the Department of Postwar Reconstruction—shared much responsibility for establishing The Australian National University. The ANU's missions were to reverse the brain drain that had kept Australia an intellectual colony; to raise the intellectual content of national policy-making; and to define for Australia a place in its Asian and Pacific neighbourhood. The Research School of Pacific Studies (always Pacific in a sense that included at least East Asia) was central to Coombs' and Crawford's conceptions of the national university, and embedded in its founding statute, which happened to be passed by the Australian Parliament in the week of my birth.

Crawford was the School's first Head of Economics and first Director. By the time I attended my first seminar he had handed over the Economics job to Heinz Arndt, who had moved across from the undergraduate school in the young Australian National University. Crawford nurtured a large Economics Department—its contributions to Australian policy and policy discussion, he once said to me, were the public justification of the Research School of Pacific Studies.

For those who knew him well, it is tempting to think of Crawford as the guiding influence on the way economics developed at the ANU and especially in the Research School of Pacific Studies. Economics was important to the extent that it was relevant to policy, in Australia, or in the international organisations that had become important in the policy discussion after the Second World War, or in developing countries. Good economic theory had value to the extent that it illuminated real problems of real economies. It was rooted in thorough understanding of history and institutions. It was tempered by realistic understanding of the political economy constraints on policy-making and economic performance. Most important of all, good economic policy, and public policy more generally, were based on rigorous analysis and research, so there was symbiosis between the academic and policy enterprises.

Why is it only tempting to think of Crawford as the source of all this? Because the other large figures in Australian economics at that time shared elements of this approach. First of all, and most explicitly, Heinz Arndt. Trevor Swan, the eminence gris on the other side of the Coombs Building, famous for his absence and disconnection as much as for his couple of brilliant contributions to economic theory and its application to policy. Coombs, when he retired as a long-serving Governor of the Reserve Bank of Australia and came to the ANU as Chancellor. Leslie Melville, who had been a substantial figure in the Australian economic policy discussion from before everything fell apart in 1929, who was present at the foundation of the postwar international financial institutions, and later Vice-Chancellor of the ANU and longstanding Visiting Fellow in the Economics Department. And, in truth, a youngish Max Corden, although Max liked to distinguish himself for being further removed from policy than his senior colleagues.

Sometimes, Crawford's acceptance of the political economy constraints on policy-making seemed to me to exclude too much that was of value. When I extolled the virtues of free trade for Australian economy and society, he would gently chide me about being unrealistic, and once commended the greater pragmatism of my undergraduate contemporary Des Ball. Sir John favoured freer rather than free trade!

Ross Garnaut with Stuart Harris, left background, and Heinz Arndt foreground, circa 1994

Arndt shared Crawford's view of the importance of policy to economics, but was not similarly close to and influential in Australian policy formation. His separation from intimate policy roles was increased by 'socialist' views through the 1950s and early 1960s of conservative political hegemony. During the 1970s, he turned right when the country turned left. For Heinz, the large Asia-related foreign policy issues of the late sixties and early seventies, rather than economic policy, were influential in his personal reorientation within the Australian political divides: the Vietnam War; the Whitlam Government's recognition of Beijing in place of Taipei as the capital of China; and the Australian left's (although not Australian Labor Governments') antipathy on human rights grounds to the Soeharto regime in Indonesia, especially after the incorporation of East Timor in 1975.

My undergraduate and graduate years at ANU covered the time when Australians were grappling with a history of racial prejudice. This involved the rethinking of what had been a central part of the national self-definition through the twentieth century. The small campus at ANU—tiny in its undergraduate dimension—was disproportionately engaged in this intellectual and political ferment. The denial of full citizenship for aboriginal Australians, the White Australia Policy, Australia's defence of the South African Government's right to manage its own domestic affairs without external interference, and the limited extent of productive economic, political, cultural and social relations with the countries and peoples of Asia and the Pacific were central to the discussion on this campus.

Humphrey McQueen was a contemporary, writing a PhD thesis under Manning Clark's supervision. Despite the central role assigned to him by the Windshuttle side of the twenty first century culture wars, McQueen's Marxist perspective was at the distant margins of students' discussion of race and national policy.

And then a much more urgent issue overwhelmed the discussion of Australian international policy and identity. There was much earnest sifting of evidence on the Vietnam War. The 'Teach-In' phenomenon, initiated in Australia on the ANU campus, had people of differing expertise and opinion spending long nights talking each other to exhaustion on the war. The Teach-Ins provided my only direct contact with Professor C.P. Fitzgerald from East Asian History. Perhaps the earnest discussion made some difference to our understanding of Vietnam. I recall a 1976 dinner party at Jamie Mackie's Melbourne home in 1976, at which the mature elite of Australian international relations and policy—most of the participants having been early supporters of the war on what turned out to be faulty premises—in which conversation concentrated on how it had come to pass that the students of the mid-1960s had been closer to the realities of Vietnam in the early stages of the war than many of their elders.

My occasional excursions across the campus to the Coombs Building in the mid-1960s contributed directly to one dimension of my career that has always looked strange to most of my colleagues in the Economics profession: my continuing interest in and allocation of time to work on and in the Papua New Guinea economy. I received a 'vacation scholarship' to spend the Summer at the end of 1966 as a research assistant at the School's New Guinea Research Unit. The Unit was a multidisciplinary centre of scholarship, across all the disciplines represented in the Research School of Pacific Studies. Ron Crocombe, a sociologist and then the Unit's Director, helped me read into the anthropology, geography and history of Melanesia, starting with Charles Rowley's *The New Guinea Villager*. I spent several weeks in a Papuan village collecting data on village industry, under the supervision of economic geographer Bob Kent Wilson. That led to my first scholarly publication, and to respect for the contributions that insights that other scholarly disciplines could make to the understanding of economic development. The experience in Papua New Guinea was rewarding enough for me to repeat it the following year, before embarking on my PhD thesis on trade in the ASEAN countries. It led to the formation of what turned out to be close lifelong friendships with several men of my own age, who then were in the first preliminary year of the University of Papua New Guinea. From that time, Rabbie Namaliu and Mekere Morauta, respectively Chairman of the Public Service Commission and Secretary of the Finance (Treasury) Department in their twenties, kept calling me back to spend some of my time and my mind in Papua New Guinea.

Early progress on a national mission (1964-1980)

Crawford led the Economics work into three areas: international agricultural research; economic policy for Papua New Guinea's independence; and relations with Japan and related issues in Asia Pacific trade policy. Much of Crawford's work on agriculture was as an adviser to the World Bank, later as the first Board Chairman of the International Food Policy Research Institute in Washington DC, and subsequently in the establishment and as first Chairman of The Australian Centre for International Agricultural Research. The World Bank connection provided the opportunity for policy work on what became the 'Green Revolution' in India, much of it with Ric Shand,

Peter Drysdale's PhD thesis on Australian-Japanese trade, under Corden's supervision, was the beginnings of the Department's research on the Japanese economy and Australia-Japan economic relations. Peter's subsequent work with Crawford in establishing the Australia-Western Pacific Economic Relations

Research Project (later the Australia-Japan Research Centre) was, in the 1980s and 1990s, to nurture the large cadre of Australian and Australia-oriented PhD graduates with deep expertise on Japan and with interests in wider Asia Pacific economic relations.

Crawford provided the high-level leadership for an extensive and influential contribution to economic policy-making for Papua New Guinea's preparations for and early independence. This included the theoretical innovations on the subsistence and early post-subsistence economies led by Fisk; work on macro-economic projections and planning by Treadgold and others; and my own pre-Independence work on economic policy for Independent Papua New Guinea from the School's Port Moresby-based New Guinea Research Unit and later as Mekere Morauta's deputy with responsibility for financial and economic policy in the Department of Finance. I would regularly give seminars back in the Coombs during my years in Port Moresby straddling self government and independence, often chaired and always attended by Crawford, by now Vice-Chancellor and then Chancellor of the ANU. For example, my work with Anthony Clunies Ross (then Professor of Economics at the University of Papua New Guinea) on mineral rents and their taxation was road-tested in seminars in the Coombs Building, before being published internationally, and applied in Papua New Guinea and then in more than a dozen other countries including Australia.

Against the erroneous better judgement of all of his colleagues at the time, Arndt established the Indonesia Project and its *Bulletin of Indonesian Economic Studies*, with the assistance of a modest grant from the Ford Foundation. The Indonesian work was commenced in the unlikely circumstances of the dying years of the Soekarno era. The graduate training in economics coupled with the development of Indonesian language expertise of Australians (and one New Zealander) were to make Australia and the ANU the world's main locus of understanding of the Indonesian economy outside Indonesia. Peter McCawley, Hal Hill, Anne Booth, Steve Grenville, Chris Manning and Howard Dick began their associations with the Coombs building over these years. These scholars retained close links with their alma mater after graduation, and after Arndt's retirement were responsible for the extraordinary and continually expanding success and influence of the Indonesian work. (Ross McLeod's PhD, like mine, was in the ANU Faculties and strongly supported by the interaction with the Coombs Building).

John Crawford at the 1970 birthday party for RSPacS

The Economics Department in these years also made large contributions to changing the intellectual base for Australian trade and industry policy. Corden's research on effective protection was incorporated promptly into mainstream Australian policy discussion through the Vernon Report to the Menzies Government in 1965 via Crawford as the Vernon Committee's Deputy Chairman. The international influence of the work on trade policy was extended through Peter Lloyd and Herb Grubel's identification, analysis and exposition of intra-industry trade, Arndt's contributions to the introduction of trade preferences for developing countries (initially through a consultancy with UNCTAD) and Lloyd's contributions to the New Zealand-Australia Free Trade Agreement, and its much more satisfactory successor, the Australia-New Zealand Closer Economic Relations Agreement. Hughes' study of early Singapore industrialisation (prior to taking up an appointment at the World Bank) and Drysdale's (now teaching in the Faculties at ANU) participation in an Asian Development Bank project led by Myint on development strategy for East Asian developing countries, gave the ANU a place at the beginning of discussion of export-oriented industrialisation.

The research on internationally-oriented development in East Asia and on trade and industry policy began to come together in analysis of Australia's emerging opportunities in the late 1970s. I returned from Port Moresby to a position in the Department at the end of 1976. My PhD thesis had been on Australia's trade with Southeast Asia, and from early 1977, Japan, Korea, Taiwan and Hong Kong were added to the economies which I introduced into my regular discussion of Asia Pacific developments and their implications for Australia. China features only in passing in my publications from this period. Rod Carnegie as Chairman and Chief Executive Officer of the mining group CRA (Later Rio Tinto) had me down to Melbourne to address senior CRA executives on developments in East Asia on several occasions in 1977 and 1978, and pushed me to say more about China. I responded that China would provide important opportunities for the Australian resources industries one day, but that sustained growth would not be established in China under the then-current inward looking trade and investment policies.

The ANU focussed quickly on the importance of the changes in China that followed the December 1978 political ascendency of Deng Xiaoping and the new strategy of reform and opening to the outside world. It was able to do this effectively for three reasons: the University's work on outward-looking growth in East Asia was known to and respected by people connected to the development and reform discussion in China; Research School of Pacific Studies academic staff outside Economics were connected to relevant Chinese policy research networks (to a considerable extent deriving from ANU historian Stephen Fitzgerald's role as Australia's first Ambassador to the People's Republic of China); and the high professional quality of Australia's diplomatic connection with China (including the scholarly Jocelyn Chey as Secretary of the Australia China Council in the Department of Foreign Affairs). These factors were instrumental in securing Chinese participation in a conference at ANU on the ASEAN economies in 1979, being the first Western academic event with mainland Chinese participation within the open policies. The paper by Luo Yuanzheng, Deputy Director of the Institute of World Economy in the Chinese Academy of Social Sciences, became a chapter in the book that I edited from the conference, 'ASEAN in a Changing Pacific and World Economy'. This was followed by a visit to China late in 1979 by Crawford, Drysdale and myself, at which the Chancellor signed Peking University's first reform era exchange agreement with a foreign University. We received detailed briefings on the new Chinese development strategy from the Planning Commission, agricultural and other ministries, and the Academy. A feature was the State Council's interest in the ANU-based discussion of Asia Pacific economic cooperation. Luo returned for several months to the Coombs Building as a Visitor to the Economics Department, where he made a weekly presentation on China's new development strategy to a small group of ANU scholars. For Chris Findlay (then working with the ASEAN Project in Economics in the School) and I, this became important background for durable research interests in the Chinese economy.

The wider focus of my work in the late 1970s pointed in two directions: internationally-oriented growth in East Asia; and implications of these developments for Australian policy and development. On the latter, several of my papers in the late 1970s argued that sustained, rapid, internationally-oriented growth in East Asia provided exceptional opportunity for Australia, should this country prepare itself through reductions in protection and more internationally- and market-oriented policies generally. Two of these papers were presented to conferences on Australian economic policy organised by an energetic Wolfgang Kasper from the Canberra-based Royal Military College (later to become part of the University of New South Wales), who had earlier come from Germany to a post in Economics in the Research School of Social Sciences. This part of my work was noticed in the Australian political process partly through my participation in several meetings of the Study Group for Structural Adjustment, commissioned by Prime Minister Fraser and chaired by Crawford. This was my first close contact with ACTU President Bob Hawke, a member of the Crawford Study Group, and thus causally related to the role I was able to play in economic policy and reform as economic adviser to Prime Minister Hawke from 1983.

The national mission to educate Australia in the affairs of its Asia Pacific neighbourhood was also substantially realised in the first one and a half decades. Staff members and graduates of Economics RSPasS began to establish beachheads of advanced scholarship in trade and development economics through the Australian University system, at first most strongly at New England (with Drake and Treadgold), then Melbourne (Lloyd, and then Dick (after a spell at Newcastle), Jayasuriya, and Zhang), and later at Adelaide (Anderson and Findlay).

The agricultural development group within the Department (with Fisk and Shand initially leading the effort) introduced a new dimension in graduate education, with a coursework Masters programme in agricultural and development economics, focussing on students from developing countries. This took the Economics Department out of Coombs for the first time since the building's construction, into 'temporary' structures between Coombs and the tennis courts.

The public education role of The Australian National University was taken into new areas by McCawley (Economics, RSPacS) and Jamie Mackie (Political and Social Change) in 1981, through the establishment of a multi-disciplinary (but with economics and politics first) annual Indonesia Update conference for scholars and interested members of the public from around Australia, with some participation of Indonesians. This grew into a large annual event, the success of which was later emulated through Updates on China (the economy), Thailand, Papua New Guinea and several of the Pacific Island countries, Malaysia and India.

The RSPacS Economics activities were important in embedding Australia in the emerging networks of economists across the Asia Pacific region, and extending the importance of those networks. This enabled Australia in the late 1980s and early 1990s to play the central intellectual and diplomatic role in building Asia

Pacific economic cooperation, and ensured that East Asian or North Pacific networks excluding Australia did not become the main organisations for regional cooperation involving East Asian economies.

The late seventies and early eighties saw the personal networks established by academic staff institutionalised in several ways. One was the Pacific Trade and Development Conference series, bringing together leading policy-oriented economists from North America, East Asia and Australasia. Crawford and Drysdale, with North American and Japanese colleagues, were instrumental in the establishment of the series and maintaining it through its first decade. A second emerged from the Pacific Community seminar held at The Australian National University in 1980 at the request of Japanese Prime Minister Ohira and Australian Prime Minister Fraser. The Canberra seminar led to the foundation of the Pacific Economic Cooperation Council, which brought together scholars, businesspeople and senior officials from all the countries that were later to form the Asia Pacific Economic Cooperation forum. The first Pacific Community Seminar was organised out of a room in the Coombs Building that is now occupied by the Indonesian Project Library, in Crawford's office when he was Chancellor. Crawford met regularly with Drysdale, Stuart Harris and me on the organising ideas and the myriad detail. A third was the ASEAN-Australia Economic Relations Research Project, established following a report by Arndt and myself to Prime Minister Fraser, after the latter had recognised the costs and risks of the absence of shared perspectives between economists and policy-makers in the ASEAN countries and Australia. The Project, with Arndt as Chairman and initially myself as Research Director, with Hal Hill stepping into the breach when I moved at short notice to the Prime Minister's Office in early 1983, brought many of the leading and promising economists of Australia and the ASEAN countries into close working relationships with each other. The relationships built through this joint work endured and were extended in subsequent years. These institutional developments located Australia and The Australian National University at the centre of intellectual discourse on Asia Pacific economic development and cooperation for more than two decades.

This all made for rich discussion in the Economics Department tearoom at the end of the first corridor, halfway between Heinz Arndt's office (since 1989, mine) and the Chancellor's. The tearoom each morning complemented the Tuesday afternoon Work-in-Progress Seminar. It was not so good for interdisciplinary exchange within the School—the latter being encouraged, perhaps at the expense of collegial coherence within economics, by migration of the morning conversation to the large Coombs tearoom in the 1980s.

Not that there was always a meeting of minds, within the Department or with colleagues from the surrounding corridors. One point of great dispute, in which Arndt and Penny were the main protagonists, was whether economic growth would (mostly) solve the problem of poverty in Indonesia, or whether the growth-oriented New Order policies were leaving large numbers of poor Indonesians behind. This was often generalised into debate about the relationship between growth and poverty. Progress on these issues was not helped when they became the main focus of a quickly abandoned experiment with joint seminars with the Human Geography Department by geographers and economists. Awkwardly, and to the great discomfort of other staff members, as Arndt's retirement drew closer, Corden, now back from Oxford, raised doubts about whether it was ever appropriate for an Economics Department to be built around focus on particular countries or a particular region.

Economics for regions or one global profession? (1980-9)

Corden followed Arndt as Head of Department. To a younger staff member who had learned a great deal from both, they shared some important perspectives on the role of economics and economists. I absorbed more of my own approach to economic analysis from Corden than from any other economist—in the sixties and early seventies when his focus was trade policy and protection, as much as the late seventies and early eighties when it was international macro-economic adjustment. Arndt had encouraged and assisted my work on Southeast Asia, and provided a role model for diligence in pursuit of academic values. This made the tension between the two through the transition years a source of discomfort, for me and for many in the Department.

One of the strengths of Asia Pacific economics at The Australian National University was the way that it was able to draw on the experience and talent of many staff members after retirement. Melville and Crawford added historical depth to the tearoom discussion of economics and economic policy. Crawford remained active in all of his interests until his death in 1986. We first became aware of the brain cancer that was soon to claim his life when, at a dinner with Prime Minister Hawke in the Scarth Room at University House, to discuss government initiatives in relations with East Asia and particularly China, Crawford repeated a page from his notes about the depth of research that lay behind advice that I had been giving the Prime Minister. We were able to organise external funding for some support and an office in University House for Heinz, establishing a congenial base for what became a model of high productivity in retirement. The Economics Division was richly rewarded through the 1990s for modest support provided to veteran analysts of development, Jamie Mackie and Ben Higgins.

Corden sought to elevate analytical rigour in the work of the Department, and was more critical of underperformance by the standard academic criteria applied by economists. He gave less emphasis to applied work on Asia Pacific economies, while not opposing it—and eventually came to value the Indonesian work.

The privileged financial position of The Institute of Advanced Studies at The Australian National University, and especially of the minority social science schools, came under serious threat for the first time in the early 1980s. This had long been anticipated by a lonely minority of academic staff. I had chaired a Faculty Board Committee in 1978 (with Professors Jack Golson (Prehistory) and Stephen Wurm (Linguistics) to examine ways of introducing greater flexibility into the funding and staffing model being applied in RSPacS, to allow a constructive response to emerging pressure on the block grant through the Institute. There was little Faculty Board interest in innovation at that time. School-wide change came only when the School faced a catastrophic financial outlook in the early twenty first century. The range of options and some of the institutional innovations being introduced in response to reductions in the block grant to RSPAS in the early twenty first century were all amongst the proposals suggested by Faculty Board's Flexibility Committee in 1978. (I had a privileged view of the slow and painful adjustment of RSPacS to financial realities, having been continuously a member of Faculty Board from my return from Port Moresby in early 1977 to my stepping aside as Convenor of the Economics Division in 2001, excepting only the seven years that I was on secondment or leave on other activities. Faculty Board was at first a source of interest through the opportunity it provided for interaction with colleagues from other disciplines. Monday afternoon in Seminar Room A became over time a monthly blank on the calendar).

Corden as Head of Department thought that the elaborate and time-consuming processes that had to be played to secure posts and funding through the School at a time of financial stringency were unproductive. This was a correct assessment, but failure to participate fully in the inefficient processes had consequences. The Economics Department's share of shrinking school finances diminished. Some of the most productive staff departed for other Universities. Corden himself accepted a senior advisory position with the International Monetary Fund that later led to a Washington academic appointment and a second departure from the ANU. Sundrum and then Barlow had periods as Head of the Economics Department, but neither for long, and both in expectation that a long-term appointment to the senior position would at some time be made.

Some excellent work continued in the Economics Department through the 1980s. The scope of high quality research on Southeast Asia was expanded with external funding, arranged late in the Arndt era, for the Indonesia and ASEAN projects. McCawley and Booth maintained the quality of the Indonesian Project; Hill stepped into the Research Director role in the ASEAN Project until its conclusion in 1985, and then took over as head of the Indonesia Project when McCawley became Deputy Director-General of the Australian aid agency. Warr established a new strength for the School on the Thai economy, alongside his established interests in agricultural economics and project analysis. Ravallion's work on famine received respectful international attention. But there was no mistaking the decline in the activity and output of economics in the Coombs. The number of PhD students fell from what had always been modest levels.

The main energy in Asia Pacific economics at the ANU moved outside the Coombs Building for a while. This was the nadir of economics in Coombs. The Australia-Japan Research Centre, now formally a centre within RSPacS, secured a significant endowment from Australian and Japanese business and government. The University established a National Centre for Development Studies (NCDS) in the School with funding from the Australian aid programme, on the foundations of graduate education that had been built through the Economics Department's Master of Agricultural Development Economics Both new centres expanded rapidly with external funding, augmented greatly by the new opportunity for recruitment of fee-paying overseas students that had been created by Commonwealth Government educational reforms in 1986.

The initiative to allow Universities to recruit fee-paying foreign students , for its part, had been driven to a considerable extent by people associated with Economics in RSPacS. Hughes, recruited back from the World Bank to head NCDS, was Deputy Chairman and Peter McCawley a member of the Jackson Committee on the Aid programme that recommended the change. I was able to move the policy process along from the Prime Minister's office, against great resistance from the Commonwealth Education Department. Hughes' and Drysdale's administrative activism allowed the ANU to respond productively to the new opportunity. AJRC and NCDS were at first accommodated in odd buildings, until brought together in 1986 in a new Crawford Building (funded from their own revenues). The expansion of student and academic staff numbers in economics in the Crawford Building exceeded the decline in the Coombs. External funding was arranged to establish a new international journal, Asian-Pacific Economic Literature within NCDS, with Arndt—his role in the ASEAN Project having concluded–as its founding editor.

Asia Pacific economies enters the mainstream (1989-2000)

My secondments to the Prime Minister's Office, and then to the Department of Foreign Affairs and Trade as Ambassador to China, were followed by a period writing *Australia and the Northeast Asian Ascendancy* (the *Garnaut Report*). I returned to the Coombs Building as Head of the Economics Department in November 1989. I came back with the focussed energy of the early forties, determined to rebuild the old strengths of Economics in RSPacS, and to extend them through use of new opportunities that had been created by international educational reform in Australia, and the shift of interest in the Asia Pacific economies into the mainstream of Australian economic policy. I was supported in my objectives by senior members of the Chancelry and the Director of RSPacS, Gerry Ward, who recognised their importance to the University and School.

Soon after my return, the Director of RSPAS replaced the Department with disciplinary 'Divisions' as the basic administrative unit within the School, and NCDS and AJRC returned to their original (NCDS) or natural (AJRC) intellectual homes as part of the Economics Division. I became Convenor of the Economics Division while remaining Head of the Economics Department.

The growth in numbers and quality of well-trained economists with deep knowledge of one or more Asia Pacific economies, to a considerable extent as a result of the first several decades of graduate education and research at ANU, made it possible to reconcile the earlier apparent conflict between excellence in the economics discipline and regional focus in research. Most appointments to the Economics Division were now expected to have both qualities in high degree. I put considerable effort into identifying and recruiting individual scholars who could make large contributions to research and graduate education in Asia Pacific economics at ANU—none more than in the attraction of Warwick McKibbin back from Brookings Institution in 1993.

The background of the academic staff working on Asia Pacific Economics changed as the success of the work strengthened the human resource base for recruitment within Australia, and as Australia's demographic face was transformed by the commencement of large-scale migration from Asia in the late 1970s and its extension to mainland China from the late 1980s. Few of the early academic appointees in Economics had had 'conventional' Australian backgrounds. Four long-term staff members of the 1960s (Arndt, Corden, Epstein and Hughes)—like Gruen in Economics on the other side of the Coombs Building—had begun their lives as children of Jewish background in what came to be known as Eastern Europe. Fisk had survived what to our generation was an extraordinary wartime experience in Southeast Asia to return as a colonial official in rural Malaysia. Donnithorne had developed an intimacy with things Chinese as a daughter of Christian missionaries. Sundrum was one of a small group of excellent economists of Burmese background, who stayed abroad when the political environment of their home country turned out to be uncongenial to academic creativity or to economic development. Bensusan-Butt was from the British Treasury and the Cambridge of Keynes and Robinson. (Arndt, but not the other refugees from Eastern Europe, shared much of Butt's cultural background: that of the highly educated European middle class). Only a small minority of early staff had spent their formative years in Australian suburbs or bush.

Arndt, in particular, had made a large and successful effort to induct Australian students into Asia Pacific economics. This was highly influential in the composition of academic staff by the late twentieth century, when for a while most appointments happened to be of people who had had Australian childhoods. The increasing component of Asian students in the best Australian and international graduate programmes in economics began to change this again in the late 1990s—especially with the appointment of scholars of Chinese background. Arndt expressed concern to me a couple of years before his death in 2003, about the small number of 'Australian' recent PhD graduates and currently enrolled students who had or were entering the pools from which later appointments of Australians would be made. This puzzled me, and I ran through a list of impressive names: Song, Huang, Meng, Yang. 'But, I mean REAL Australians', Heinz said. 'They ARE real Australians, just like you, Heinz', I responded. We both grinned. The quality of the ANU's economic work on China, and increasingly on South Asia (Premachandra Athukorala, Kali Kalirajan and Raghbendra Jha) and Indonesia (Resosudarmo), has been built on Australia's old genius for turning people of many backgrounds into real Australians.

In one way, the assimilation of the new generation of immigrant Australian scholars was more complete than that of the founding generation. Arndt used to say: 'There are times when I feel thoroughly assimilated to Australian life, and then someone starts talking about cricket!' In the early 1990s, we began a pre-Christmas annual cricket match between the economics groups in the Coombs and the Crawford Buildings. Males and females born in Australia, China (both the mainland and Taiwan), India, Pakistan, Indonesia, Sri Lanka, Bangladesh, Malaysia, the Philippines, England, Japan and Thailand have played with enthusiasm. But there were limits to the assimilation of Australian sporting traditions beyond cricket. The Tuesday afternoon seminar always continued through the distractions of the first Tuesday in November. But some scholars responded to the events outside the seminar on the Tuesday that marks the boundary between the Southern Australian Spring and Summer. The leading Philippines economist Balisacan Arsenio once told a Conference of East Asian Economists about the strange academic customs at the ANU. 'Twice I have given seminars at the ANU,' he said. 'And both times many of the participants walked out half way through, explaining that they had to watch a horse race.' It was the random succession of circumstances rather than intelligent design that caused Arsenio again to bump into Melbourne Cup day when he gave a third seminar in 2005. Another point of tension between the traditions of Economics in the School and of the host nation was the holding the Indonesia Update on the last Friday and Saturday of September. It took a long while for Australian traditions to prevail, but recent Indonesia Update programmes have not extended into the Saturday afternoon, and the 2006 Update is scheduled for the week before the Australian Football League Grand Final.

The 1990s took Asia Pacific economics at the ANU into the mainstream in a third sense. It had been part of the purpose of my 1989 report to the Prime Minister and Foreign Minister, *Australia and the Northeast Asian Ascendency*, to bring discussion of Australia's relations with Asia into the main channel of Australian policy discussion, out of the realm of exotic area studies. (It is an indication of the magnitude of the task that the ANU's Asian Studies Faculty had carried the name 'Oriental Studies' until the 1970s, and East Asian History was still 'Far Eastern History' in 1989). I expressed in the Report the objective that a new generation of Australians should grow up in 'comfortable familiarity' with their Asia Pacific neighbourhood. The main issues in education or economic or other policy towards the Asia Pacific would be the main issues in education or economic or other policy more generally. So the main policy recommendations in *Australia and the Northeast Asian Ascendency* related to general Australian policy—removal of protection, strengthening the educational base for Australian development, raising the skills component of the immigration programme—and were debated and largely accepted in this context.

This was the right time for this shift in the locus of Australian discussion of Asia, from the margins to the centre of Australian political discourse and policy-making. The success of reform in China from 1978, the acceleration of internationally-oriented growth in Southeast Asia from the mid-1980s and the massive structural adjustment in Japan, Korea and Taiwan after the exchange rate appreciations following the Plaza Accord in 1985, together greatly expanded Australian opportunity. The formation of Asia Pacific Economic Cooperation (APEC) through Australian diplomatic initiative, with the inaugural meeting in Canberra in the month of the launching of *Australia and the Northeast Asian Ascendency*, elevated the political and public focus on Asia

Pacific relations and diplomacy. It was widely recognised that the ideas and the networks upon which APEC had been built had had their origins in Economics at The Australian National University, after Crawford's death through Peter Drysdale, Stuart Harris and myself, and with Economics Department PhD graduate Andrew Elek pulling the strands together as Director of the Economics Division of the Department of Foreign Affairs and Trade. Before 1989, it was rare for discussion of the Asian economies other than Japan to feature in the main public documents from the Australian Treasury or Reserve Bank. After 1989, it was increasingly rare for the Asian economies not to feature centrally in discussion of Australian economic choices and prospects.

All of this supported efforts to expand resources available internally and externally for research and graduate education in Economics. I aimed to increase research productivity (as measured by publications output, weighted for quality of journal and publisher), restore the Economics share of University-funded research posts in Economics as closely as possible to the levels of the Crawford and Arndt years, and to use this secure long-term funding as a base for maintaining the quality of a greatly expanded quantum of externally funded research. Alongside these developments, continued rapid growth in fee-paying student numbers, again with a focus on quality, would expand the resources available for research as well as for graduate education.

By the mid-1990s, these objectives had been realised and more ambitious goals could be set. Access to external research funding had been particularly successful, despite the exclusion of the ANU's Institute of Advanced Studies at that time from the Australian Research Council's funding system. A new agreement with the Australian aid agency on the funding of the Indonesia Project allowed the number of research posts allocated to work on Indonesia to be raised to three. A bequest from Professor Sir John Crawford allowed the establishment of the J.G. Crawford Chair in Agricultural Economics, to which Peter Warr was appointed. Grants from the Australian Centre for International Agricultural Research allowed Peter Warr to expand the work on general equilibrium modelling of Southeast Asian economies, and Andrew Elek to restore the Division's former strength on the Papua New Guinea economy. The Australian aid agency contributed to the restoration of research effort on the Papua New Guinea economy by funding two posts in NCDS. External funding from several sources allowed new appointments for research on Chinese economic development. A university-level commitment of funding of three posts, permanently added to the base budget of RSPAS, complemented a replenishment of the endowment and general funding base of the AJRC, for work on Japan and Asia Pacific economic cooperation.

A chance encounter with eminent Indian American economist Jagdish Bhagwati on a flight from London to New York in 1992 sparked a renewal of quality research on the Indian economy. Bhagwati had been a pessimist on Indian economic reform and development. 'This time, its happening', he said to me. 'I've just spent a few months in New Delhi, and Manmohan Singh's reforms are real and extensive, and they're going to last'. We spent much of the seven hours of the flight going over the evidence. On my return to Australia, I met the Education Minister, Kim Beazley, himself with longstanding interests in Indian development. Beazley committed the Government to funding the equivalent of two posts in the Economics Division for research on the Indian economy, so long as equivalent commitments were made from the University. The counterpart resources were provided through the return of Ric Shand to one of his former research territories, as Director of the Australia South Asia Research Centre, and the reallocation of Kalirajan's research emphasis to the Indian economy. Strong research appointments were made, and the Centre embarked on a period of high output and national impact. From this base, fund-raising for a Rajiv Gandhi Chair in South Asian economics was commenced.

An innovation in allocation of research support funds within the Economics Department—on the basis of quality and quantum of publications—was surprisingly effective in re-focussing effort towards publications of substantial academic impact and on volume of publications.

The increase in numbers and quality of graduate students was similarly marked. Graduate student numbers—especially in NCDS, but also in the Economics Department and AJRC at PhD level—rose to the point where the Economics Division of RSPAS—one of five Divisions in the School—came to account for something like one third of the graduate students in the ANU's Institute of Advanced Studies. The lifting of graduate student numbers and quality in the Economics Division RSPAS provided the base from which the ANU could be built as the home of Australia's one world class graduate programme in economics.

Naturally, this expansion in economics gave rise to territorial conflict. The corridor containing Seminar Room B, occupied by Economics in the early years and surrendered in the 1980s, was reoccupied. Space elsewhere in the Coombs was found for the Australia South Asia Research Centre. Most of the expansion of activity occurred in the Crawford Building.

The growth of the Economics Division raised questions about whether RSPAS (now the Research School of Pacific and Asian Studies, RSPAS) was still the best institutional home for the economics work. Several of my colleagues pressed the view that an independent structure within the university would support the Asia Pacific economics work more effectively. There were disadvantages in domicile in RSPAS: the antiquated financial and academic management arrangements diminished the response to the new research and educational opportunities; the absence of any sense of opportunity cost in the management of the School would, sooner or later, precipitate a financial crisis that would damage all of the School's parts; a separate School or Centre would be able to develop an incentives structure that was much better suited to the changing funding model for Australian universities (and in particular for the ANU's Institute of Advanced Studies); and we would be free of pointless tension over intra-School resource allocation.

I resisted these views for a considerable period. One reason for doing so was sentimental: the old RSPacS had provided a home for good work over a long period, and I, and some others, valued contact with colleagues from other Divisions. One was inertial: some members of the old Economics Department feared that institutional change would lead to challenge to the research-only posts that they occupied. Like Prime Minister Menzies and the White Australia Policy, many recognised that change had to come, but could see no need for the pain of change to come during what remained of their own professional lives.

More fundamentally, there were real dilemmas in defining the ideal institutional model for work on the Asia Pacific economies. There would be synergies in having one Economics School at ANU, but the perspectives of traditional economics would not support the exceptional strengths that had developed at the ANU on the Asia Pacific economies. An Asia Pacific economics-only research and graduate school would have a natural constituency neither amongst the supporters of Asia Pacific Studies, nor amongst those whose concern was to maintain and to extend the strength of economic theory and technique independently of its applications.

My own acceptance of the need for change was precipitated by the RSPAS leadership's response to financial crisis in 1997. Neglect of opportunity cost in establishing desirable new activities, and more generally the accumulated effects of a long period of poor financial management, at a time of declining real financial receipts from the block grant, finally caught up with the School. A large reduction in the School budget was required over a short period. The then Director explained to me that a budget cut that focussed disproportionately on Economics, which was seen as being well funded from external sources, would be politically more acceptable than any alternative approach. The proposed cuts excluded South Asia from a more restricted view of regional priorities.

A long and enervating struggle followed. The compromise that emerged from conflict embodied the formation of the Asia Pacific School of Economics and

Management (APSEM), reporting directly to the academic leadership of the University, and comprising the Economics Division of RSPAS, the National Graduate School of Management with its MBA programme (established by the Vice-Chancellor and given a home within RSPAS because its success would depend on it having an Asia Pacific business focus) and the Graduate Programme in Public Policy. The Economics Department component of the old Economics Division of RSPAS was considered to be in two Schools—RSPAS as well as APSEM. The Economics Division agreed to share proportionately in any budget adjustment required in RSPAS, and the University guaranteed that the Economics share of RSPAS research posts funded from the block grant would remain at 23%, the level at the onset of budgetary crisis. A new fiscal constitution was negotiated for APSEM, that was appropriate for a School drawing most of its revenue from student fees and external research grants. The APSEM fiscal constitution of 1998 remained in place in 2006 for its successor, the Crawford School of Economics and Government (CSEG).

The negotiations to establish these arrangements took about 20 months from the time the University decided to establish the Asia Pacific School of Economics and Management. I was Director during that transitional time, but declined an offer of a longer term appointment. Many elements of the new arrangements were a large improvement on what had gone before. But there were flaws. In my view, the key to expanding success in research and graduate education at the ANU was to integrate productively the (gradually diminishing) block grant for research, with the externally funded activities of the School. This would be rendered difficult by the location of the RSPAS-funded Economics Division in two schools, despite the guarantee on economics' share of RSPAS posts. The difficulties were compounded by the Vice Chancellor's continued intervention in the management of the MBA programme, effectively insulating those activities from changes that I thought were necessary to lift its work to ANU standards. I declined an invitation for a long-term appointment as Director, and advised the Vice-Chancellor and the two Schools that I would take my first and only period of sabbatical leave, and would return to half time employment as a Professor in the Economics Division of RSPAS. I would continue to chair the China Economy and Business Programme, and the editorial boards of the journals *Asian-Pacific Economic Literature* and *Bulletin of Indonesian Economic Studies*. But beyond that, my formal leadership roles at ANU had been completed.

An Asia Pacific future for Economics? (The twenty-first century)

The post-2001 institutional arrangements for Asia Pacific economics were untidy, fragmented and awkward. But the strength of the people, the agreed protection of the Economics Division's share of RSPAS resources, and the new incentive structure in APSEM allowed each of the components of the old Economics Division of RSPAS to prosper in the early years of the twenty first century.

The growth in access to external funding had continued through the establishment of APSEM, in the short period in which I was Director. Appointments were made to mainly externally funded chairs in Japanese economics (Corbett, jointly with the Faculty of Asian Studies and de Brouwer), Asia Pacific international economics (Findlay), South Asian economics (Jha as the Rajiv Gandhi Professor), and environmental economics (Bennett).

Ron Duncan, who had succeeded Hughes as Director of NCDS, became Director of APSEM, and McKibbin continued as Convenor of the Economics Division. Over time, the MBA programme was relocated into the Faculties, and the Economics Division again became a unit only of RSPAS (with the guarantee of 23% of School-funded research posts remaining in place). A new Director with a political science background, Andrew MacIntyre was appointed to CSEG in 2003, Hill became Convenor of the Economics Division in 2004. These changes separated the block-funded activity within RSPAS in the Coombs Building, from the large group of graduate students and academic staff working on Asia Pacific economics in CSEG. While this created practical difficulties for graduate education and for some research (especially in relation to China), it was time for all to get on with their work.

By now, the economics work and RSPAS as a whole had well and truly outgrown the Coombs Building. The budget and academic staff of CSEG, almost entirely funded by fees and research grants and endowments, were now as large in real terms as the whole of RSPAS had once been. CSEG was looking for a new home. The Coombs Building was extended, and still was not large enough for what remained of RSPAS.

The institutional arrangements for Economics and Asia Pacific Economics at the ANU still look untidy in 2006. One lesson from the story of economics in the Coombs Building, is that ideal institutional arrangements are not necessary for high achievement in research and graduate education in Asia Pacific economics. But another lesson is that better arrangements would have helped. In the past, the Australian and international competitive environments allowed Asia Pacific economics at the ANU to carry some deadweight costs and still to be better than any other in the world. It is unlikely in today's more competitive world with its higher standards in economic analysis and Asia Pacific Studies, that the ANU can carry large imperfections in institutional design and remain the world's most important centre for graduate education and research on the

Asia Pacific economies.

Reform can make things better, but the institutional arrangements will never seem right to everyone. There is inevitably tension when an academic enterprise draws its strengths both from being embedded in a scholarly discipline, and in the study of the world's most populous and dynamic region. But the establishment of a College of Asia Pacific Studies, and a Review of the Research School of Social Sciences in 2006, create an opportunity for improvement.

CHAPTER 16

Reflections of a Defence Intellectual

Desmond Ball

Intellectuals, as Karl Mannheim explained, tend to have special difficulties separating their work and domestic domains. Thinking does not stop at home in the evenings or at weekends; many of the Coombs Building's researchers do most of their writing in their studies at home. Conversely, the university provides a social and cultural environment for personal activities. Over time, the 'office' becomes as much a part of life as the residential address; together they shape the intellectual product.

I have worked and lived in the Coombs Building in a series of capacities, from PhD student to Professor and Head of Centre. I even had a short stint as a research assistant, in 1967–68, at the end of my Economics degree, when I worked for Sir John Crawford on Asia-Pacific Economic Cooperation. I was a PhD student in the Department of International Relations in 1969–72, where I relished the supervision of Hedley Bull, Geoffrey Jukes and Arthur Burns. Hedley was brilliant, but he could also be paternalistic and arrogant. When I went to the United States on my first fieldwork in 1970 he arranged for my stipend to include funds for me to buy a suit and a new pair of shoes for wearing when I conducted interviews. He could be devastating in seminars, puffing on his pipe between acerbic comments. At a conference on Australian defence policy, he intervened in a heated discussion about alternative defence planning methodologies to dismissively opine that the whole subject was a waste of time; there were many more momentous issues in the world warranting academic inquiry than defending Australia. He did not really believe this, and in fact wrote several articles about Australian defence, but he enjoyed sniping.

I also relished the companionship of Nancy Viviani, Robyn Lim, Kevin Foley, Paul Keal, Gunther Patz, David Armstrong and others in a remarkable stable of PhD students at the time. Several of them were appointed to Chairs in the 1980s and 1990s. They were a collegially competitive lot, always watching closely the productivity of their compatriots, but also engaged, more I think than their successors, in seemingly continuous rounds of picnics, barbecues, drinking sessions and parties, often stretching the social conventions. These were, after all, the days of 'sex and drugs and rock-and-roll'. I began a regime of working odd hours, sometimes sleeping in my office when writing the final drafts. In those days PhD students often had their own rooms, where they would sometimes sleep, after returning from fieldwork or while in between digs, for days or weeks. The floors were not very comfortable, but the showers in the bathrooms near the foyer were pretty good.

I joined the Strategic and Defence Studies Centre (SDSC) as a Research Fellow in July 1974. The Centre had been set up by Dr T. [Tom] B. Millar, a former Australian Army officer, in 1966, when he was a Senior Fellow in the Department of International Relations, to 'advance the study of Australian, regional, and global strategic and defence issues'. It was initially funded by a grant from the Ford Foundation, and was an independent offshoot of International Relations. It was for two decades the only academic centre concerned with strategic and defence studies in Australia. Several others were established in the late 1980s and the 1990s, but SDSC has remained pre-eminent in terms of international reputation and research productivity. Tom later became Professor of Australian Studies and Head of the Sir Robert Menzies Centre for Australian Studies at the Institute of Commonwealth Studies in London (1985–90).

Desmond Ball with former US President Jimmy Carter

The Centre had been headed since 1971 by Robert O'Neill, who had also been an Army officer and who was also a Senior Fellow in International Relations. He presided over the Centre's expansion and rise to international recognition. In

1974 he secured financial support from the Department of Defence for two Research Fellow/Senior Research Fellow posts, and was later able to move the Centre into the University's staffing and budgeting system and obtain 2-3 University-funded posts. Bob moved to London to head the International Institute for Strategic Studies (IISS) in 1982. He was recognised internationally for his leadership qualities, adeptness at collegiate and Foundation politics and immense personal integrity as well as his intellectual work. In 1987 he became the Chichele Professor of the History of War at All Souls College at Oxford University, where he stayed until his retirement in 2001.

I received one of the first two Defence-funded posts, beginning a relationship with Defence that we both often found uncomfortable over the ensuing years. The other post, for work on regional security issues, went to Peter Hastings, the pungent and waggish and quarrelsome journalist, who worked on political and security issues concerning Indonesia and Papua New Guinea. He enjoyed regular access to the office of the then Director of the Joint Intelligence Organisation (JIO), as well as conviviality and good wine. He married Jolika Tie, who had been our research assistant, in 1981. Two other key members of the Centre at this time, when a critical mass was being put together, were J.O. [Jol] Langtry and Billie Dalrymple. Jol, another lover of good wine, was the Centre's executive officer from August 1976 to December 1988. He was a former Army officer who had worked in JIO and Army combat development areas, whose ability to think of novel strategic and operational concepts was inspirational. Billie was the Centre's secretary from 1977 to 1989. As Bob said when she retired, Billie was the crux of a hive of activity, working unstintingly, 'with her own special flair and style, smoothing down ruffled feathers when others became agitated, cheering those under pressure and dealing with the outside world with charm and panache'.

The largest proportion of the Centre's work in the second half of the 1970s and in the 1980s concerned the defence of Australia. The Centre was at the forefront of the conceptual revolution in Australian defence policy from 'dependence on great and powerful friends' to 'greater self-reliance' and from 'forward defence' to 'defence of Australia' which occurred during this period. It contributed to the development of new ideas concerning command and control of the Australian Defence Force (ADF), such as the establishment of 'functional' command arrangements; reorganisation of the Defence portfolio, such as establishment of the Defence Council, recommended by Tom Millar; greater utilisation of the civilian infrastructure, especially in defence of Australia contingencies; greater appreciation of the challenges of lower level contingencies in northern Australia; and particular force structure issues.

Members of the Centre were credited with an influential role in the Government's decision in 1981 to acquire the F/A-18 as the RAAF's tactical fighter aircraft. Costing $4 billion, this was the largest capital program in Australia's history, and has turned out to have been the right choice. The core people involved in this work on Australian defence were Bob, Jol and myself, together with Ross Babbage, initially as a PhD student in the mid-1970s and later (1986–90) as Senior Research Fellow and Deputy Head of the Centre, but we relied greatly on a stream of Defence-funded Visiting Fellows, including mid-career ADF officers, for their operational and planning expertise.

Many of the ideas, especially those relating to northern defence, were incorporated in Paul Dibb's *Review of Australia's Defence Capabilities* produced for Defence Minister Kim Beazley in 1985-86, and described by Mr Beazley as 'the most important appraisal of Australia's defence capabilities since the end of World War Two'. Paul had joined the Centre as an SRF and Deputy Head in 1984.

The field trips around northern Australia during the 1980s, using Coastwatch or RAAF aircraft, 4-wheel drive vehicles and river barges, mapping the local civil infrastructure and vital national installations, proffering novel operational concepts for northern defence, and seeing these being tested in large-scale defence exercises, were exhilarating affairs. My daughter Katherine, born in 1984, was named in part after the township 320 km south of Darwin, which we had identified as the focal point for the defence of the Top End, and where the first squadron of the new F/A-18 fighters would soon be based. One of the particular northern infrastructure projects for which we became leading proponents was construction of an Alice Springs to Darwin railway connection, and it was very pleasing to be invited to Darwin in October 2003 to see the first train come up the line.

The second large area of work in the Centre, which brought us to international attention, concerned the strategic nuclear balance between the United States and the Soviet Union. My own work focussed on the operational aspects of strategic nuclear targeting and the controllability of nuclear war, and showed that the mechanisms needed for controlling a nuclear exchange degraded rapidly after only several tens of detonations or a day or so of operations, leading inexorably to full-scale nuclear war. These were heady days, involving sojourns to underground missile silos, the warning centre under Cheyenne Mountain near Colorado Springs, the Pentagon, the United States intelligence agencies and the White House. I sat only feet away from the 1.2 Megaton nuclear warheads atop the Minuteman ICBMs at Whiteman Air Force Base, each about a thousand times more powerful than the bomb which destroyed Hiroshima in 1945. I was in West Berlin on 9 November 1989, when the Berlin wall was demolished, watching the panicked Soviet intelligence officers based in the Soviet Consulate desperately reacting to the loss of some of their covert technical equipment.

I had become Head of the Centre in March 1984, but I was spending lengthy periods overseas, at the Centre for International Affairs at Harvard University, the RAND Corporation in Los Angeles and the IISS in London, as well as various places in Washington, D.C., and was soon having to contemplate moving to the United States. In March 1987 I was awarded a personal Chair, one of six 'special professorships' created in the Institute of Advanced Studies 'in recognition of a high international reputation for distinguished academic work'. I had really wanted to stay at the ANU, both because I much preferred living in Canberra to any major city in the United States, particularly now I was married and having children, and because of the opportunity to devote a lifetime to academic research in the Research School that the personal Chair offered.

I was honoured that, in addition to my academic referees, former United States President Jimmy Carter and former Secretary of Defense Robert McNamara graciously agreed to provide references on my behalf, even though I had been one of the harshest critics of their strategic nuclear policies of 'controlled' nuclear war-fighting. Defence Minister Beazley said that my 'work on global strategic issues is acknowledged internationally as outstanding', and that: 'It has been an interesting experience as Defence Minister to hold discussions at the highest levels in the capitals of our allies and to have him cited to me as an authority (to be supported or opposed) on an array of defence matters'. He said that appointing me to a personal Chair 'would do the nation a substantial service'.

The third broad area of Centre research concerned regional security. We had a succession of 2-3 year appointments on various aspects of regional security, some of them funded by Defence and others by the University. They included Lee Ngok, Don McMillan and Denny Roy who worked on China, Paul Keal and Peter Polomka on Japan, Greg Fry and David Hegarty on the Southwest Pacific, Sandy Gordon on India and Alan Dupont on Indonesia. Their names are associated with standard reference works in their respective areas. Several of them found longer term homes in the Coombs Building.

Some of our work was intensely controversial, as befitting pathbreaking scholarship on major national and international issues. Some senior Defence and intelligence officials regarded my own work on United States installations in Australia, such as Pine Gap, with great suspicion. While I argued that it was necessary in a democracy for the public to know the purposes and implications of these facilities, a proposition now taken for granted, Sir Arthur Tange complained that I was dangerous and irresponsible, opening up matters which 'successive American and Australian Governments have deemed it a national interest' to keep secret. It was reported in 1980 that our offices had been searched and bugged, our diaries photographed and our telephones tapped by ASIO. Surveillance of this sort probably happened on other occasions in the 1980s and 1990s.

On the other hand, we were also accused by political activists of various sorts of being agents of the 'military-industrial complex'. We had demonstrations against many of our conferences, sometimes directed at the participation of particular Ministers or overseas speakers and sometimes at our subject matter. On two occasions, hundreds of protesters tried to physically break up the proceedings, once in the Coombs Theatre in November 1989 when the subject was *New Technology: Implications for Regional and Australian Security* and the other in the Law Theatre in November 1991 on *Australia and Space*. They were misplaced affairs, given the broad and fundamental nature of the conference agendas and the reputations of the overseas participants as leading critical thinkers, and really quite insipid compared with protests against the Vietnam War or nuclear weapons that I had been involved in organising.

The working environment in the 1970s and 1980s was more relaxed and sociable. There was more time for informal discourse between colleagues from different parts of the School, and indeed the University, perhaps lubricated by good wine on the lawns of the old Staff Centre (Old Canberra House). The contemporary research projects and publications tended, as a result, to be broader and more multi-disciplinary. Books published by Centre members in the 1980s included chapters by Rhys Jones in Prehistory, John Chappell in Biogeography, Andy Mack and Trevor Findlay in the Peace Research Centre, Hal Hill in Economics, Richard Higgott in International Relations, and Jamie Mackie and Ron May in Political and Social Change. The discussions with Rhys led to one of my favourite edited books, *Aborigines in the Defence of Australia*, in which he and Betty Meehan wrote a chapter on 'The Arnhem Salient'.

By the end of the 1980s the Centre was being consistently ranked among the top 15 or 20 strategic studies centres in the world. In 1990, the Review of the Institute of Advanced Studies, chaired by Sir Ninian Stephen, cited SDSC as an illustration of 'how well parts of the Institute's research have met the goals of those who created the ANU'. The Vice-Chancellor, Professor Laurie Nichol said it 'is one of this University's major success stories'. The Governor

General, the Honourable Bill Hayden, said in 1991 that the SDSC's influence extended 'well beyond academic cloisters' and that 'this kind of interaction between scholars, policy makers and the broader community was in fact the inspiration behind the establishment of the Institute of Advanced Studies in 1946'. Defence Minister Beazley called the Centre a 'national asset'.

Paul Dibb succeeded me as Head in July 1991 and became its longest serving Head. I had become frustrated with administration, which was probably less arduous than in more recent times, but for which I was clearly unsuited. I was also anxious to spend less time wearing a suit and tie and more time fulfilling the research commission of my personal Chair. In addition to authorship of the *Dibb Review*, Paul had served as head of the National Assessments Staff (NAS) in the JIO, the forerunner of the Office of National Assessments (ONA), Director of the JIO, and Deputy Secretary of the Department of Defence responsible for strategic policy and intelligence. He had also had two previous tenures in the Coombs Building. He was a Research Fellow in the Department of Political Science in RSSS in 1967–69, and a Senior Research Fellow in the Department of International Relations in 1981–84 and then SDSC in 1984–86, where he had written the prescient study of *The Soviet Union: The Incomplete Superpower* and served as Deputy Head and oft-times Acting Head. Sir Arthur Tange said in support of his appointment that he had 'rare versatility' and that on defence policy issues 'there is none inside or outside the Defence Community better equipped at present to understand the issues in contention and the policy choices'. I might add that Sir Arthur could not resist using his reference for Paul to make some caustic remarks about myself, saying that I had evinced 'some imbalance in the choice of subjects for study', particularly concerning United States installations in Australia, and expressing relief that I would no longer be heading the Centre.

Paul's accession to the headship coincided with the collapse of the Soviet Union and the end of the Cold War. He had to manage a wholesale transformation in the Centre's research agenda. The post-Cold War issues were more disparate and diffuse. A new core academic staff was assembled, consisting, in addition to Paul and myself, of Coral Bell, David Horner, Alan Dupont and, since 2001, Ron Huisken and Clive Williams. Coral Bell became a Visiting Fellow in SDSC in 1990. Truly indefatigable, she had been Professor of International Relations at the University of Sussex in 1972–77 and had returned to Australia to spend the next eleven years as a Senior Research Fellow in International Relations, pursuing her passion for comprehending and explaining the fundamental power dynamics of the international system. In the decade and a half with SDSC she has produced more than half a dozen insightful books and monographs, most recently *A World Out of Balance:*

American Ascendancy and International Politics in the 21st Century (2003). David Horner, a former Army officer with wide command and staff experience, is Australia's leading military historian. He joined the Centre as its executive officer in September 1990, transferred to a Fellow in 1994, and Defence-funded post of Professor of Australian Defence History in 1999. David had won the J G Crawford Prize for the best PhD in the University in 1982. Ron Huisken had been a Visiting Fellow in the Centre in 1976–77, and returned as a Senior Fellow after more than two decades in the Department of Foreign Affairs and Trade and the Department of Defence, where he was responsible for arms control issues and the Australia-United States defence relationship.

About half of the Centre's work became devoted to Asia-Pacific security matters. Paul produced the classic studies of the balance of power in the Asia-Pacific region and the Revolution in Military Affairs (RMA) in Asia, as well as the United States-Australia alliance. We developed many of the original practical proposals for regional security cooperation, a lot of which were quickly adopted by the new ASEAN Regional Forum (ARF). The Centre was one of the 10 regional strategic studies centres which in 1992–93 founded the Council on Security Cooperation in Asia Pacific (CSCAP), the premier 'second track' organisation in this part of the world, which now has 22 Member Committees in 22 countries (with the Australian Committee served by a secretariat in SDSC), and which through its Steering Committee meetings, Study Groups and General Conferences provides an institutionalised mechanism for continuous activity for promoting regional security cooperation.

Centre members also explicated a broader conception of security to encompass economic, environmental and other so-called 'non-traditional' threats in addition to the traditional military focus. Alan Dupont's path-breaking book, *East Asia Imperilled: Transnational Challenges to Security*, analysed over-population, deforestation and pollution, global warming, unregulated population movements, transnational crime, virulent new strains of infectious diseases and a host of other issues which could potentially destabilise East Asia. There was increasing appreciation of the importance of 'human security' as opposed to State security as reflected in some of my own work on security issues in the Thailand-Burma borderlands. Travelling in these borderlands has been fascinating, whether meeting in jungle hide-outs in with leaders of the ethnic and pro-democracy groups fighting the Burmese military dictatorship, in poorly demarcated border areas often patrolled by Burmese Army units, or talking with Thai para-military personnel and villagers about the local security concerns. On one occasion in 2003 I was going by long-tail boat up the Salween River between Thailand and Burma with one of the resistance leaders, accompanied part way by a hitch-hiking Thai Army Ranger, while another boat carried weapons and supplies to a guerrilla base up-river and a Burmese Army battalion moved up the riverside to their camp opposite Mae Sariang district.

The Centre took some hard knocks in the 1990s, although its international reputation was not dinted. It suffered from the vicissitudes of dependence on external funding from external sources, and especially the Department of Defence, which at its height at the beginning of the decade amounted to more than half of the Centre's budget. More painfully felt were cuts in the Centre's University funding and a shift in School priorities which decimated much of its work on Australian defence. It was severely damaged by the move off-campus to Acton House in 1992. This occurred partly at our instigation, as we had PhD students and Visiting Fellows spread around several buildings and were desperate to bring everyone together. In practice we found sub-standard premises and intellectual isolation. In October 1999 we moved to the Law Building, which at least had the great benefit of bringing us back onto the campus and fairly close to the Coombs Building. There was a palpable air of exuberance when we returned to Coombs in September 2004. It was a real home-coming. We were excited about the prospect of daily encounters with colleagues who we had too rarely seen; the closer interaction has already brought cooperative research initiatives and joint publications between SDSC staff and other Coombs members.

The return to Coombs coincided with other major Centre developments, producing a sense of regeneration. We have accorded a high priority to educating and training a new generation of strategic thinkers, which has involved greatly expanding our PhD program and developing a new Masters program, directed most ably by Robert Ayson, who himself did an MA in the Centre in 1988–89. Paul Dibb reached retirement age in October 2004 and became an Emeritus Professor. Hugh White was appointed Head in November 2004. He had previously been Deputy Director (Civilian) of the Defence Intelligence Organisation (DIO) and Deputy Secretary of the Department of Defence (Strategy and Intelligence). He was the primary author of the Government's Defence White Paper published in 2000, and he had been the founding Director of the Defence-funded Australian Strategic Policy Institute (ASPI) in 2001–04. He had been attracted to SDSC by our international reputation but also by the intellectual freedom enjoyed in academia and the depth and breadth of expertise about our region that avails in the Research School.

Strategic and defence studies are not popular areas of academic activity. To some critics, the study of war is macabre. Some of our former colleagues in the Coombs Building used to refer to members of SDSC as 'bomb-fondlers', not always in jest. Work on defence planning is regarded as antithetical to the universalism of scholarship. Policy-relevant work is regarded by some as serving the interests of defence and foreign affairs bureaucracies and military establishments, and supporting State power more generally. We have been called 'prostitutes', in academic papers, by colleagues elsewhere in the University. Some critics have argued that the Centre should be moved from the University to the Department of Defence.

However, we could not do our job in the Department of Defence. Compared to the Coombs Building, we could expect more luxurious facilities and fabulous resources. But we are at heart 'defence intellectuals'. I would simply find it unbearable to work in Defence or under any direct or indirect official instruction. The majority of my colleagues in the Centre have spent large parts of their careers in the higher echelons of Defence or the intelligence agencies, but they come to SDSC because of the freedom to think and write independently, critically and objectively, untrammelled by prevailing government policies or bureaucratic interests. Strategic and defence issues are among the most vital issues of public policy; defence capabilities are also enormously expensive. They warrant intensive and rigorous scrutiny and informed public debate at least as much as health, economic, welfare, environmental or other national issues. The Centre remains the leading academic centre in Australia capable of proving this systematic scrutiny and informing debate. But we learnt the hard way that the extent to which we really excel is very dependent on our direct participation in the intellectual life of the Coombs Building.

CHAPTER 17

Political and Social Change
Not the Research School of Politics and Sociology

R.J. May

RSPAS, as I once had to explain to an overseas colleague, is not an acronym for Research School of Politics and Sociology. In fact, until 1978 RSPAS, surprisingly, undertook no systematic, ongoing research into the contemporary politics of the region. The Department of International Relations occasionally produced work on domestic politics of regional countries, but its focus was global. Some historians wrote about contemporary history, but without a specifically political viewpoint. But there was no part of the School working comparatively on domestic politics. In 1973, it was decided that the time had come to rectify this, and in a triennium submission to the Australian Universities Commission, Vice-Chancellor Sir John Crawford and RSPAS Director Oskar Spate proposed the establishment of two new departments—in Sociology and in Political Science. What came out of this was the establishment, under incoming Director Anthony Low, of single department, with the innovative title, Department of Political and Social Change.

In a review of RSPS 'structure and functions' in 1972–73, it was reported that 'The school is in the process of establishing' the new department. But things did not happen quickly. In 1975, after Low had left RSPAS to become Vice-Chancellor, the incoming director, Wang Gungwu, noted in the School's annual report that the Department of Political and Social Change had not got off the ground 'largely because of the financial stringencies imposed for 1976'. Financial stringencies continued to place a constraint on the expansion of the Department once it had been established. Academic staff numbers were severely limited in the early years—which might have been just as well, since the department, being the last created in the School, also suffered from an acute shortage of office space.

In due course, a Chair of Political and Social Change was advertised and Professor J.A.C. ('Jamie') Mackie, then Research Director of Monash University's Centre for Southeast Asian Studies, was appointed. He took up his post in 1978. I had been appointed in 1972 as field director of the ANU's New Guinea Research Unit and had overseen the transfer of the NGRU to the Papua New Guinea government in 1977, I was invited to join the new department and arrived in Canberra shortly before Jamie Mackie. Coincidentally, both foundation members of the department had backgrounds in economics as well as political science, a factor which facilitated the close association the Department established with the Economics-based Indonesia Project.

Ron May in his 'document dreaming' office, Coombs Building 2003

A third foundation member of the department was former prime minister, Gough Whitlam, who had been appointed Australian Fellow of the ANU following his retirement from politics in 1978. Notwithstanding his great eminence (and the special security measures that brought—a button on the underside of his desk which could summon Coombs security), Whitlam was an active and collegial scholar (provided one didn't mention East Timor) and a regular visitor to the Coombs tea room. He took special delight in serving for a few days as acting head of department; our advice, when he sought a briefing on what to do in the event of a crisis, was to leave everything to the departmental secretary (as the position was in those days), Jan Bretherton. (Jan had previously worked with me in Port Moresby and later became the secretary to the Director, RSPAS).

The Department's early academic strategy was to concentrate on the strengths of its initial appointees, which in geographical terms meant Indonesia, Papua New Guinea, and the Philippines. The Department's first non-tenured appointment was a Cornell-trained Indonesianist, Bill O'Malley (who later worked with the Office of National Assessments). O'Malley, notwithstanding his American origins, was notable, amongst other things, for his ability to turn up on a Monday morning and give a detailed critique of the weekend's football matches in both rugby league (NRL) and Australian Rules (AFL). Indonesian-born scholar M.A. Nawawi, whose interests included Indonesia and the Philippines, was transferred across from the then Development Studies Centre to become the department's fourth academic staff member. Virginia Hooker, now a professor in the Faculty of Asian Studies, was the Department's first research assistant. In 1979 the Department acquired its first PhD scholars, John Nation (an Australian writing about Fiji) and Rico Tsuda (a Japanese working on the Philippines).

The School's annual report for 1978 recorded that

> The work of the Department will be focused initially on Southeast Asia, with East Asia, Papua New Guinea and the South Pacific Islands as secondary interests. The emphasis will be mainly on the domestic political processes and social dynamics of change in the various countries of this region, thereby complementing work being undertaken elsewhere in the School.

The Department's core geographic interests have broadened over the years, to include Malaysia, Thailand, Vietnam, Aboriginal Australia and more recently North Asia, but Indonesia, Papua New Guinea and the Philippines have remained major foci of the Department's work.

In terms of academic discipline, early appointments came from a variety of backgrounds: O'Malley a historian; Indonesianist Colin Brown a historian; Filipinist Brian Fegan an anthropologist; Filipinist Francisco Nemenzo a political scientist; Australian Aboriginal specialist Jon Altman an economic anthropologist; Filipinist Ben Kerkvliet a political scientist; Indonesianist Ken Young an historian and anthropologist; Indonesianist/Malaysianist Harold Crouch a political scientist; Thai specialist Kevin Hewison a sociologist; Indonesianist Terry Hull a demographer; Filipinist/Melanesianist Mark Turner a sociologist; Pacific specialist Stephen Henningham an historian. All comfortably spanned disciplines and related well to colleagues in other parts of the School. In terms of thematic interests, the Department covered a broad range, from rural social change, government-business relations and the role of the military, to democratization, elections and ethnic conflict. When once asked about the Department's dominant theoretical paradigm, Mackie responded, 'eclectic'. In fact, the field of comparative politics has been less susceptible to changing fashions of 'grand theory' than some other branches of the social sciences, and with their varied backgrounds scholars in Political and Social Change have mostly employed a range of 'middle level' theoretical approaches, with perhaps a bias towards the structural-functionalist but a strong admixture of the culturalist, informed by extensive fieldwork.

The politics of Indonesia has been a major focus of the Department's work, including graduate training, since its inception. In conjunction with that of colleagues in the Indonesia project and other parts of the School and the Faculties, this has given the ANU international prominence as a centre for the study of contemporary Indonesia. An early research focus, with support from a School 'New Initiatives' scheme, was on long-term processes of social change in Java, with some comparisons with Central Luzon. This project was conducted in collaboration with Indonesian colleagues from the Regional and Village Research Center at Gadja Mada University. Currently, the Department includes three of Australia's foremost Indonesianist specialists, who have been conducting research on the Indonesian military, Islamic movements in Indonesia and the conflict in Aceh.

With the closure of the ANU's New Guinea Research Unit in Port Moresby, Political and Social Change also became a major international centre for the study of contemporary Melanesia, hosting a series of annual seminars, publishing several books and monographs, and attracting a number of distinguished visitors and PhD scholars from the island Pacific. In 1995 Political and Social Change was involved in a successful bid to the University's Strategy Committee for support to establish a research project on 'State, Society and Governance in Melanesia', which looks at processes of state formation and state weakness, conflict and peace making, and other issues in the contemporary Pacific. Subsequently, of the three people appointed to this project, two— Anthony Regan and Sinclair Dinnen—were located in Political and Social Change. Regan has served as adviser to the Bougainville delegation in the successful Bougainville peace process and Dinnen has had the challenging task of advising the Papua New Guinea government on its Law and Justice Sector program.

In the early 1980s the Department's work on the Philippines, initiated by myself, Nawawi and Fegan, was strengthened by the appointment of Nemenzo, former dean of the Faculty of Arts and Science at the University of the Philippines and a political activist who had been detained during the Marcos dictatorship. In late 1983 (while Marcos was still in power) Nemenzo and I organized an international seminar on 'The Philippines After Marcos'. Shortly before the seminar Nemenzo received intelligence from the Philippines that one of the keynote speakers, Philippines opposition spokesman Jose ('Pepe') Diokno might be the target of an assassination attempt while in Australia (this, it must be remembered, was shortly after the assassination in Manila of opposition leader Benigno Aquino). DFAT and Australian Federal Police were notified, and it was later confirmed that a suspected 'hitman' from the Philippines had booked a flight to Australia coinciding with Diokno's visit. AFP personnel maintained a discreet watch on Diokno during the seminar and during a social gathering in suburban Wanniassa, and Diokno was able to return to Manila safe and sound. The proceedings of the conference were published the following year and enjoyed brisk sales when Marcos was ousted by the People Power revolution in early 1986.

The change of regime in the Philippines, followed by the Fiji coups of 1987 and the uprisings in Rangoon in 1988 and Beijing in 1989, gave rise to another Departmental initiative, with the launching of a 'Regime Change and Regime Maintenance in Asia and the Pacific' (RCRMAP) project in 1989. A residue of funding from the New Initiatives scheme enabled the Department to offer Vietnam specialist Carl Thayer a secondment from the Australian Defence Force Academy. The project linked a number of Australian and overseas scholars, and over the next ten years produced several workshops, four books and twenty-four working papers, which contributed to the debate about regime change, regime consolidation and democratization, revived in recent years by Samuel Huntington, Larry Diamond, Juan Linz and others.

With the appointment in 1983 of Jon Altman, and my own involvement in a study of the first election after self-government in the Northern Territory, the Department took on a brief engagement with Aboriginal Australia. However a 1987 review and some RSPAS colleagues apparently had difficulty with the idea that a politics department should devote scarce resources to Aboriginal issues, and when Altman was seconded to set up the ANU's Centre for Aboriginal Economic Policy Research this line of research lapsed (though in 1999 I returned briefly to Darwin as acting director of the North Australia Research Unit).

In reporting the decision to create the Department of Political and Social Change in 1973, Professor Low spoke of the close interaction within the School in the study of the natural and cultural history of the region but observed, 'If there has been less interaction between departments at "the other end" of the School, this is largely due to the absence from our midst of political scientists and sociologists concerned with national developments in the countries of our region'. With its multi-disciplinary orientation, and the background of its two founding members in inter-disciplinary centers, Political and Social Change was well placed to provide something of a bridging role, and indeed in a submission to a review of the departments of International Relations and Political and Social Change and the Strategic and Defence Studies Centre in 1987, the then head of the Anthropology Department, Jim Fox, said, 'the Department of Political and Social Change has provided a critically important catalyst for interdisciplinary work within the Research School. From its inception it has quickly developed to become a crucial "linking" Department in the School'. (Fox also commented—wistfully it seemed—on the congeniality of the Department of Political and Social Change.)

In 1983 the Department co-sponsored (with the Indonesia Project in the Department of Economics) the first of what has become an annual series of Indonesia Updates, which have attracted widespread recognition for their authoritative assessments of contemporary developments in that country. Following the 'Philippines After Marcos' conference, a 'Philippines Under Aquino' conference was held in 1986 and the first Philippines Update (with support from DFAT) in 1990. In 2004 the Philippines Update was conducted by video linkage with the Asian Institute of Management in Manila. The Department also organized the first Burma Update in 1990, with eminent US Burma specialist Joseph Silverstein as keynote speaker, and took part in establishing the annual Vietnam Updates in 1990. The first of a series of annual thematic conferences on the Pacific began in 1979, with early seminars on West Papua, social stratification, political parties, women in politics, law and order; provincial government, and foreign policy. A subsequent School report commented that 'These seminars are performing a unique function in maintaining a point of focus for work on Papua New Guinea throughout the University now that some departments are reducing their involvements in that country'. In 1990 the Department organized a conference on the Bougainville crisis, the first of three such conferences/workshops which not only helped to educate a wider public to the complexities of the Bougainville situation but helped to create dialogue amongst Bougainvilleans engaged in the conflict.

Notwithstanding the virtues which many saw in the Department's multi-disciplinary approach, the review of the Department in 1987 recommended that it should 'reinforce its identity as a political science department'—a process the review committee saw as already under way—and extend its work into North Asia (an attempt to recruit a Korean specialist in the early 1980s had failed to attract a suitable candidate). Subsequent to this, Jennifer Amyx was appointed to work on Japanese politics, and a position on Chinese politics has been shared with the Contemporary China Centre. But in a period of limited financial resources, expansion into North Asia could only be achieved by restricting the Department's established geographic focus on Southeast Asia and the Pacific.

As early as 1979, the Department had launched a publications program intended to disseminate its research, engage with other scholars, and raise its profile. Its first Working Paper, an edited collection on 'The Vietnam-Kampuchea-China Conflicts', from a conference organized by RSPacS and the Asian Studies Association of Australia, came out in that year, and the first Political and Social Change Monograph, on *Micronationalist Movements in Papua New Guinea*, edited by myself, appeared in 1982. By 1998 the Department had produced 25 Monographs and 13 Working Papers (as well as the 24 RCRMAP Discussion Papers). Such an output would not have been possible without the dedication and tolerance of series of support staff, among whom Claire Smith and Allison Ley have been salient. Successive School reviewers (especially those from North America), however, tended to denigrate all publications produced within RSPAS as 'in-house' publications—notwithstanding their international authorship, international reviewing process and international distribution—and eventually cultural cringe and editor-weariness (on my part) prevailed: following the path of the ANU Press, the series were discontinued.

Apart from the various Updates, the Department has, from its beginnings, been actively involved in a range of outreach activities and public commentary. Its members have served as consultants to a range of clients, including AusAID, the World Bank, OECD and the Australian and Papua New Guinea governments; they have provided briefings to a variety of visiting missions, Australian personnel about to be posted overseas, and the diplomatic community in Canberra; and they have appeared regularly as media commentators in Australia and overseas—notably at times of crisis like the 'People Power' revolution in the Philippines, the 'Sandline Affair' in Papua New Guinea or the demise of Indonesia's President Suharto—sometimes placing the prospects of future visas in jeopardy. Following the demise of Indonesia's President Suharto, Harold Crouch, who became the Department's third tenured appointee in 1987, spent two years in Jakarta establishing the Southeast Asian office of the International Crisis Group, an influential organization headed from Brussels by former Australian Foreign Minister Gareth Evans.

From two PhD scholars in 1979, the number had risen to eight by 1984 and for most or the 1990s and early 2000s there were more than twenty—giving the Department one of the highest PhD scholar/academic staff ratios in the School. Of the 38 PhDs completed in the Department, 35 per cent have been by women. The review of 1987 noted that, 'Students in DPSC, unlike some other departments, have generally praised the academic staff for regular consultation and close supervision....and the general intellectual stimulus which staff members freely provided'. In return, the Department's PhD scholars have lent it a certain character. One of the Department's early scholars, a Fijian rugby international, returned to Fiji to become a high-ranking chief and head of the University of the South Pacific's School of Social and Economic Development. Another, a Malay Muslim from Thailand who wrote about Muslim separatist movements in the Philippines and Thailand, was named in 2004 as the leader of an umbrella organization of (essentially moderate) southern Thai separatist groups, and is now in Sweden. Continuing this radical tradition, a West Papuan activist came to the Department from exile in Sweden to complete a PhD on the West Papuan struggle (while continuing to serve as an international spokesman for the Organisasi Papua Merdeka). As against these, the Department's first Burma scholar was inclined to be somewhat defensive of his country's government. An Australian scholar working on the Philippine military left Manila at short notice after finding that his apartment had been searched in his absence—never knowing whether the perpetrators were military intelligence, failed coup plotters, or members of the extreme Left. More recently, a Solomon Islander who was working on his PhD as his country was heading towards a violent internal conflict, was rumoured to have briefly conducted affairs of the Isatabu Freedom Movement from his Coombs office. Some research scholars have followed more conventional paths to successful careers in academia, government and, in a few cases, the private sector.

The Department of Political and Social Change, while deciding not to introduce yet another graduate coursework programme in the School, has contributed courses to graduate programs in the National Center for Development Studies and the Department of International Relations, and undergraduate courses in the Faculties.

Over the years a large number of distinguished visitors have also contributed substantially to the intellectual life of the Department. Among them have been prominent Indonesianist scholars Bill Liddle, Ruth McVey, Dan Lev, Mochtar Pabottingi and Miriam Budiardjo; Philippine Communist Party founder Jose Maria Sison, prominent Filipino journalist Amando Doronila, and Canadian Filipinist David Wurfel; Malaysian scholars K.J. Ratnam, J.M. Gullick, Lee Poh Ping and Mavis Puthucheary; Singaporean Chan Heng Chee; James C.

Scott of Yale University; and Pacific specialists Alan Ward, Bill Tordoff, Michael Oliver, Yaw Saffu, Nau Badu and Terence Wesley-Smith.

Jamie Mackie retired in 1989, though he is still a familiar figure around the corridors of the Coombs Building. He will be remembered by some for his uncanny ability to seemingly sleep through a seminar, but then ask probing (if sometimes lengthy) questions during discussion. I took over briefly as head of department in 1988 before Ben Kerkvliet, a former research fellow in the Department, was recruited from the University of Hawai'i to take up the Chair in 1992. I retired in 2004, to be remembered, if at all, for my achievement in transforming an empty office into a 'document dreaming' site, a place of pilgrimage for those defying the prophesy of the paperless office. With my departure, and the creation of a separate entity for the State, Society and Governance in Melanesia Project (SSGM), the Department's commitment to the island Pacific, carried on over the years by scholars such as Stephen Henningham, Mark Turner, Randal Stewart and Bill Standish, will come to an end, ironically coinciding with Australia's increasing engagement in the region.

PART IV

Running the Coombs

CHAPTER 18

Sue's Story

Sue Lawrence

I started work in the H.C. Coombs Building on Monday 17 December 1973. I clearly remember my interview for the position. A friend and I were just graduating from the Metropolitan Business College in Civic and were told there were positions available at the ANU. We were told to walk over and see the ANU Staff Office and fill out a form. I knew the general direction of the campus but really had no idea where to go. The ANU didn't have a very public face in Canberra then and I knew very little about its activities.

Together, my friend and I set off in the general direction of the university, asking people where to go along the way and, eventually, we made it to the staff office. We had been told to ask for Mr Brown who greeted us and gave us a form to fill in. Looking at the pile of forms and papers on my desk today, I'm amazed by the simplicity of that document—it had space for our name, address, date of birth and qualifications. No referees, no selection criteria, no duty statement; we were able to fill it in then and there.

After checking the forms Mr Brown told us that there were two positions in the H.C. Coombs Building 'School Services' that he thought we might be suitable for. Not knowing what the Coombs Building was or what 'School Services' did, we could only agree that we thought we would be very suitable! He walked with us over to the building and introduced us to the Assistant Business Manager Mr Ian Horsburgh. We were interviewed together by Mr Horsburgh and were told there were two positions available, one in the Typing Pool and the other in the Business Manager's Office. My friend immediately said she would take the typing pool position and I was taken to the Business Manager's Office for another interview.

In those days the two research schools of Social Sciences and Pacific Studies were generally referred to as the Joint Schools, sharing the same location in the H.C. Coombs Building and the same administration. Peter Grimshaw was the Business Manager for both schools. Our interview consisted of Mr Grimshaw asking me what courses I had done at the MBC, what my father did for a living, where I had been to school, what it was like living on a farm and what magazines I read. I must have answered something right because after about 20 minutes he stood up to usher me out and as I got to the door he said 'So, we'll see you on Monday then'.

Sue Lawrence (seated) with Gladys O'Sullivan, Doris Slater (now Whitby) and Myriam Bonazzi, 1974

It all seemed perfectly natural then: two short conversations on a Friday afternoon, one brief form, and I had landed a job—continuing no less—to start on the following Monday. I remember being delighted, excited and scared. Less than a fortnight before Christmas and I was starting my first full-time job. I couldn't imagine how I would ever find my way through the campus each morning, let alone navigate around the amazing honeycomb Coombs Building.

I was appointed Junior Stenographer in School Services on the princely wage of $3,000 p.a. A professor on the top of the range was earning the, to me, huge amount of $25,964. I was pretty happy with the weight of my paypacket; and, like everyone, I looked forward to payday. When I first started and for a number of years afterwards staff were paid in cash. On payday, members of the University Accounts section (accompanied by an armed guard) would travel across campus at set times to each Building. In the Coombs Building a table would be set up, just outside the tea room—where the drinks machine is now—and all the staff would line up to receive their fortnightly salary and sign-off to confirm they had received the correct amount. That line was a good way of getting to know people throughout the school—people were always in a good mood in that queue; it was payday, after all. One canny member of staff worked out a way of making the most of his cash payment. He devised a system to raffle off his paypacket. He would sell about 30 tickets at $5.00 each and whoever won would receive his pay of about $100 and he would take home $150. An easy way to boost your income!

In the 1970s, administrative work was very different. The equipment we had then seems so old-fashioned and inefficient now. I know, though, that at the time I thought my electric typewriter was absolutely state of the art. And I didn't even try to get my head around the newly installed mainframe computer—the DEC 10—located in the Coombs basement. As far as I was concerned, computers had nothing to do with me!

I suppose, because things took a lot longer to do then, we had a lot more staff to do the various administrative tasks. Each department in both schools had a secretary and in most cases at least one typist who were supported by a general school typing pool of up to 12 typists (women, of course! I don't recollect ever meeting a male typist). The typing pool took on any overflow of work from the departments as well as general school material and their fingers flew as they worked on normal correspondence, seminar and conference papers, publications, statistical material, work from Dictaphones and anything else that might be sent their way. I thought the typists were extraordinary: not only did they have to be incredibly accurate in their work as photocopying was expensive and most reproductions were by carbon copy, they also often had to decipher the handwriting of the original document—at times this was more like code-breaking than clerical work.

The staff in the typing pool would change fairly regularly—I always thought it was a particular head of department's (who shall remain nameless) handwriting that did for them in the end!—as they would apply for higher-level positions within the School as they became vacant. Thus we had our own training ground for Departmental Secretary positions.

The school also had its own stationery store that employed three members of staff. They ordered and stocked the stationery for the whole school—you could go down to the store to collect your order or, if you were feeling lazy, someone from stationery would deliver it to your office.

There were three staff on reception as well, a receptionist and two others who sorted and delivered mail directly to each department. Mail would arrive promptly twice a day and you would know they were coming by the sound of the mail trolley trundling down the corridor.

Of course, the focus of the Coombs Building, then and now, was the tea room. This was a very different affair in the '70s and '80s compared to the way it is run now. Then, there were three tea ladies (everything seemed to come in threes in Coombs!) A service station was set up at each end of the room and from there, teas for morning and afternoon sessions and any seminars or meetings happening throughout the building, would be served. There have been many tea ladies over the years, all of them with strong personalities and particular ideas. It always made for some interesting tension at morning tea time, watching a tussle of wills between the ladies about the best way of going about things.

Most areas didn't have a photocopier and the majority of the school's duplicating was dealt with on the ground floor in a room with a large photocopier and a Xerox machine. For a time, this service was run by the formidable Mrs B. A product of colonial India, she ran the business with an iron will and the discipline of the Raj. She called all the women staff 'girlie' and hid a heart of gold behind her gruff exterior. Everybody knew to tread carefully around Mrs B.

Coombs also had its own printery, long since dismantled. Books, conference proceedings, reading bricks, and so on, were printed on site. The printery had 6 staff with numerous casual staff who were called in when needed. One of the more memorable staff members was also a member of Emergency Services. During bush fire season he would appear at work dressed up in his emergency services jump suit and a big coat with numerous pockets with compasses, clip boards, terrain maps and toilet paper all hanging out of pockets. He did look quite funny wondering around the Coombs corridors. He loved people's looks of amazement and their curious questions.

Nowadays, one of the most essential school services—cleaning—is done long after hours, when everyone has gone home. Back then, we had our own cleaning staff who were much more visible and a big part of the school team. There would have been about 16 staff all up, with a supervisor. While the majority of them started at 4a.m. and finished at eight, the rest worked on until noon. Each cleaner was responsible for a particular area of the school and they were all familiar with each area's requirements. For some sections, a spit and polish did the trick; others, of course, demanded a much more thorough job. Unfortunately with the increasing salary and worker's compensation levels across the campus the University decided that all cleaning on campus should be done by contract and so we could no longer have staff directly employed by the School.

In the Assistant Business Manager's office there were, not including the manager, three (again!) staff members in the office that processed general staff payroll and personnel media, took all the seminar room and lecture theatre bookings, held petty cash, took care of maintenance reports and occupational health and safety issues and handled general enquiries. In those days, payroll/personnel matters for academic staff and all student affairs were looked after by the Assistant Registrar who, although located in Coombs, was a member of the university Registrar's Division. Of course there was also the Accounts Section that had six staff with one of these people being responsible for just the purchasing!

The Business Manager's Office consisted of his administrator and two other staff.

In the early days we had a telex machine in the office and sent hundreds of messages a week. The first machine we had needed to be connected to the receiving machine while you typed, so you had to be a fast and accurate typist or the call would be expensive. The next generation of telex machine had a facility where you could produce the message on a strip of paper about 10mm wide. As you typed out the message the machine converted it to a series of holes punched into the paper. When you sent the message through the machine, it read the paper and sent it at a higher speed than could be typed. If it was a long message, however, we would end up with metres upon metres of tape that could be ruined by the smallest of tears or creases. I spent many hours in tears of frustration at having to retype what seemed to me to be the silliest of messages.

After the telex we got the first fax machine in the building—oh happy day! Fax messages for all the departments in the two schools were sent and received from the Business Manager's Office As you can imagine hundreds were sent every week and the staff were kept occupied sending and receiving messages as well as doing all the financial accounting for messages sent. Clearing paper jams and redialling busy numbers became a part of every day. Now, fax machines are one of the least expensive pieces of equipment in the office, and most departments have their own—and electronic mail is making even them obsolete.

Well talk about history! Since RSPacS, or RSPAS as it is now, started there have been seven Directors, Professors Crawford, Spate, Low, Wang, Ward, Ricklefs and Fox. I have worked with the last five. As well, there have been so many other outstanding colleagues and friends whose faces are still vivid to me—especially because quite a few are still wandering the corridors and still actively involved in the School today. I treasure the wonderful memories of those who are gone.

Professionally, the person who had the most influence on me was Peter Grimshaw. After that first, casual interview, he and I ended up working together for 25 years—a long time in anyone's book. Peter was devoted to his work and, in particular, to the Research School of Pacific and Asian Studies. He came to the Joint Schools from the Snowy Mountains Hydroelectric Scheme in 1964 as the Finance Manager (later changed to Business Manager) and remained in that position until RSSS appointed their own Business Manager in 1995. Peter remained as Business Manager for RSPAS until he retired at the end of 1997 so he served this School for nearly 34 years.

I think he had a particular affinity for RSPAS because he spent some of his childhood in Papua New Guinea. Peter's father was Police Commissioner in Papua New Guinean and so they lived in Port Moresby for a number of years.

Peter was a tall, rather large man and was quite imposing. He always knew where the money was and could always find more for someone who had just come up with a special project or needed that bit extra to invite a special visitor or to buy a 'just released' piece of equipment. He was always interested in learning what work the academic staff and students were doing and if a bit more funding for fieldwork was needed then he would usually be able to find it.

Across the campus, Peter was famous for his memos. He always went back over the history of what he was writing about and usually provided scenarios of the different outcomes arising from the options presented. As a result, there were very few brief memos that left his office—they went on for pages. He also made sure that relevant people and files received copies and so each memo had a large distribution list. I can remember typing these with up to 8 carbon copies—you had to be accurate or you would end up spending the rest of the day erasing errors with whiteout. Some days I went home looking like a house painter with my hands—and hair—covered in whiteout.

Peter was always admired and in some cases feared for his memory. You could never promise to send him something or get away without responding to one of his memos because he would always remind you. He did have a great memory but he also had a great re-submit system that he used to remind himself of outstanding matters. (I hope that is not a myth buster.) I looked after this system for a number of years and there could be hundreds of documents rotating through his office as reminders of papers he was still waiting for or that needed action on a particular date.

Peter Grimshaw, Business Manager of RSPacS for 34 years, circa 1970s

Peter was very generous with his time and if anyone went to him with a problem—be it work related or personal—he would do his best to help. He was also heavily involved in activities outside work that included P&C committees, the board of the Credit Union, The Administrative and Allied Officers Association, Industrial Relations Society and the Journal of Aboriginal History. He also taught a course in Industrial Relations at CITE and did a BA and a MEdAdmin, all while working full time. Peter's stamina was extraordinary. Although he was in the office from 9a.m. until about 6p.m. he always took home two briefcases full of work (and his portable typewriter) He would arrive each morning with mounds of work for me that he had prepared the evening before. Sometimes I wished he watched just a little bit more television and went to bed a bit earlier.

He was never worried about getting his hands dirty either. The school had several houses and a research centre—the North Australia Research Unit (NARU) in Darwin that were wiped out by Cyclone Tracy in 1974. Peter and some staff from Facilities and Services went to Darwin and started trying to salvage as much of our equipment as possible. They also searched for research records belonging to academic staff and surprisingly were able to save quite a bit. A few years later he helped build a covered veranda off the main office area at NARU.

I think most people would agree that the New Guinea Research Unit and NARU would not have been the successes they have been if it was not for

Peter. He put an enormous amount of effort and planning into finding the funding to support the essential research being done in these areas. He was always thinking of the best ways of using available funds and his dedication to the future of the school was fundamental to its success.

To me, the Coombs Building is a strange and unusual place that is never short on entertainment. Over the years we have had to explain many things to the public, or just the central university administration, about some of the funnier (strange or amusing, depending on your interpretation) incidents that have taken place. Some of our questions, such as 'How do we put a pig—a gift to the school from a chief in the Highlands of PNG—on the inventory?' or answers to their questions 'Yes, there is a big lizard that likes to have a daily swim in the NARU pool but, no, we don't see it as an OH&S problem' must surely have caused quite a stir in some quarters. Somehow though, whether we're explaining the purchase of bush materials to build a house in PNG; or reporting on the sinking of a barge, with the school's 4WD vehicle on board; or requesting funds to buy rifles for use in case of crocodile attacks on field trips, or adding a catamaran (for fieldwork!) to our insurance policy: the school keeps ticking over and the work gets done.

As with any community, or family, the fun and laughter have been mixed with sadness and grief. We have lost friends and colleagues and we have celebrated the birth of children and the making of new friends and colleagues across the world. We have dealt with accidents and injury to staff and students and we have applauded the international recognition of our colleagues for the quality and range of their research.

Have things changed? Sure they have but I don't think we can look back and say that the '70s and '80s were the 'good old days'. Things change and so do people. When I got lost on campus in 1973, I had no idea I'd be here more than 30 years later or that, despite new faces, new machines and new structures, I would be familiar with every nook and cranny in Coombs. And I'm happy to be part of this community that continues to grow and change.

CHAPTER 19

PAMBU, the Islands and the Coombs

Ewan Maidment

Brij Lal once said to me, the Canberra school of Pacific history was a faith, with a shrine (the Coombs Building at the ANU), a prophet (Davidson) and an Island orientated theology.

Doug Munro, 'The Isolation of Pacific History', *Journal of Pacific Studies*, Vol.20, 1996: 47

Before you come in the front door of the Coombs Building have a look to your right at the Kiribati canoe hidden in the scrub under the eve. Go past Seminar Room A along the administration corridor, its walls lined with Roger Keesing's and Ian Frazer's photographs of comfortable-looking Solomon Islanders. Before you climb the staircase roping around the lift have a glance at the Melanesian artefacts on display in the glass case opposite the Coombs Lecture Theatre foyer. Meander along the Coombs corridors past Melanesian artefacts once lent from the now-vanished Institute of Anatomy. Find your way, if you can, to the top floor quarters of the Division of Pacific and Asian History, its walls lined with Polynesian images, worn tapa hangings and the signed fine-mat commemorating Professor Davidson's participation in the drafting of the Samoan Constitution. You will find the Pacific Manuscripts Bureau at the end of the corridor, at the highest point in the building on the edge of the precipice above the invisible divide separating the Research School of Pacific and Asian Studies from that other research school which occupies the Coombs building.

Perhaps the Pacific Manuscripts Bureau too is a remnant of a glorious scholarly past. The longest running international joint copying project in the world: Pambu is certainly a survivor; protected by outside funding and the necessity to help preserve Pacific archives, manuscripts and rare printed material. It was established in 1968, in the heyday of Pacific studies at the ANU, as part of a comprehensive effort 'to locate, catalogue and copy manuscript material relating to the Pacific Islands.' Gordon Richardson, the NSW State Librarian, had revived an idea, first proposed by Floyd Cammack in 1963 when he was Assistant Librarian at the University of Hawaii, for combining library resources to locate, preserve and share Pacific Islands documentation. With Richardson's encouragement and the support of Jim Davidson, Harry Maude developed the proposal in his report, *The Documentary Basis for Pacific Studies* (1967), which laid the foundations for the formation of the Pacific Manuscripts Bureau in 1968. Maude also head-hunted Robert Langdon from the staff of the *Pacific Islands Monthly* and oversaw his appointment as the Bureau's first executive officer.

Robert Langdon circa 1970s

Maude's enthusiasm for systematic preservation of Pacific documents was evident even in the early 1950s when as executive officer of the SPC Social Development office, working with Ida Leeson, he organised programmatic microfilming of unpublished Pacific linguistic materials. Maude maintained this enthusiasm throughout his long career, ultimately conceiving of the Department of Pacific History as 'the world centre of document-orientated study concerning the people of the Pacific islands.'

Archival advocacy was a key aspect of the Research School of Pacific Studies. The School initiated and partially funded the appointment of the Dorothy Crozier as the first government archivist in Fiji where she established the Central Archives of Fiji and the Western Pacific High Commission in 1954. The Department of Pacific History was one of the two original sponsors of Phyllis Mander-Jones' survey of archives and manuscripts in Great Britain relating Australia, New Zealand and the Pacific Islands. A regular manuscripts section was incorporated in the *Journal of Pacific History*, from its first issue, to report news of newly discovered documents, publish check lists and critical notes on older accessions.

Modelled on the Australian Joint Copying Project, the Pacific Manuscripts

Bureau was subsidised by a consortium of specialist Pacific research libraries, initially formed by the National Library of Australia, the Mitchell Library, the State Library of Victoria, the Alexander Turnbull Library and the University of Hawaii Library. (A few years later the State Library of Victoria dropped out of the consortium and the Library of the University of California at San Diego joined up.) In its early days, when Robert Langdon was Executive Officer, the Bureau located and microfilmed personal papers, such as diaries and correspondence, linguistic materials and the records of non-government organisations, especially missions. Langdon made many fieldtrips using a portable Hirakawa microfilm camera to copy documents and the acronym, *Pambu*, became well known throughout the Islands.

After Bob Langdon's retirement School funding for the Bureau ceased and no provision was made to continue the Pacific Manuscripts Bureau. However a number of Pacific historians, particularly Dorothy Shineberg and Niel Gunson, lobbied to revive the Bureau. Gunson prepared a document for the RSPAS Faculty Board outlining some of the work that still needed to be done and other reasons for reviving the Bureau. Six of the libraries agreed to form a consortium to fund all the Bureau's wages and operational costs, while the RSPAS supplied accommodation and support services. A management committee was established consisting of representatives of all the member libraries, Pacific Regional Branch International Council on Archives (PARBICA) and Pacific scholars in the Research School, chaired by Gunson.

For the next seven years, under two Executive Officers, the Bureau was exiled from the Coombs Building. Most of the microfilming was contracted out. Microfilm production dwindled. The Bureau went into debt. Support staff was minimised. Following the resignation of the previous Executive Officer, Gillian Scott, the PMB's secretary, agreed to take on the position of Executive Officer, at a reduced salary and on a temporary basis, in an attempt to restore the PMB's viability. Despite the difficult circumstances, while Gillian was Executive Officer the Bureau consolidated and published its complete catalogues, developed and started a productive new microfilming program and recouped earlier losses. When Gillian resigned in 1993, the NLA intervened to appoint its own manager, Adrian Cunningham, for one year, and Brij Lal took over the chair of the PMB Management Committee. The Bureau returned to the Coombs Building. Production increased as the new microfilm program bore fruit. Adrian Cunningham began a re-invigorated program of preservation microfilming in the Islands. The Bureau's work was re-orientated toward documenting contemporary Pacific Islands politics and Island-based organisations. In 1996 and 1998 two new libraries, the University of Auckland Library and the Yale University Library, joined the PMB consortium.

Ewan Maidment at work in the Pacific Manuscripts Bureau, 2004

Over the last ten years, guided by an international management committee of expert librarians, archivists and scholars, working from a hot-house of Pacific studies specialists, stabilized and energetic, the Bureau has reached out from the Coombs Building, to develop collaborative Pacific archives preservation projects with many individuals, organisations and curatorial institutions in Australia, New Zealand, the Islands and beyond.

The Bureau works closely with hundreds of individuals to identify, organise and preserve their Pacific Islands papers, audio recordings and photographs: the last kiaps and other Islands civil servants, missionaries, business people, trade unionists, scientists, journalists, politicians, activists and researchers, and their families. Over the last decade, drawing from a vast database of indexes and archives listings, the Bureau has handled thousands of reference inquiries from researchers all over the world. With the assistance of Coombs IT experts, the Bureau has developed a web presence and on-line searchable catalogue of its microfilm series, including web-accessible reel lists itemised to document level.

In accordance with the current notions of archives preservation reformatting best-practice, and in the face of strong pressure to conform to a popularised digitisation industry, the Bureau has maintained its commitment to analogue photography as its primary method of reformatting. Microfilm is a far more stable means of long term preservation for bulk textual materials than digitisation. At the same time the Bureau has developed a capacity, in collaboration with the most advanced micrographics studio in Australia, to automatically scan very large amounts of high quality digital images from microfilm on demand at far less cost than direct digitisation. In conjunction with its digitisation projects, the Bureau has been at the forefront of development of digital content management, standard metadata systems and long-term digital storage repositories at the ANU.

Much of this work is accomplished on fieldtrips in the Islands, away from the Coombs Building, with its concomitant long hours, day after day, in front of the computer screen. PMB projects are selected by the management committee in accordance with a strategy of broad geographic coverage, while maintaining flexibility to develop specific projects in response to particular circumstances. Each project is clearly negotiated with the owners or custodians of the original records well in advance and endorsed by the management committee. However the implementation is often far less routine. Having worked in the PMB office up to the departure deadline to clear the decks, having packed the camera, film and associated gear (against a check list written in remorse on an Air NZ serviette after one trip where I forgot an essential piece of equipment), I usually leave the Coombs in the dead of night, drive to Sydney in the old Pug, say a brief hello-goodbye to my family (I am an exiled Sydneysider), get a lift to Mascot, negotiate the over-weight baggage, take the plane and sleep.

Arriving in the Islands, usually in the middle of the night, you have crossed the beach, as Greg Dening puts it, even if in 500 tons of Boeing. The pace changes at once. The balmy night settles me, the stars, the distant sound of the reef, the shadowy coconut trees along the street. Discussing the local news with the taxi driver on the way to the guesthouse, I am no longer a denizen of the Coombs Building, I am a whiteman, a palangi, a visitor in a foreign land. PMB field projects are in some of the most exotic places on earth: Port Moresby, Madang, Goroka, Mt Hagen, Wabag, Losuia, Honiara, Yandina, Colonia, Pohnpei, Majuro, Tarawa, Nauru, Port Vila, Noumea, Nadi, Lautoka, Suva, Nuku'alofa, Apia, Alofi, Avarua, Papeete.

Waking up in the Aitutaki Hostel last year, after a chat with Maria the warden and Mata her offsider, I would walk through the back streets of Avarua to the corner occupied by the Cook Islands Trucking Company and then along the lane beside the creek, past mango trees and taro gardens, to the Cook Islands National Archives nestled high up the valley beneath Te Ko'u mountain. It is one of the most pleasantly situated and well-protected archives repositories in the Islands. There I would spend all day microfilming, under the strict supervision of George Paniani, the National Archivist. Working beside his staff, Kanny Vaile and Ake Willie, I helped them receive two large transfers from the Ministry of Justice and they helped me with re-arranging some of the disordered documents for microfilming. It was the third stage of an on-going PMB project aimed at microfilming the NZ Resident Commissioner's Office correspondence with the Resident Agents in the outer islands, 1900–1970. During the second stage my colleague, Barry Howarth, had contracted a bad case of dengue fever, was hospitalised for a week in Rarotonga, and subsequently barred by his doctor in Canberra from any further trips to the Islands. However this trip went smoothly, making 17 rolls of microfilm of correspondence with the Islands of Atiu, Mauke, Mangaia, Penrhyn and Manihiki. In the evenings, back at the Aitutaki Hostel, there was much gossip, eating and singing with the residents, including a group of Fijian nurses attending the South Pacific Nursing Forum.

On 5-6 January 2004 Cyclone Heta caused severe damage in the Cook Islands, Samoa, American Samoa, Niue and Tonga. In Niue at Alofi South, the main government centre, winds of up to 350km/hour were followed by massive sea surges at high tide which crashed over the cliff-line, flooding areas more than 40 metres above normal sea level. One woman and her child were killed; many residential, commercial and government buildings in Alofi South were destroyed or damaged, including the hospital. Most of the contents of the Huanaki Museum and Cultural Centre were destroyed. The National Archives and Library building was damaged and much of its contents was water damaged. The offices of the Department of Justice, Lands and Survey were also badly damaged; some of its records were destroyed and most of the remainder was water damaged. PMB microfilming of surviving lands records after the cyclone was carried out inside a shipping container parked outside temporary accommodation allocated to the Ministry for Justice. Working in the container was stifling and not improved by the strong smell of mould, as the container was used for storing saturated records. Although the facilities were less congenial than in the Cooks, the hospitality was just as warm, and the gossip just as intriguing.

One of the very few times on PMB fieldwork in the Islands in which I encountered anything other than hospitality was in Honiara in 2001 during a lull in the civil unrest. People in the street were tense. Bedraggled and a little dazed after a heavy stint microfilming a dirty batch of records of the Solomon Islands

National Union of Workers, taking a break out to buy a soft drink, a chap took a flying kick at me for the heck of it! I got pretty sick on that trip too: some militants had damaged the Honiara water source, clean water was hard to find and there had been rats nesting in the archives! The kick was a shock though. Previously Honiara had been a safe and friendly town. The street lighting was so poor that passers-by would sing out to each other on dark nights to avoid colliding, but no one felt threatened. One of the most interesting pastimes during fieldwork in Honiara was to sit on the balcony of the United Church Rest House, overlooking the main wharf, gossiping with the residents and watching the shipping movements, including speed boats coming into Honiara Hospital with wounded militants from Bougainville.

Angau Lodge in Boroko, Port Moresby, was also a good place for meeting people and conversation. The caretaker, Moro, and his family protected the Lodge and its residents. It was the last of a number of RSPAS owned facilities in PNG, originally established by Mr Grimshaw, and the base for PMB fieldwork in PNG until the School's New Guinea Field Services were closed down in 1999. The Lodge and its two rather shabby vehicles, emblazoned with ANU insignia, gave the University a presence in Port Moresby and enabled researchers to reciprocate hospitality. Relegated to prison-like hotels and the latest model hire-cars, which are prime targets for raskols, fieldwork in Port Moresby is now a lot more lonely and dangerous.

Returning to Canberra from the Islands is always another culture shock: the sheer conspicuous materialism of western urban society is alienating. However, arriving back at the Coombs Building, laden with exposed negative, is much less jarring. The relatively Spartan conditions of the Coombs Building are not too distant from the Islands. Island emblems decorating the Coombs corridors are familiar. Islands news is the main topic of conversation amongst colleagues in the Coombs Tea Room, picking up many of the themes being discussed in the Islands guest houses, work places and news media. And, most important, Coombs scholars continue to give seminars and publish on the Pacific Islands. The PMB office routine reasserts itself: the microfilm negative has to be processed, edited and documented; positive prints duplicated and distributed; the backlog of correspondence and research inquiries has to be addressed; reports and articles to be written; in-house archival projects demand attention; the next projects have to be organised. Nevertheless there is a brief sense of satisfaction in having contributed to Islanders' efforts to preserve their documentary heritage, in having produced research materials which complement and contribute to research efforts of scholars in the Coombs Building, and in being able to make those research materials accessible to scholars worldwide through the PMB member libraries.

Although the Pacific Manuscripts Bureau concentrates its main efforts outward to the Islands, it has also looked inward, within the Coombs Building. In recent years, with the retirement and death of many of the post-War Pacific studies scholars, the Bureau has recognised that their research papers may be as much at risk of loss and destruction as archives and manuscripts in the Pacific Islands. Some key record groups, such as the papers of Jim Davidson, Derek Freeman and Roger Keesing, have been sold or donated to institutional custody. However no regular arrangements have been made to assess and preserve the research materials generated by the majority of Pacific academics and visiting fellows associated with the School. Over the last few years, the Bureau has collated, and in some cases, microfilmed and stored, records of about 20 Pacific scholars associated with the School, such as Alan Ward, Sir Colin Allan, Peter Sack, Sione Latukefu, Dorothy Shineberg (including her database of indentured labourers in New Caledonia), Dorothy Crozier (including her collection of the papers of Rev. Shirley Baker), Ric Shand, Scott MacWilliam, Donald Denoon, Don Laycock (including his collection of the papers of Richard Thurnwald), Robert Langdon, Stephen Wurm (in conjunction with PARADISEC), and Rev. Neville Threlfall.

These records under PMB control, and other research materials still in the hands of active and retired ANU academics, are only part of the School's research resources. Loosely controlled cartons of research materials, many generated by the Department of Human Geography, are stored in the Coombs courtyard garages. Further papers and publications are held in cages in the Acton Underhill Tunnel by the Division of Pacific and Asian History (PAH) and the Department of Political and Social Change. The Department of Linguistics has many hundreds of audio recordings of Melanesian languages and related documentation which are only just being brought under control. The Coombs Cartographic Unit has a magnificent collection of Pacific maps. Established record repositories are maintained by PAH, and the Departments of Anthropology, and Archaeology and Natural History. Together with the resources of the Pacific Manuscripts Bureau, and combined with the strong Pacific holdings of the ANU Library and extensive Pacific business and labour holdings of the ANU's Noel Butlin Archives Centre, this vast body of records constitutes the raw material for, in Harry Maude's terms, a world centre for Pacific Islands documentation.

NOTE

Material on the history of Pacific Manuscripts Bureau is taken from Harry Maude's letters in Bob Langdon's file on the early days of the Pacific Manuscripts Bureau; Susan Woodburn's book *Where Our Hearts Lie: A life of Harry and Honor Maude in the Pacific Islands*; and the *Journal of Pacific History* (volume 20).

CHAPTER 20

EGW and me

Claire Smith

In 1980 I applied for a job as part-time stenographer in the Research School of Pacific Studies and to my surprise I was appointed. Perhaps two years living in Singapore got me the job, but I had no previous experience working in Academe and the Pacific was no more than a large ocean dotted with various islands. I had brushed up my German-based Stolze-Schrey shorthand, phonetically adapted to English, which had the advantage that nobody else could read it, often including myself. I was convinced that working in the rarefied atmosphere of great intellects would inevitably rub off on me and somewhat overawed by so many great brains. On the other hand, I was puzzled how so few of them could cope with a jammed photocopier, repair a stapler which got stuck or deal with an unresponsive fax machine.

Those were the days of IBM electric typewriters, multiple carbon copies and Tippex to erase mistakes. On my first day, the secretary of the department, who had a strong Scottish accent and a brisk manner, handed me a list of staff and students. It was an impressive list of PhDs and students aspiring to such a degree, with one other name at the end of the list: E.G. Whitlam, National Fellow. Slightly alarmed, I asked whether it was THE Mr Whitlam. Maybe there was someone else but an ex-prime minister by that name?

EGW soon made one of his weekly appearances. The department had allocated the biggest, best room to its illustrious visitor. It had a fine teak desk, a vast green armchair and bookshelves with timber edges. The secretary's job was to organize Gough's diary, schedule meetings between the big man and students and staff who sought his advice and turn away those who wanted his presence at openings of various events. Students soon found out about Gough's sweet tooth and one particular young man appeared with a whole tray of what looked like home-made baklava. On another occasion, the very attractive young woman, who was at that time writing a book about another labour leader, presented Gough with several enormous cream buns which he proceeded to eat with gusto, sugar-dusting the front of his immaculate suit coat in the process.

Gough Whitlam with H.C. Coombs at the launching of Coombs' book *Trial Balance: Issues of my working life* (Jack Golson and Anthony Low in the background)

I was given some of Gough's typing jobs, often from handwritten notes in a fairly illegible scrawl. Gough, with his love of all things Italian, was at that time involved with the Dante Alighieri Society. With my very basic background of the Italian language, I was asked to type his hand-written draft of an address to that society, a text liberally sprinkled with quotes in Medieval Italian which, combined with his spidery scrawls, presented a considerable challenge. I was convinced I had made a real mess of it, but Gough was appreciative of all my efforts. He called me 'the Hun'.

'Comrade' was the way Gough addressed members of staff. Some days Gough could be convinced to come to the Coombs tearoom where he would hold court, with his minions gathered around him, listening to his rhetoric on the state of the nation. He was utterly charming to us, the secretarial staff, and displayed a quaint old-fashioned gallantry. In his typically demonstrative way he once went down on his knees to kiss the boots of the secretary, a rather disconcerting sight in the confined space of room 5101.

With an ex-prime minister in the building, security became a concern and it was decided that an alarm system would be appropriate. This consisted of a button fixed under the desk of the secretary, alerting the reception area on the ground floor. I don't think it ever needed to be used while Gough was in the department. Later on, when I had moved into the position of the secretary, I once or twice accidentally pushed the alarm button while moving from side to side at my desk, whereupon after several minutes one of the elderly mailmen came panting and gasping up the stairs to assist in the emergency. The alarm system was then dismantled. After Gough's departure, the biggest and best room became cluttered with printers, photocopiers and ergonomic furniture. The vast green armchair was swiftly claimed by a staff member who found that it allowed him to almost fully recline and thus greatly enhance powers of concentration.

CHAPTER 21

Editing Reflections

Maxine McArthur

I liked the Coombs Building the first time I saw it, in 1996. In the courtyard parrots chattered, magpies warbled, and huge trees shed welcome shade. It seemed an oasis of sanity after busy Civic, and I found myself quite desperate to get the job for which I had come to be interviewed.

The job was a research assistant's position, to work with Morris Low, then a research fellow in the Division of Pacific and Asian History, on the production of a Historical Dictionary of Japanese Science and Technology. I had just returned to Australia from a long residence in Japan—16 years—and felt confident in my ability to read Japanese material, although less confident in my ability to be part of this very scholarly setting. As it turned out, however, my worry was unfounded (at least, on my part).

After a couple of wrong turnings I knocked timidly at the door of what seemed to be an administrative office, where several people were chatting and drinking tea. An elegant and gracious lady introduced herself as the administrator, Dorothy McIntosh and escorted me to the interview room. I don't remember a great deal about that interview, so little that in writing this essay I had to consult the file to remind myself who was there. I think Mark Elvin and Morris Low asked most of the questions, but Elizabeth Drysdale and Tessa Morris-Suzuki also attended. I do remember that everyone was most un-fearsome and considerate, which made the usual post-interview despair (that one has acquitted oneself badly) even more poignant; I really wanted this job!

To my delight, I got it.

The work itself was fascinating, and in the early stages required mainly reading and note-taking. I had my own office, opposite Morris's room and next to the kitchen, which also housed the photocopier and printer, so when I left my door open people would often mistake it for the kitchen and drift into my room dreamily holding a cup, or rush in brandishing papers to be photocopied then stop dead in embarrassment. I also followed with interest the imprecations of a certain academic who fought a running battle with the photocopier. Although the machine performed like a lamb for most of us, when this person required its services it would stop, chew paper, print wrong-sided, run out of ink, or just sigh and give up completely. It Knew.

I grew to know and admire the other general staff who worked in the Division at that time—Marion Weekes, Jude Shanahan, Julie Gordon, and Oanh Collins. They never made me feel less than totally welcome and my initial impression of the Division as a wonderful place to work was confirmed.

The building itself was another matter. I still liked the courtyards and the window in my office, but there were other aspects of the Coombs Building's 'personality' that proved harder to cope with. I evolved basic survival routines: always use the same entry and travel the same corridors to your office, otherwise you will arrive to work late through getting lost on the way; ditto always use the same route to the tea room; never try to find a seminar room alone (I still keep this rule); never trust those cryptic maps at the head of stairwells.

It was after I spent an afternoon trying to find Cartography that I came up with the layer theory. The Coombs building has layers, like a lasagne. The most obvious layers exist in space; as the trails inside a beehive or the shelves in Borges' library, so are the corridors in the Coombs building. Labyrinthine and venerable, they have a multi-dimensional quality; you are seldom on the layer you think you're on. The building is always full of surprises: I have opened a door off the car park and come upon storerooms full of books with alluring titles (Pandanus Books), greedily fingered useful-looking boxes stacked carelessly next to a service exit, peered into dark alcoves that lead nowhere (unless their original destination had been boarded over in a *Cask of Amontillado*–like frenzy), relaxed in comfortable chairs on verandahs overlooking those wonderful courtyards that provide a refuge from the glaring computer screen (all comfortable chairs in Coombs gravitate from offices to verandahs), and been comforted by the night watchman as we waited for the NRMA to come and restart my car at midnight. The nice thing about the building is that there is always somewhere to go when you are tired and sick of your office. Take a walk—with luck, you'll be back by tea time.

It is a pleasant fantasy to see the design of the Coombs Building as a metaphor for academic research: that is, you should never theorise ahead of your material and assume you know where you will end up. You can't see too far ahead, and the easy straight line sections are very short; corners come quickly. Then, somehow, you arrive.

Maxine McArthur in East Asian History Library, Coombs Building 1997

The emphasis in the building's design is on horizontal layers; corridors spiral around the three hexagonal blocks and, unlike more modern buildings that diffuse the outside into corridors through skylights and huge windows, the corridors of Coombs very properly keep the outside at bay, as if anxious to preserve peace and quiet for the academic activities within. The stairwells provide a vertical connection, as do the shutters, which allow windows to be shaded in summer for at least half the day, and thick walls divide rooms on one side from those on the other. It is a design eminently suited to Canberra's climate, and ensures that rooms are cool in summer (provided you close your window to keep out hot air) and warm in winter (provided the heating is turned on).

Each corridor is different. Some have photographs of people and research subjects, some boast maps and glass-fronted cabinets to entice you to stop on your way through. Some boast resolutely cheerful seminar and departmental notices, often combined with large clear name labels on doors. Some are quiet, all doors closed, while others hum with conversation and people tracking from room to room in deep discussion.

Each discipline, of course, regards itself as the centre of the layers, but surely that honour must go to the tea-room. The tea-room is itself an example of multi-dimensional space—it is a place for work, relaxation, and socialisation. It sprawls outside onto the verandah, an extension of the world inside; it is a symbol—of how academic life is a holistic pursuit reliant on coffee.

The longer I worked at the Coombs building, I began to realise that it also has layers in time. Occupants of these previous layers glower at you from portraits hung on corridor or office walls as you make your daily pilgrimmage from tea-room and parking lot. Collections of artwork, too, tell of the activities and taste of those who used the building before we did. Some of the names on doors are those who now play a less active part in the running of the building, but their work built the foundations of present-day activities. The large trees in the courtyards must have been saplings when Coombs was first built.

And there are layers in the activities within the building, overlapping and complementing each other: students, academic staff, general staff, support staff. The Coombs Building to outside eyes may seem to 'be' the research activities of the departments within, but in fact it needs all kinds of activities to function. Although essential (and extremely tasty), this outermost and most obvious layer of sauce and cheese does not by itself a dish make.

Although my work on the historical dictionary finished in 1998 and Morris Low left us for a post in Queensland, I stayed on in the Division of Pacific and Asian History, and in the years since my job has become largely editing. Now, editing also has layers. There is the grilled cheese-type editing done at the end of a project, that is, proof-reading, which involves checking punctuation such as missed periods or footnote numbers, page numbers, missing quotation marks, consistency of citation etc. Consistency of format is extremely important in academic writing, and is something many students do not spend enough time on until the very end of their thesis or project. Despite advice to leave plenty of time for proofing and printing, there have been occasions where running off a thesis and getting it to the university printers has been a highly athletic exercise.

Students are not the only ones guilty of inconsistency, or of being just plain busy. I have been handed 200-odd pages of collected papers by a senior academic with the comment 'I think it's ready' (to go to the printers as camera-ready copy), only to find that there was at least a week's worth of proofing and formatting work still to be done. God is in the details.

Then there is the bolognese sauce-type editing, AKA 'copy edit' or 'it's nearly ready to print, can you look at it before I send it to my supervisor' editing. Most of my work is done in this layer, mainly with students whose mother tongue is not English. It involves more invasive editing, in that sometimes I have to try to guess what the writer means and tweak the grammar accordingly. Occasionally this requires telepathy-like powers to decipher the writer's intent, and if there are two or more possible readings I refer back to the writer. What do you make of: 'To be free needs to defend other people's freedom'? Or: 'The vision will fruit less without permeation, therefore the process should be investigated'? The most satisfying part of this job is to see some students actively learning from this process to produce a polished draft that can stand beside native speakers' theses.

Rarely do I work on deeper, how-many-eggs-have-we-used-for-this-pasta editing issues, such as structure of chapters or the thesis as a whole. These issues should be resolved before I see the work, although some cases are tougher than others. On one memorable occasion a student brought me a chapter upon which one of her supervisors had carefully noted many times on the first few pages every incomplete sentence (and there were many), then by page 5 had given up and only pencilled the occasional sulky 'delete' for certain phrases. After much discussion and hard work on the student's part, she got the hang of sentences, after which we revised paragraphs…and so on.

Students are generally content to accept minor alterations. I stress that it is their choice whether to accept corrections or not—it is their name on the thesis, after all. I have had arguments at times, as with the native English speaker who would not accept that I found his sentences incomprehensible. I am often frustrated by my own ability to explain grammar, for example, when to use the definite and indefinite articles, which is a problem common to many Japanese speakers when writing English. Why did I correct 'a' in one place but 'the' in another? Some cases are clear, but in others it is a matter of preference, and I find it difficult to explain why I think there should be 'the' instead of 'a' or even nothing at all. I am always learning—correcting others' grammar makes me pay more attention to my own; and a huge bonus of working in such an interesting place as the research school is that, to me as a fiction writer, the content of theses and papers often offers fertile pickings of exotic and unusual information, and of concepts that I would not have encountered elsewhere.

While writing this essay I have reflected on my years at Coombs in Pacific and Asian History, and it has made me realise anew how lucky I am to be able to come to work and be confident that the day will bring subjects of interest, pleasant interactions with intelligent people, and the sound of birdsong from outside my window. I would rather work in this circuitous, textured, and above all *layered* building than just about anywhere else.

CHAPTER 22

Finding Nuggets in Coombs

Allison Ley

My first glimpse of the Coombs Building filled me with apprehension. Even the familiar scent of eucalyptus on the pure Canberra air did nothing to relax me. After the Jakarta heat, the chill on my hands should have reminded me I was home in Australia, but all it did was make me feel more nervous. It was August 1988, and after more than seven years in Indonesia, I was about to be interviewed for a position as a research assistant in the Department of International Relations.

Entering the building brought no relief. Its separate hexagonal structures and labyrinthine corridors with winding staircases leading to different floors soon had me totally lost, only adding to my list of worries. Of course, I later discovered that all first timers, including some of the world's greatest intellects, lose their way when they enter the building; which is ironic, as the one thing the committee advising Coombs' architects wished to avoid were corridors that were 'attenuated and confusing'. Finally, after several attempts and helpful directions, I managed to find my way to the department, where Barbara Owen-Jones, secretary, sat me in the library for ten minutes.

As I re-read my curriculum vitae, I tried to suppress self-doubt. What kind of person was the ideal candidate for the position? An editor? Well, yes. I had edited the Bandung Hash House Harriers weekly newssheets and yearbook, which mostly meant putting red lines through four-letter words and censoring nude photos. Would that skill be required here? Probably not. What else? Experience in Indonesia? Yes again, but would they see experience in International schools and with nappies, baby food and play groups as relevant? What else? Bahasa Indonesia? I could buy mangoes and bargain for batik tablecloths with the best of them, but what if I had to discuss Indonesian politics? We had been told to keep out of local politics, although I did once attend a meeting of the Dharma Wanita … Oh dear. All in all, not a lot of experience in the academic world. I looked around the departmental library and seemed to be surrounded by dark leather bound journals, *Australian Journal of International Affairs, International Security, World Politics, Global Governance.* Was sitting me here simply to remind me I wasn't up to the job?

John Girling and Robyn Ward interviewed me. They were softly spoken, and asked me how I would go about putting a publication together. A bit of luck. Familiar territory. Perhaps the Hash House Harriers experience could be relevant after all. I managed to list each step in the process and began to relax a little. They asked me what I would bring to the job. I remembered and sketched some Indonesian experiences with serious purposes. It was going better than I expected, so I decided to joke my way through any questions which may have revealed my shortcomings.

From left: Beverley Fraser. Allison Ley, Anne Robinson, and Claire Smith on the Coombs Tea Room Balcony, circa 1992

As the interview progressed, I began to form an impression of what it would be like to work in this building. John Girling's office had two floor-to-ceiling windows and a balcony overlooking a courtyard with gum trees, native shrubs and birds. It was like a den in an Australian country hotel. Smiling people wandered through the courtyard gardens in casual clothes. John and Robyn seemed as polite and patient as hotel assistants, and somehow I imagined myself as a tourist in Canberra, resident in the Coombs Building and those I met on that crisp August morning, were part of my holiday adventure. Perhaps that fantasy helped me. To my surprise, I was offered the job and began work in October 1988.

I soon discovered that I needn't have worried about my lack of academic experience, or the limits of my Bahasa Indonesia, as my first task as a research assistant was to learn to drive a bus to take a group of Russian visitors to and from a conference venue. And my experience of being given totally unfamiliar tasks certainly wasn't unique.

International Relations had been in existence for more than three decades before I began there. One of the first research assistants in the department was Rosemary Brissenden, who arrived in the late 1950s, when the department was still temporarily housed in a weatherboard cottage in Liversidge St. Rosemary had been a tutor in political science at Melbourne University, and was invited by Arthur Burns, head of the department, to work on Indonesian politics as part of the newly-formed program on South East Asia. Having spent time in Indonesia as a NUAUS student, Rosemary was fluent in Bahasa Indonesia and well-versed in Indonesian history and contemporary politics. So naturally, she assumed she was going to publish on Indonesian politics. But her first task turned out to be writing a chapter on Nehru and neutralism for a book on SEATO, funded by the Ford Foundation.

Judith Wilson, one of the longest-serving RAs in the school, began working in the department of Anthropology and Sociology in 1962, when it was in the Old Nurses' Home of what had been the Canberra Community Hospital. Conditions were basic. To quote Judith

> The 'tea facility' was the nurses' old bathroom with a sheet of masonite over the bath and an unreliable electric jug; I don't remember a frig. Only the Director and senior academic staff ... had telephones. The rest of us including PhD students and visiting academics, shared a wall phone in one of the corridors. I remember queuing up with Economics staff, all waiting our 'turn' and trying as nonchalantly as possible NOT to listen to others' conversations.

It's hardly surprising, then, that when Judith moved to the Coombs in 1964, the year Sir John Cockcroft opened the building, she found it 'well-planned, even luxurious'. She was given her choice of rooms, a luxury rarely if ever offered to professors these days. Unlike Rosemary, Judith was given tasks considered normal for RAs in the 1960s. Judith again

> ... sometimes referred to as 'detective work'—lots of foot-slogging, long hours in libraries, winding microfilm until one's eyes crossed or donning the compulsory white gloves to search through fragile book or manuscripts at the National or Mitchell libraries or elsewhere. 'Put on your trench coat', one professor used to declaim when suggesting one of these projects.

Judith worked for Professor Bill Stanner on Aboriginal matters; she read microfilm and hard copy reports and collected information for his 1968 Boyer Lecture on 'After the Dreaming'. Later in 1977 she became an editorial assistant for the journal, *Canberra Anthropology*, now the *Asia Pacific Journal of Anthropology*.

Not long after its opening, the Coombs Building was full, and departments had formed separate groups. The need to meet across disciplines grew. A few cross disciplinary bodies emerged in the 1990s. I was part of one of these, the Pacific Islands Group, or PIG as it was known (an acronym endorsed by our colleagues from the Pacific, especially those from Papua New Guinea, for whom pigs are highly valued). PIG activities covered different Pacific islands, communities and disciplines. Take these seminars, 'Tahiti in crisis', Karin von Strokirch (historian/peace research); 'Bougainville peace process', Ruby Mirinka (nurse); 'Praise the lord and pass the ammunition; Rascal group surrender in PNG', Sinclair Dinnen (restorative justice scholar); 'US and the South Pacific', Professor Henry Albinski (International Relations); 'Customary law in the Pacific islands', Hon John Muria (Chief Justice, Solomon Islands); 'Pacific resources on URICA', Colin Steele (Menzies Library), as examples. We publicized films in our newsletter: Joe Leahy's *Black Harvest* and Dennis O'Rourke's *Cannibal Tours* and piggy-backed on the success of others, featuring Chris Owen's award winning *Man Without Pigs*, a film which captured the conflict between traditional and Western values. Most of the administration of PIG fell to me as an RA.

By 2002, the building had been fully occupied for nearly four decades and Luke Hambly, who joined the department of anthropology as a research assistant that year, thought it was showing its age. While growing to appreciate its certain charm over time, his first impressions of Coombs were of 'a dowdy, tatty, mouldy, stained old relic' which evoked the image of 'a cold Orwellian bunker'. Then, Anthropology was one of the largest departments in the school with 36 academic staff members (including departmental visitors) and 35 students. High staff and student numbers generate considerable administrative work. Luke, a team player, undertook a variety of tasks, apart from the usual of searching for literature, compiling bibliographies and editing articles for publication. He bought, sold and shifted furniture, catered for functions, and counselled students.

Individual academics shape our working conditions. We try not to judge them harshly while accommodating their idiosyncrasies. 'You had to go in arms waving' was how Geoff Jukes' assistant described the best way of entering his room, so thick was the smoke from the cigarettes he smoked incessantly. Ron

May's office was wall-to-wall floor-to-ceiling stacks of books and papers. Into the impossibly small space left over was squeezed a desk, chair and computer. To find a reference in his room meant clambering over piles of books to locate it.

Most of our tasks are more mundane, though. Checking text for errors is what we do. We're paid to be pernickety. I was reminded of this when I came across the original typed copy of Professor Sir Leonard Huxley's speech for the official opening of the Coombs Building. He had dictated

> The whole field of Pacific studies awaits fuller development than it has previously received in Australia. Our relations with the East, with the Americas, with the East Indies, New Zealand, New Guinea and all the Pacific islands must be carefully studied in order that they become friendly and fruitful, as they must if our future is to be safeguarded and if we are to make our full contribution to the counsels of the nations.

At the end of this quotation, the word 'counsels' was struck out and 'councils' put in its place. But was this change correct? If he meant 'councils' in the sense of assemblies or congresses, it was. (But if he meant 'counsels' in the sense of recommendations or deliberations, it wasn't. You be the judge.) This kind of fussy correction is the bread-and-butter editorial work of research assistants. I once spent three hours in the National Library locating and checking a quotation, which resulted in a change in the position of a comma. An expensive comma.

These are exceptions of course. The tasks we generally do, such things as compiling and annotating lists of references on a subject; finding and photocopying articles; writing chapters; editing text; checking the references and quotations; formatting documents and taking them through the steps of publication, all reduce the burden for academics, supporting their efforts and allowing them to concentrate on their research work.

We also assist students. Some PhD candidates demonstrate peculiar writing traits. I remember taking out the word 'political' eight times in one sentence of a dissertation. Another used quotation marks indiscriminately in the text. After seven chapters of "this", I began to wonder whether my unadorned text was "somehow" "lacking".

*****

When the Coombs Building was opened in 1964 the then Vice-Chancellor, Sir Leonard Huxley, likened its structure to 'a basic hexagonal seed crystal upon which infinite expansion and growth can take place in the future'. He was seeing the potential for the school's development. By 1966 the three hexagons were full and already the number of Coombs researchers and visitors had outgrown the building's capacity. It wasn't until 2002 that the Coombs extension was built to house the ever-increasing numbers of staff and students.

New technologies have expanded and developed the nature of academic work over the decades. Since 2003, films, CDs and electronic publications have been listed in annual reports. Growth has occurred in publications across the range of disciplines. In 1973 the school published its first annual report. It lists 236 publications, consisting of 16 books, 8 more edited, 63 book chapters, 132 journal articles and 27 working papers. Three decades later, in 2003, members of the school produced a total of 572 publications comprising 49 books, 25 more edited ones, and 149 chapters in books, 218 journal articles, 59 working papers, 11 chapters in conference proceedings, 14 reports, 31 book reviews, 23 electronic publications and 24 microfilms CD titles. These figures show both an increase in traditional publications and an expansion into new academic media. And there's more ... Student dissertation numbers show the same escalation.

What does this increasing crop of academic material mean for the small band (twenty-six, twelve of whom are part-time) of research assistants who work in the Coombs building? For every one of those publications you can be sure some of the raw data will have been collected by an RA; quotations verified by another; chapters edited and proofread, references checked, bibliographies compiled by someone else.

In my time in the Coombs Building, I have come to appreciate the skills needed to support research and publication. I don't recall having had to strike out four letter words in any publications, but I have shifted furniture, built websites, driven buses, returned videos, catered for dinners and collated papers for conference folders. I have even climbed mountains (well, of books) for relevant material.

But RA skills are broader and more indepth in the 2000s. Early in 2004, I was on a selection panel to appoint an RA in the school. There were 73 applications from highly qualified individuals from different career strains: librarians, archivists, first-class students, one of whom had won a history prize, one applicant had worked on the theatre production of the 'Vagina Monologues', another had worked in the food industry. We short-listed five for interview. On the day of interview each applicant arrived promptly, was well-dressed and poised. Unlike my interview, in which Robin and John coaxed the relevant information out of me, the selection panel I was on required ten detailed answers to specific questions. I was given three questions to ask, one of which was six sentences long and loaded with acronyms like KINETICA and

FACTIVA. I stumbled reading the question and would have struggled to answer it.

If the selection process works, the new breed of RAs, through balancing teamwork with independence and defining their work priorities, will (take a deep breath): launch new projects; undertake broad literature searches, uncover specific material in the quest of furthering research. They will annotate bibliographies; edit internationally refereed journals; correspond with obstinate authors; organise conferences, and leap over piles of books in a single bound...

Great changes have occurred over the two decades since I started to work in Coombs. But my sense of the accommodating character of the Coombs Building refuses to budge. Perhaps that is why I have stayed so long. Though workday routine has eroded my original fantasy of a tourist hotel, a few treats remain. I can gaze at the bright red and blue parrot on the bottle brush just outside my window; am free at lunchtimes to walk through gardens to a restaurant; and regularly go for coffee with friends. Inside the building people tend not to hurry, lest they lose their way. An appropriate habit of mind, when you think about it, for those in a research institution.

Note: I gladly acknowledge Judith Wilson, Rosemary Brissenden, Robyn Ward, Helen Glazebrook, and Luke Hambly for their helpful comments on this chapter. ANU Archives supplied the files for the historical information on the discussion with Coombs Building's architects and the opening of the building.

CHAPTER 23

The Fly on the Wall of Room 4225

Jude Shanahan and Julie Gordon

From 1989–2000, Julie and Jude sat at their desks with their backs to each other on opposite sides of room 4225 on the top floor of the Coombs Building, in the corridor that belonged to the Division of Pacific and Asian History (PAH). Their desks faced opposite walls and they each had a window to one side—Julie's left; Jude's right. Between them were two small filing cabinets, a telephone, telephone books and a noticeboard. They were like bookends in the room.

From their bookend positions they could simultaneously word process; answer the phone; converse; order stationery; monitor corridor conversations (the mail box was placed strategically outside their door); interrogate, converse with or pass messages to anyone who entered the office. People collecting mail would often sort their mail at the long bench in room 4225 and they would stay and chat. Hank Nelson was one of those who regularly did this; and if Bill Gammage was also present Julie and Jude would be treated to their mock verbal duelling. Niel Gunson was another and he had many stories to tell of the early years of Coombs and the ANU. For example, he told of an ex-Prime Minister who, whilst still a postgraduate student, took a midnight skinny dip in the University House fish pond.

Julie made it her business to see that anyone who entered the room was up to date with all events of PAH, and that every member and associate, of the division, knew every other member and associate of the division—even if that meant being introduced twice, or as was the case with one PhD student, several times to the same person. Julie and Jude's duplicate antennae picked up much of what was taking place on that upper floor of PAH. They might hear the baritone voice of Tony Reid; Jim Griffin's deep voiced rendition of a song; David Marr muttering that he was late for a meeting, as he hurriedly grabbed a writing pad from the stationery cupboard or some in depth academic discussion taking place around the mail box. A divisional wit once likened the mail boxes to the village well.

Room 4225 was a central place of activity within the Division; people came to get stationery, stamp mail, type and gossip. Personal and Divisional landmarks were often celebrated there, e.g birthdays, departures and most importantly the celebration of newly acquired PhDs. Dorothy, Marion, Oanh and others regularly joined Julie and Jude in their office for morning and afternoon tea. Academics and students would regale the general staff with their fieldwork experiences and many other stories were shared on those occasions. For example Brij Lal reported his experiences in Fiji when travelling with the Constitutional Commission. The Commission attended village meetings to consult with the locals on the new constitution. Brij recalled the problems associated with juggling the obligation to drink some kava, at each of these meetings, and the necessity to be abstemious in order to remain clear headed. There was often discussion of past events and people within the division, for example the fact that at one time there was a departmental suit that could be borrowed by any of the 'suitless' academics who found themselves in need of some clothing to impress. Although, by all accounts this dated suit wasn't destined to impress. If walls could talk an anecdotal history of the Asia Pacific region could be told by room 4225, not to mention the odd bit of Coombs' gossip.

Jude and Julie in Room 4225 with a summer vacation scholar, mid-1990s

Julie's Coombs experiences, however, commenced eight years prior to Jude's. She recalls 19 enjoyable years with PAH. Julie was always concerned with marking and celebrating special occasions and creating a community. She recalls one incident from this earlier period (1980s) concerning the issue of whether to collect for a wedding present for one of the young academics, 'I approached the Head of the Department armed with a list of reasons and great trepidation as to why this should go ahead, as this was quite a rare occurrence! People had either been married for years and years or were students who had their career in mind, and not matrimony! The Head listened very gravely to my arguments, then after considerable thought, agreed. I later realised he had derived much amusement from this exercise!'

The Department Head at that time was Gavan Daws and Julie considered herself very privileged to have been there during his reign. He encouraged interesting departmental visitors such as husband and wife filmmaking team Bob Connolly and Robyn Anderson (Robyn now sadly passed away). They made a series of documentaries on Papua New Guinea: *First Contact*, *Joe Leahy's Neighbours* and *Black Harvest*. *First Contact* was the film they made as visitors to the Department; they also authored a book of the same name. Another visitor was Dennis O'Rourke, who made *Half Life* a chilling documentary about US nuclear testing in the Marshall Islands; and Andrew Pike (owner of Canberra's independent cinema, Electric Shadows), who collaborated with Gavan Daws and Hank Nelson to produce *Angels of War*, a film about 'the experiences of Papua New Guinea villagers who lived through some of the most brutal fighting of the Pacific campaign [WWII].' (Ronin Films catalogue). This film won the Best Documentary—1982 Nyon Film Festival in Switzerland and Best Documentary in the social sciences—ATOM Awards. Geremie Barmé was also involved in filmmaking, and we were given the opportunity to preview his film on the history of Tiananmen Square.

Over the years the Division had some very notable academics and visitors, among them, Oskar Spate and Rev. Sione Latekefu. While Bill Gammage was a visitor to the Department he undertook a couple of expeditions that followed historical trails in the rugged Papua New Guinea terrain. Later Chris Ballard, another member of the Division, together with other members of RSPAS made a similar expedition, and this time through the advancement of technology, ie digital cameras, laptops and satellites, Chris and his colleagues were able to email back digital images of their adventure, including close ups of their feet stricken by trench foot.

Julie also recalls the unpredictability of the Canberra climate. She recalls 'a departmental lunch at O'Connor, roughly about the end of October. After enjoying our meal, we walked out and much to our surprise, found that—at that time of the year it was actually snowing!' and 'Yet another occasion which was a workshop held at the Old Canberra Inn, Lyneham, with all staff attending. In theory it was supposed to be a pleasant, balmy spring day, with barbecue facilities under wisteria-covered pergolas. However after we got there the weather became colder and colder (typical Canberra), and finally some of the staff who lived nearby went to their homes to return with as many parkhas and windcheaters as possible, as well as small heaters! This unexpected cold snap didn't exactly sharpen our minds with what was on the program for the day!'

Julie and Jude shared some chores, e.g word processing, answering the telephone, collecting and sorting mail but other chores were divided. Julie took care of stationery, seminars, organized social occasions, accommodation bookings, and handed out the photocopying bills. Jude looked after the Records Room and assisted people with using computer software. Probably one of her most intriguing experiences on the computing side was teaching a visiting Pacific Island dignitary, Vakatora, how to manipulate the mouse. He had always had a secretary to do such things, and he told Jude that he'd only used a computer to look at his golf averages. However, he very good naturedly took on this challenge, but those large fingers found it difficult and Jude never worked out a satisfactory strategy for teaching such a thing.

Julie and Jude dealt with the shared duty of answering the telephone by using a simple roster system. Julie answered the phone in the mornings and Jude in the afternoons. When something of importance was taking place in the Asia Pacific region the phone would be ringing constantly. For instance they were both kept busy taking calls during the 2000 Fijian coup. At that time the media and Fijian VIPs all wanted to contact Brij Lal who had served on the three-member Fiji Constitution Review Commission. So Julie and Jude were often able to witness, vicariously, history as it happened. And speaking of Fijian coups, Sitiveni Rabuka, leader of the 1987 Coup, also numbered amongst the interesting visitors to the Division. At that time he stated that he regretted his part in the coup; he was a charismatic person, with a modest and thoughtful demeanor.

As well as answering the phone Julie and Jude were often asked to place calls to overseas locations. In the 1990s this could be quite a trying experience when calling places like Papua New Guinea or Indonesia; there were only so many lines going into these countries, and sometimes it might take hours even days to make contact. Jude reflects 'Making these calls also connected us to those different and exotic worlds. I remember once having to put through a call to an important person—prime minister perhaps—in the Kiribati parliament. The switchboard person at the other end responded to my request by saying, 'I think he's in today, hang on I'll just go and see if I can see his car parked outside'. This immediately put into perspective for me the small island nature of the Kiribati parliament!'

Wildlife was another part of their expertise. Over Jude's desk was a large poster identifying the various Australian parrots, many of which visited the window sill. These birds were of particular interest to overseas visitors: king parrots, gang-gangs, galahs, crimson rosellas, eastern rosellas and even sulphur crested cockatoos would come to collect the birdseed that was spread across the window sill. [Names of the spreaders will not be mentioned here, as this was an illegal activity in the Coombs building.] The crimson rosellas became so confident that they would tap on the window at a certain time in the afternoon. On a couple of occasions young birds would come into the office, and then panic when they couldn't find their way out. But Julie or Jude usually managed to assist them, sometimes enlisting the help of some passing academic and wildlife handler such as Bill Gammage. Somewhere on disk there may even be some academic papers with input by a crimson rosella. Jude recalls entering the office one day to find a rosella running up and down her keyboard, 'when I looked at the screen it was filled with all sorts of interesting parrot language.'

Birds aren't the only wildlife in the Coombs building. Possums are quite an attraction for the overseas visitors. On one memorable occasion Christine Weir, a PhD student at the time, reported the presence in her office of a mother possum with her little baby on her back. The possums huddled on the window sill as they unwittingly posed for the many photographs that were taken by overseas visitors and locals alike as they traipsed through Christine's office.

The Coombs experience is one not to be forgotten, and if you hang around long enough you become part of an extended family, with all its good and bad points. During the period when Julie and Jude worked at RSPAS there were great changes in technology. Word Processors, as some general staff were called in those days, went from using main frame computers to personal computers, and the internet began to dominate. Paper memos became a thing of the past, and emails all pervasive. Academics began to type their own work and technology opened new opportunities for general staff and there was a gradual breaking down of formalities between general and academic staff.

CHAPTER 24

Fieldwork and Fireworks: A Lab Assistant's tales

Gillian Atkin

The lab wing is a mystery to many working in the Coombs. It is made up of offices, archives and about a dozen laboratories. What happens therein? In brief, we analyse material collected on fieldwork. How do we go about fieldwork? Crudely put, we travel to remote parts of Australia and overseas, set up camp and collect sediment, soil and bones.

In this short essay, I will tell some fieldwork stories, in which my technical colleagues wrecked a brand new car; drove the wrong direction in the Strzelecki Desert for a day and a half; lost a trailer load of equipment and unwittingly set fire to Coombs. Not all in the one episode. Details later. First the lab wing.

I started working in the laboratories of the Coombs Building in 1982. In the 1980s there were a quite a few technical officers in the Department of Archaeology and Natural History, now there is one, me. My expertise is the extraction of fossil pollen from sediment cores to enable palynologists to reconstruct past environments.

The ground floor labs are largely used for archaeological work, which involves the treatment and analysis of stone, bone, pottery and wooden artifacts. Our department also sources obsidian, a volcanic glass, excellent for making stone tools. We link it to an original source, which gives us clues to ancient social connections. The ground floor also accommodates an expensive microwave oven for cooking up soil samples in chemicals leaving only plant-derived silica particles called phytoliths. This enables the identification of plants associated with archaeological sites. We also have an extensive animal bone collection used to identify bones from archaeological sites.

Before the geomorphologists were driven from the school during the dismemberment of the department in 1997, the middle floor labs were used for soil chemistry and analyzing sediments. Around the time the geomorphologists were axed, our resident chemist disappeared in the bush and was never found. The chemistry lab sat somewhat like the *Marie Celeste*, deserted and abandoned, for many years. In 2004 more than 500 obsolete chemicals were disposed. Though some sedimentology is still done in the department these labs have become general-purpose labs for the use of students and staff.

Gillian Atkin 2003

The top floor is for pollen analysis and other microscope work. In general the only nasty chemicals now used in the lab wing are in the pollen prep lab on the top floor. We keep and maintain an extensive pollen reference collection, microscope lab and pollen preparation lab in this area. Cores are collected from field sites, sliced into small sections then analysed for pollen, phytoliths and diatoms. Radiocarbon dating and examination of microscopic particles give insights into past environments. Pollen is tough so extracting it from sediments involves cooking samples in very strong acids and alkalis to eliminate everything else until only the pollen is left, which is then identified microscopically.

We examine material from overseas and Australia collected on field trips. Fieldwork provides lots of adventures. Max Campion, a technical officer with whom I worked for many years, assisted in the field and spent most of his time driving around Australia. 'Aussie larrikin' describes Max's personality. Keith Fitchett, another colleague, was a meticulous cartographer with endless enthusiasm for detailed work. Whilst collecting geomorphological data on a South Coast Beach, Keith and Max bogged a brand new school vehicle in the sand. They spent hour after hour trying to free the 4-wheel drive but, in the end, all they could do was sit on a dune in the sunset and watch as it disappeared into the incoming tide.

With its winch cable, they had tethered the vehicle to the dune and then spent the night watching it slosh around in the surf. The following day a bulldozer hoisted it out and they hosed out the seaweed and driftwood, as best they could. A mechanic managed to start the vehicle and Max and Keith drove back to Canberra to admit their folly. The vehicle was a write-off. You can image the sensation, some weeks later, when they claimed 'overtime' for the night spent on the dune!

Max also traveled around Australia with the late Gurdip Singh (world renowned biogeographer). In many an outback pub, Max introduced himself and Gurdip as 'pollen trappers' or himself as a 'palynologist's labourer'. Gurdip and Max both had strong wills. Gurdip was a formal academic, and a gentleman, seldom seen without a shirt and tie. Max was the larrikin technician famous for his approach to any crisis: boil the billy, have a cuppa and sit and think things through. Gurdip was stubborn and pedantic. Max would take his time. There's a story they disagreed on which track to take in the Strzlecki Desert one morning. To break the standoff, Max eventually gave in and agreed to go Gurdip's way, insisting he would keep driving until Gurdip admitted he was wrong. They traveled in silence for the next day and a half in the wrong direction. Finally Gurdip admitted he *may* have been wrong; and they returned to the intersection, the scene of the original dispute, after three wasted days of desert travel.

My own experiences in the field have led to interesting times too. In this tale the location was idyllic, a perched lake on Fraser Island. All of the field crew were women including an academic, student, research assistant and a technician. We were monitoring lake conditions over a 24-hour period, taking temperature readings every couple of hours from the middle of the lake. We had had dinner including wine. The mood was jovial as we rowed out. I rowed out to the center of the lake for the 10 pm reading, then the others took measurements and samples. Work done, it was time to head back so I began to row shoreward. It was a warm, starry night so we gazed for some time trying to make out the various constellations; there was no hurry to get back. Time seemed to stand still as I looked towards the shore then gazed up into the night sky. I had the impression we had been out for quite a while, but onward I rowed. I was getting tired of rowing and the shore wasn't getting any closer. My colleagues advised me to keep going whilst they enjoyed the experience. Eventually they too began to think we had been out for a long time. Judy casually leant over and pulled on a chain and said 'I forgot! I put the anchor down when we started taking measurements'. We were thankful that a group of fishermen who were around the lake earlier had not witnessed our performance. By the time we got back to shore it was just about time to go out again. I made one of the others row.

I also went on field trips to central Australia assisting with surveying, collecting eggshell for dating, sampling sediments and digging and logging sections of shoreline around Lake Eyre. I was one of three technicians on these trips. Two of the other technicians were on the excursion to drill into the lake sediments and extract cores for laboratory analysis. The logistics of getting all the food, water, fuel, and equipment including a drill rig through the dune fields of the Simpson Desert were challenging. We were in the field for six weeks at a time with one trip out to re-supply. I kept a diary of these trips and one day stood out in my memory.

We had been in the desert for about six weeks, the boys with the drill rig had set off a day earlier leaving two of us to pack up and break camp. Packing up took all morning—much longer than anticipated. It was a hot windy day so bundling our gear was difficult and uncomfortable. We decided to shower before leaving using the last of the available excess water. Because wind was so blustery, showering involved dancing under the precious drops falling from a bush shower hoisted up a tree. This was our first shower for 7 days, a luxury, so after mine I refilled the bush shower and hoisted it up a tree for John. Whilst drying myself I heard a splosh and @#&*!!!&*%$#@!! as the bucket of water hit the ground. It was my fault; I was never very good at tying knots. So John went without his first shower in a week.

This was just the first of many mishaps to come. We didn't get away from camp until after 1.00pm even with a 6.00am start. We had a car full of equipment plus a fully laden trailer to haul over the dunes, but at least we were on our way home. Twenty or so kilometers along the track I looked out to my left to see a fully laden trailer passing us by, heading for the bush. I thought 'Where did that come from?' Silly really as traffic in the Simpson desert tends to be scarce and trailers travelling unassisted even less common. I could only assume ours had become unhitched. Not good news for the driver. I pointed this out as the trailer overtook us and headed down a sand dune. It came to an abrupt halt, hitting a tree. Great.

We took a close look. The A-frame of the trailer had snapped off and there was no way of towing it. There was nothing we could do without welding equipment so we resigned ourselves to a return trip into the desert to rescue the trailer later.

Then our vehicle coughed, spluttered and ground to a halt. An overworked fuel filter, which kept blocking in the dusty and windy conditions, was the cause of our breakdown. So every 20 km we had to stop and manually blow out the fuel filter. This was beginning to feel like a very long day. We were not going to get out of the Simpson Desert easily.

About 30 km from the nearest homestead the Toyota developed a puncture. We stopped again. It was dusk and we still hadn't gone more than 50 km. Then we discovered the car jack wasn't working and there was no jack handle. (It was in the vehicle with the drill rig.) Lying beside the vehicle on the dusty road, using a screwdriver as a jack handle, we jacked the car up centimeter by centimeter. I reminded John that the shower he missed would have been wasted anyway. He was not amused.

We were hungry too. After picking the mouldy bits from the bread, I made sandwiches. At least the meat wasn't fly-blown. We were not smiling. In silence we changed the tyre and were on our way again. By this time, blowing out the fuel filter was routine. Finally we arrived at the homestead. It had taken six hours to travel about 80 km; a trip that normally takes less than two.

The drilling crew, who had left a day earlier, along with our jack handle, had left more gear at the homestead for us to transport. There were serious doubts whether we could shift all this equipment back to Marree even with a trailer. As the trailer was still back in the desert this was not of immediate concern.

We departed the homestead after dark with the Toyota bulging from the excess field gear, a mere 400 km drive on dirt road toward Copley and bitumen road. We were exhausted; but now faced the flooded Cooper Creek in the dark. Night herons lined the gravel piles marking shallow water so we went through hundreds of metres of floodwater in the dark, using night herons as markers.

Having successfully negotiated the flooded Cooper, John said 'Nothing can stop us now.' Two minutes later we had the other flat tyre. The only other spare was under the vehicle; getting at it meant sliding under the car in the dust, winding it down with help of our screwdriver. John managed to cram an arm between the tyre and underneath the vehicle and slowly lowered the tyre down bit by bit. Once the tyre was down we started the process of jacking the car up with our makeshift jack. We were both covered in dust and dog-tired but we managed to change the trye.

The bright lights of Marree appeared on the road ahead, an oasis in the desert. We found accommodation at the pub, even though it was 1.00 am. Rooms with beds, showers and no flies – BLISS. Next day seemed easy. Up, get the tyres fixed, find a welder and traipse all the way back to rescue a trailer. No problem. Just two more days of work in the desert.

*****

Twenty -sixth of February 1996 was a routine day in the lab wing but for one step in the pollen preparation. One of the chemicals we use has a very high freezing point which means it is a solid at room temperature. We warm the chemical to melt it. It is also very flammable. To speed up the melting process we decided to put a small bottle of the chemical in a saucepan of water on a heating element and slowly raise the temperature. We had a bottle of flammable chemical in a saucepan of water on a stove. A phone call distraction. Then we're off to lunch.

On returning from lunch we heard fire alarms. Ho hum. Fire drills were common in those days. We approached Coombs car park and saw smoke which appeared to be coming from the roof. Lunch group speculation: an electrical fault?

The heating up procedure was not routine and the smoke was coming from the roof of the building we still made no connection with the pollen lab.

Then, as they say, the penny dropped. Suddenly I knew exactly why the smoke was coming from the roof. In the lab we have fume cupboards designed to flue gases out of the building. The saucepan set up was in a fume-cupboard. I realized that not only did we have a hotplate on which was sitting flammable liquid, we had unwittingly set up a chimney sucking in air to fuel the fire. And below that particular fume-cupboard we store one of the most dangerous chemicals used on campus, hydrofluoric acid.

I alerted the fire brigade to the hydrofluoric acid store under the fire. They sent for chemical disposal backup. There was mild panic developing but the smoke seemed to be receding. A soft solder had been used in some of the water pipes in the ceiling above the lab. The fire had melted the solder and the water pipes had burst, dousing the fire. The fire had put itself out.

Though the pollen lab was destroyed the fire damage to rooms close by was minimal. Smoke damage was a problem. Smoke is corrosive and has a deleterious effect on computers so information was backed up and new computers purchased. Smoke also destroyed lenses on microscopes. The cleanup of the lab wing took more than six months. When the new lab was opened it had safety features, including sprinklers in the fume cupboards and a new saucepan. We have never used the flammable substance that caused the fire again.

Damage to the Lab wing after the February 1996 fire

CHAPTER 25

Coombs Administration

Ann Buller

I entered the Coombs Building back in the 1970s, direct from the Canberra Technical College (CTC) as it was then called. I was one of about six young people the University offered positions as we were completing our courses at CTC. No hunting for a job in the Classifieds for me. No written application. No interview. Just a direction to turn up at 9.00am on my first day and start work. What a lark this job-hunting process was I thought. Little did I realise that in 2005 I would still be in the Coombs. Perhaps it is just a case of never having found my way out of the famed Catacoombs. Or perhaps it was the most marvellous piece of luck I had so long ago.

The life of an administrator in the Coombs Building three decades ago was daunting for a young woman. I commenced my administrative life being moved from one department to another across the building filling in for departmental secretaries (yes, secretaries, not the now-politically correct administrator) who were on leave. I was thrown into academic disciplines I had never even heard of such as the History of Ideas; I was required to type papers with words so long they surely must be full of spelling errors—certainly my schoolgirl dictionary didn't contain many of them!

I recall working for a visiting professor in the Department of International Relations for six weeks. From 9am to 12.30am (no tea break with other administrators in the tea room) he would dictate chapter after chapter of his developing book and I would frantically put into practice the shorthand skills I had learned over the previous twelve months at CTC. Then from 1.30-5.00pm each day I would type all the morning's work up on a manual typewriter with a carbon copy! Heaven forbid if it wasn't ready and waiting for the professor the next morning when we started on the next section. I was eventually rescued from this situation by two very strong women colleagues, one American, the other a Scot. They were both union members and threatened to go the union and organise a strike if things didn't change. I was horrified by this, imagining Mr Grimshaw would sack me on the spot. But instead the American decided to take my place one morning, and simply announced to the visiting professor at 10.30am that she was now off for her regulation tea break, and departed.

Simple as that. I had so much to learn.

This phase only lasted a few months and then I was permanently settled into a position within a department. What a most wonderful change. Suddenly I was actually part of a department, considered now to be part of that department; one of 'them' and so treated with some respect and consideration. I was given my own duties to perform. Initially it was fairly basic activities such as typing letters and reports; dealing with mail; ordering stationary. But as time passed, experience was gained, members of the department began coming to me for advice and assistance, seeking me out. My name started appearing in 'acknowledgements' in articles and books. I felt so incredibly proud.

Once I joined the department, it quickly became apparent that there were two real sources of power and authority in the building. Firstly, there was Mr Grimshaw, the Business Manager of the Research School of Pacific Studies (as it then was) and the Research School of Social Sciences. He appeared to hold the overall authority in the Joint Schools, not the Directors who were people administrators very rarely interacted with and who were rarely seen. If anything required attention, then it was Mr G who would organise it, whether it be supplementary funding, more office space, encouraging some embassy to speed up the issue of a visa, arranging the use of a 4-wheel drive vehicle for a fieldworker's use. It probably took little more than a month for me to learn this lesson.

And secondly there was the Head of the department. In 'my' department, the Head at this time was both physically and intellectually a very large man. For an administrator there was no room for levity with this professor. Letters and documents had to be typed perfectly first time; budgets had to be monitored daily; tea, coffee and biscuits were to be served in a lady-like(!) and very quiet way at seminars every week; tea and lunch breaks were monitored by him to the minute. I recall once asking the hot water kettle to 'please hurry up boiling' (I was running short of time). This was overheard by my professor, who proceeded to lecture me for the next 10 minutes (there went my tea break) on how a kettle was an inanimate object and could not understand what I was asking it to do. There was, therefore, he instructed me, no point in talking to it!

But most people in the department were a delight and fun to work with— academic staff, students and visitors alike. The department had a lovely corner where everyone gathered for morning and afternoon tea, a marvellous place to get to know each other, to discuss the work of the department and to enjoy the never-ending stream of birds visiting the trees immediately outside this area. The American members of the department in particular loved the parrots. One American student was absolutely dumb-founded when he first saw a pair of sulphur-crested cockatoos sitting on the balcony, and could only comment 'they would cost $10,000 back home!' It was also the area where my many games of tennis and squash were arranged with colleagues including students James Masing, Taro Goh, my boss Roger Keesing and documentary film-maker Patsy Asch.

Ann Buller 2006

There were the usual administrative activities to be undertaken of course—booking travel; maintaining diaries; filing; typing. But it was a fieldwork department and so there were all sorts of out-of-the-ordinary things to deal with. I had to become familiar with purchasing, using and repairing all sorts of equipment: Uher and Tanberg reel-to-reel tape recorders; cameras and their lenses; survey equipment. I had to arrange to send the most extraordinary supplies to the fieldworkers while they were away (often for period of 12 months or more): jars of Vegemite had to be sent on request to a student in the remote Highlands of Papua New Guinea (an American student I hasten to add)—apparently Vegemite was the only thing that satisfactorily varied the taste of sago, the main staple of food for breakfast, lunch and dinner for this individual; a particular type of toothpaste to a fieldworker on an island of Indonesia; toilet paper to another (no other fieldwork ever asked for toilet paper in all my years of working with fieldworkers!—perhaps they really do use leaves of local plants?).

I became expert in dealing with government customs and quarantine departments and organising the clearance of patrol boxes being returned from fieldwork sites prior to their owners return to the ANU, patrol boxes often full of not only dozens of field notebooks, but also, for example, wooden Papua New Guinean masks decorated with possum skin and fur—a quarantine nightmare. And I still go cold when I recall opening one patrol box in the customs area and my hands and arms were immediately covered in a tidal wave of small beetles swarming out of their unwanted home—the customs officers were not amused, and during the next 15 minutes there was pandemonium while we all rushed around the room stamping on and spraying every beetle in sight.

And while students were on fieldwork it was up to the administrator to help find ways of storing their personal possessions back here in Canberra. Thankfully I had a very understanding partner, as more often than not the department ran out of space and the area under my house would be used. For years there was little room for our personal odds and ends as row upon row of department cardboard and wooden boxes slowly gathered dust and cobwebs. I worked with this department in a number of different positions on and off over a very long period of time.

Visiting Fellows always played a major role in the life of the department and School, and departmental administrators usually oiled the wheels of their visit—booking air tickets, arranging accommodation, organising the school enrolment for the visitors with children. Visiting Fellows came from all over the world, both developed and developing. After months of planning, I recall finally meeting a visitor from the remotest part of Borneo. The lady had never been out of her jungle region and her village let alone overseas. I could not imagine what she would make of travelling the long distance to Kuching, getting onto an aeroplane and flying across the vast ocean to a country so completely different from hers in culture, environment and scale. But I need not have worried—she, through an interpreter, told me that it was just like one of the myths of her people, nothing different, all explained. She thoroughly enjoyed the experience of flying; she enjoyed trying the different foods people in Canberra had access to; and she particularly enjoyed going to the cinema.

In 1984 I had my daughter Claire and took a year off work. I had planned to return to full time work after this period, but when the time came I simply could not face putting her into full time care. So I broached the subject of job-sharing with my Head of department. He supported the idea, so long as I was able to find someone the department approved of and I was able to arrange it within the University system. The woman who had acted in my position while I was on leave was also looking for part time work, so that part was easy. However, it took considerable negotiation with the personnel office as the proposed arrangement had not happened before with administrative staff. However, we finally were able to arrange it, and for four years we worked as a very successful team—she working Thursday and Friday, me working Monday and Tuesday and each working one Wednesday in a fortnight.

As the years have passed the administrators job changed in many ways, but perhaps the most marked was as a result of changes in technology: the introduction of photocopiers; telegrams being gradually replaced by telex machines, which in turn were phased out in favour of fax machines—and fax machines quickly being overtaken by computer scanners and email; manual typewriters being superseded by the IBM electric typewriter; then the Rainbow electronic typewriter; followed by the Dec10 mainframe; which was then phased out as personal computers started to appear in the mid-80s. Apart from the obvious change in the way documents were produced, the changes also resulted in shorthand no longer being used; letters being typed not by the administrator so much as by the academic themselves. And typing theses - which I often had to do—there was no more 'cutting and pasting' resulting in little bits of paper and glue all over the office. Now the changes could be made so easily, paragraphs swapped around, new sentences inserted. Carbon paper and Tippex became collectors items only.

In 1990 the Research School of Pacific and Asian Studies' Faculty Board had decided to adopt the recommendation of the report of an external review of the School and to restructure the School, developing a divisional structure partly with a view to rationalising support services and to facilitate the allocation of resources to research within the School as well as to encourage more interdisciplinary research activity. Much debate followed the announcement that this was to happen, many feeling that it was just another layer of bureaucracy. I was one of those. But the change did proceed, and quickly.

By the middle of 1991 I was in another new position, that of Divisional Administrator (DA) of Society and Environment. So much for objecting to the new structure, I was now to help implement it. The 'office' coordinated the largest division within the School, a division consisting of a wide range of disciplines, but all with a fieldwork orientation. I quickly learned that the role of a DA, as they became known across the School, is much more regulatory than that of a departmental administrator. Professor Harold Brookfield was the first Convenor of this Division, and set the governance structure that remains to this day—that of a federation of departments and centres. A Divisional Committee was formed consisting of Heads of each unit within the Division.

The Divisional Committee decided the allocations of funds for fieldwork research, for conference attendance and for equipment purchases. Scholarship applications were considered and ranked Divisionally. Discussions took place on staffing priorities across the Division, particularly when there were financial pressures and vacated posts were not being filled for some time.

Like a creeping glacier, gradually over the past decade the demands placed on administrators (at all levels) have increased. There are the organisational demands which have increased a hundred-fold. Forms, more forms, and yet more forms seem to dominate everybody's lives these days. There are forms to ask for extra funding; forms to spend that funding; forms to report it to government. Forms. Think of any activity within the Research School and there will be a form for it. Every administrator, academic and student dreads the email which arrives announcing the instigation of yet another form, which, of course, will need umpteen people to sign, countersign and authorise it. But we are assured that they really are necessary and help the efficiency of the overall administration of the university! Ummmmmmm. There are ever increasing office space issues which probably cause more anxiety and contention than just about anything else within the school. There is the increasing number of students to assist through their course. The loss of core funding has lead to the continuous search for outside funding. Thankfully, the Division of Society and Environment has been particularly successful in winning Australian Research Council and other external grants in recent years. But the downside of this is that there are now approximately 150 separate budget accounts to manage, an immense task not only for the DA but for departmental administrators as well.

But there is still fun to be had—just ask anyone who has afternoon tea in the Coombs Tea Room which table has the people who are inevitably trying, usually unsuccessfully, to stifle their laughter as yet another story about some extraordinary activity within the building is being shared: it will be the table with the administrative staff sitting at it! And so it will probably be another few years before I finally tire of helping to administer the world of Pacific and Asian Studies and decide to leave the wonderful-sited office I occupy in the Coombs Building, an office with a balcony, looking into an ever-green courtyard, filled with birds, and end the many games of tennis still being played with colleagues from around the School.

CHAPTER 26

At the Leading Edge: Computer Technology in Coombs

Allison Ley

Sean Batt has always had a vivid imagination. Even as a two year old, visiting the Coombs Building with his student father in 1967, he would stand at the top of the open circular staircase, hold onto the metal railings, and place his feet close to the edge, just to experience the thrill of being an inch away from falling three stories. So imagine his reaction when, as a thirteen year old with a fascination for science, he returned to Coombs to discover the Mainframe Digitial Equipment Corporation (DEC) 10 supercomputer.

By today's standards, the DEC 10 was a digital dinosaur. Users connected to it by plugging their terminals into a patch board (a grey metal box, attached to the wall with circular sockets, one of which still remains downstairs in room 2014 RSSS), its only present-day relic. Although its functions included processing statistics, dataset manipulation, linguistic analysis and text-based functions, users had to learn a complex language of mark-up symbols just to make it go. Phrases like ^nM; r n#;name nC;purge#^ were at the interface of this new technology. To complicate matters, access was limited to 30 users at once. Woe betide anyone who unplugged someone else's connection before they were finished!

But to thirteen year old Sean, the DEC 10 was a thing of awe and mystery, like 'HAL 9000' in Stanley Kubrick's movie, *2001: A Space Odyssey* or an infernal machine from Dr. Who. It was huge, occupying the space of five normal rooms under the tea room balcony. The whole area was secured under lock and key. The man in the white coat who looked after this grand, new supercomputer could have come straight from a James Bond film. No one bar him was allowed into the DEC 10 area. He, and only he, was entrusted with the responsibility of vacuuming the secure computer room to keep the atmosphere dust-free. He was the one who put magnetic tapes in cupboards as big as 4-door filing cabinets and ensured the air conditioning worked continuously. And if that air conditioning were ever to break down, the DEC 10 had to be turned off or it would catch fire. Users and inquisitive teenagers could peer through a small glass window at the enormous machine; but that was as close as they were permitted to get. No wonder Sean would soon leap at the chance to learn to program this monster.

Despite its limitations, the DEC 10 was the first crucial step in the march towards computerization for social sciences in Coombs. In the 1970s, the physical sciences dominated computer usage. In academic institutions everywhere, social sciences had to bid competitively against physics and chemistry for access to computers. The prevailing attitude was, 'Why would people who study the migration of Pacific Islanders need a computer?' When the Joint Schools (Research School of Pacific Studies and the Research School of Social Sciences) used a government grant in 1974 for 3/4 of a million dollars for the installation of computer technology in Coombs to purchase the DEC 10, they were trailblazing entry into computer technology by the social sciences in Australia.

Courtesy of Yvonne Pittelkow, a friend of his mother's, Sean became the Coombs Computing Unit's regular visitor. In those days, opportunities to learn about computers were rare for adults, let alone teenagers. The same buzz of being at the edge of something big that had seized the adventurous two-year old revived as he learnt to program on the terminals in Coombs, which were, for their time, at the leading edge of computerization.

Sean Batt, 2006

Even from its early days, the DEC 10 was connected to plotters and electric typewriters to produce 'camera ready' copy and by the early 1980s, academics had started to use it for document formatting (a primitive type of word processing). Computer technology was advancing fast, and so was demand. Applied research grew to such an extent in the 1980s that its magnitude and direction wrought major changes in the way academics and students used computer technology. One department head described the change 'Eighteen months ago there were 5 people who used the computer at all. Today [1981] there are 15, most of whom are intensive users.' Frustration levels with limited access were high. The same head of department describes the time wasted by a research assistant trying to access the DEC 10. 'The time she spends monitoring the queue at the communal terminals could be usefully employed [elsewhere]'. The recognition of how efficient computers were in processing word-based documents was drawing more and more people to the DEC 10, but its limited capacity was becoming a problem. Its greatest memory upgrade was 1.6 gigabytes (a lap top computer in 2005 has 80 gigabytes). By the mid 1980s, some academics had personal computers. Sean returned to the Coombs Building in 1986 and assisted Coombs personnel to learn their use. Demand had outgrown the capacity of the DEC 10. A Joint School's committee decided the solution was to give each employee a mini-computer. The DEC 10's days were coming to an end. It was decommissioned in 1989 and an era passed.

Things were moving fast, and this was no time for nostalgia. In 1986/87 the Schools advertised a tender for purchase and installation of mini-computers in Coombs. Perhaps the $$ figures led to the decision to accept the cheapest quote for IBM clone 286 Computers (CCS) from a Queensland company with no guarantees and no quality record. Not surprisingly, the computers turned out to be unreliable. Many did not work at all. Merv Commons, employed by the department of Human Geography to assist with the computerization of cartography, recalls, 'the motherboards malfunctioned ... users suffered 'downtime' due to faulty video cards and hard disk drives ... the situation was so bad they sent a Queensland technician to Canberra for six months to fix them'. They sent a truckload of faulty computers back to Queensland at the height of the problem, too.

Next the School purchased NEC computers. A big improvement. They worked but were 'proprietary' computers, i.e. you could only replace NEC bits with original NEC spare parts. Merv said 'replacements parts cost an arm and a leg'. The smallest part cost four times the price of the 'clone' equivalent. This was not a viable long-term option.

Then on advice taken from Merv, the Joint Schools purchased PCs from a Canberra-based company which had already secured several government contracts. They were reasonably priced and reliable. Installation ran smoothly. Soon most people in Coombs had their own PCs and the Computing Services established network systems. Given the problems experienced as the DEC 10 reached its limit, Merv's comment 'We started to get things working with networks and printers the output was pleasing' is quite an understatement.

PCs carried promise of increased efficiency. It was said, in the future, academics would type up and edit their own material on computers. The corollary was the threat of redundancy for typists and research assistants. A quotation from Committee papers advocating PCs illustrates this point

> ... we conservatively estimate that equipping one of us with a micro computer would enable him to dispense with all the typist services and at least half of the research assistance he currently consumes.

There was little concern for those in the firing line, as this memo headed 'Elimination of typist time' shows: 'Our statement about the elimination of our claim on typing resources was not a hopeful projection. It was a firm commitment.' Almost twenty years later, we no longer have 'typists'. Many in Coombs who began as such stayed on, however, and developed their skills to become high-level administrators (see chapters by Lawrence and Buller).

Redundancy applied to equipment too. The dot matrix printer, 'glorified typewriters', according to Sean, was one of the first casualties, once Coombs employees had access to the sharper/slicker laser printers. A memo soliciting material for the Annual Report in 1988 underlines this point. It said unequivocally, 'DO NOT USE DOT MATRIX'.

But other, equally useful technologies were emerging. Merv recalls that the need for electronic copies of academic papers led to another requirement. 'We had to transfer hundreds of type-written documents to computers.' Enter the scanner. The ANU's Computing Centre's original scanner, although costing $20.000.00, could only read seven fonts and even introduced errors. For example: "Avoiding the Scanning Blues" might end up as ^{11}Au0idin8 tne Scahhin8 B1ucs$^{!!}$. Merv witnessed Christine Tabbart and other academic assistants trying to fix up scanned papers of up to 8,000 words, many of them jumbled. On his advice, the department of Human Geography purchased Omnipage, an Apple optical character recognition package and a scanner into which you inserted A4 pages. He remembers 'We had people queuing up to use it... it saved the department time and money', and those like Christine Tabbart, grey hairs.

Soon nearly everyone was using computers but their assimilation into the work place was troublesome. For many older academics basic skills were lacking. Sean reflects 'we used to sit down with some professors and teach basic typing and formatting. For others more advanced courses were necessary.'

Early viruses created problems from nuisance to heartache. Sean recalls a PhD student in Anthropology who was in the writing up stage of her dissertation when her computer contracted a virus which deleted years and years of original work. Sean felt responsible. 'I worked incredibly hard to resurrect the situation'. The student could only exclaim. 'It should be easy to get everything back. There should be an anti-virus program that will solve it.' What could Sean do? The 80s viruses were more destructive and it took days, even weeks to update anti-virus software.

The 80s viruses caused physical damage, too. For example, there was one virus which instructed your computer to read track 85 and there were only 80 tracks on the floppy disk. The computer would go to the end of the range and keep on trying, literally grinding away to locate track 85. Sean found that 'in one case we had to replace the floppy disk drive.'

In the late 1980s, with nearly all Coombs employees using computers and bearing increasing workloads, there was an epidemic of Repetitive Strain Injury (RSI). According to Sean, RSI had, 'as much to do with bad job design and the pressure of unreasonable deadlines, as the position of the mouse or the screen and keyboard height'. Whatever the complex combination of factors that cause RSI, Merv worked with Professor Harold Brookfield to combat the conventional understating of it in the Department of Human Geography. They financed wind-up desks and monitor arms and ergonomic chairs for all staff and students. According to Merv 'It took about a year but we surmounted our RSI problems, setting the standard for the University's Occupational Health and Safety Unit'. A brochure on RSI around at the time perhaps tells us something of how people's spare time activities have changed. It read: 'when resting, operator should avoid activities involving fine movements of the hands, for example, knitting.'

The next major change, in the mid-1990s, was controversial. It was the decision to go with Microsoft. For Sean, Microsoft was not the best product for all computer functions at the time the choice was made, but he concedes it was correct in the long term. For Merv, academic Microsoft products have always been cheaper. Coombs computing unit has stayed with Microsoft products since the decision was made. About the same time too, people started using computers mainly for communication.

Throughout all of these changes Sean and Merv have been in the engine room, and occasionally at the helm. Sean has been part of the story of Coombs computing since its beginning. He programmed on the DEC 10 as a teenager, studied computer science at the ANU and returned to Coombs to manage data. He went on to assist and advise on computer purchases and installation and troubleshoot technical problems. In the 2000s he became the manager of Computer Services, RSSS. When you talk to Sean his eyes light up at the mention of new technologies and the potential for even more sophisticated computer output, as they must have done when he first saw the DEC 10 and the man in the white coat. He uses the word 'gorgeous' to describe the visual quality of computer produce. He has a full set of *Byte* and *Wired* and reads futuristic novels, which have as their backgrounds innovative technologies. He predicts the personal digital assistant (PDI) will be as ubiquitous as the mobile phone in 10 years time. In short, he has a passion for computer technology that goes beyond the workplace and Coombs is lucky to have someone like Sean.

Merv Commons receiving 1996 Council Medal for General Staff Excellence

*****

Coombs was also fortunate to have had someone of the caliber of Merv, who retired in 1997. Imagine the attention to detail required as he converted hand-drawn maps in cartography to electronic versions using rudimentary Adobe software and a scanner. Concurrently, and more importantly, he helped hundreds of people in Coombs with their problems. Merv's average day spanned 7.30 am to 8.30 pm because 'some academics started early, others late; students came in at 5.00pm and needed assistance too'. He was regularly called in on weekends ... Once he even came back to Canberra from Newcastle over Christmas. He accepted calls at midnight much to the dismay of this family. When he retired from the University after 28 years of service, he was awarded the University Medal for general staff.

Sean, Merv and their colleagues in the computing unit, working at the user-end of the Information Technology hierarchy, and upwardly managing, have kept Coombs Computing at the leading edge.

PART V

Across Coombs

CHAPTER 27

Have you got a title?
Seminar Daze

Hank Nelson

When I arrived at the Coombs Building at the end of 1972, I reported to my new head of department, John La Nauze, in the Research School of Social Sciences. An Australian who had been at Balliol College, Oxford, in the 1930s, La Nauze seemed reserved and English. 'And, what are you going to do, Nelson?' he asked. I told him that I was going to write a book. I was just about to launch into a summary of the astounding soon-to-be book, when he said, 'That's good, Nelson. Some people come here and they just go to seminars or do photocopying. I'm glad you're writing a book.' With that the meeting ended and I was out in the still unfamiliar Coombs corridors. I thought, he has lived up to his name, 'Jack the Knife'. Later, I was to appreciate La Nauze's scholarship and generosity. As I should have known, his learning, craft as a writer and understanding of his fellows were all apparent in his two-volume biography of Alfred Deakin.

La Nauze was right to warn of the time-consuming danger of seminars. In an ordinary week there are about 55 seminars in the six seminar rooms of the Coombs. On Mondays there might be eight or nine; they peak on Tuesdays, Wednesdays and Thursdays in a flush mid-week harvest of a dozen-a-day seminars and decline to nine or ten again on Fridays. And in most weeks the Coombs seminars spill over into University House, where departments sponsor one or two day conferences, and the Chancelry, where they exploit executive meeting rooms. Before the opening of the annex, Coombs academics were holding some 65 seminars a week. That's well over 2,000 in a year. During the 33 years that I have been around the Coombs, perhaps 50,000 nervous or confident, novice or experienced academics have presented seminar papers.

Seminars flourish in spite of doubtful utility. It takes longer to listen to 6,000 words than to read them, and reading is more likely to lead to careful assessment. Most people going to seminars retain little. They have just a general interest in the topic, and they note details only when they are relevant to their own work. Beyond that, they might be stimulated by the scholarly method, the way material is organised, or sources of data. Two days after the seminar, they would be lucky to recall five out of 50 minutes, and in a week that might be reduced to two. The seminar survives as a social occasion, a test before peers, and a commitment to a date that forces production. The seminar paper will have a second life as an article or a chapter.

John La Nauze circa 1970s

Like others, I remember more of the occasion and particular incidents than the content. It was always good to sit alongside Bob Langdon. Bob had had no formal tertiary education, but he was not intimidated by real or pretended expertise. In his own search for learning, he asked frank and searching questions, and in reply he demanded clarity. He also had a special weapon. Having gone from school to the South Australian public service and in 1942 into the Australian navy, Bob worked his way to postwar England as a merchant seaman. Down and out in London, he revived his school shorthand by pawning his watch and typewriter, took a course at Pitman's College and spent his spare time on lightning phrases and transcribing his *Concise Oxford Dictionary* into shorthand. Soon his shorthand speed was fast enough to apply for a job as a Hansard reporter. Instead he went to Bolivia, and later exploited his shorthand as secretary and journalist. In Seminar Room E, Bob always listened intently, but would appear to take down just a quick casual note or two. At the end of the seminar he would preface a question with a statement such as:

'When talking about Queen Emma in Rabaul you said ...'. The astonishment of many a stranger to the Coombs grew with each verbatim sentence quoted back. Suddenly, the presenter realised he might be held to account for every word.

It was different sitting next to Oskar Spate. He had come to the history department after a career as geographer and Director of the Research School of Pacific Studies. As he listened to the speaker, he would draw a contour map. Gradually a landscape emerged: promontories, deep gullies and winding streams: the density of contours indicating steep slopes and much danger of erosion. He would also pen witty couplets and limericks. On the back of a filing card on which was typed 'Tate, Vernon, Spanish Documents relating to the Voyage of the Racoon ...' he once scribbled:

> A chesty young lass of Mount Hagen
> Believed in straight talk and no jargon
> 'I want two hundred pigs
> ten shells and twelve wigs,
> and even at that I'm a bargain!'

A good listener and sharp critic, Oskar sometimes made it hard for those beside him to give full attention to the speaker. I kept the card on which he had written of the Mount Hagen lass, and later used it as a bookmark in his autobiography, *On the Margins of History*.

Derek Freeman could be a more disconcerting seminar companion. When new to the Coombs, I went to an Anthropology Department seminar and sat next to Derek. Even before the seminar began he had taken out the Oxford University Press edition of *The Poetical Works of William Blake,* and was soon immersed in the 'Songs of Innocence and Experience'. As the speaker began, Derek turned away so that his shoulder and most of his back were towards the head of the table. Every now and again Derek demonstrated his commitment to the power and simplicity of Blake's lines by making a note in the margin. Distracted and uncomfortable at this display of apparent indifference to what was being said, I missed much of the seminar. But as soon as the chairman asked for any questions and comments, Derek put his book down, corrected a couple of points of detail in the presentation and then fluently and without rancour destroyed the basis of the paper.

In Coombs seminars, careers have been made and ended. I chaired two ends. In one, words that should have been seen to be empty in writing were obviously so when spoken. It was then clear that the speaker would never write a publishable book. On another day I chaired C. Hartley Grattan who had by then retired from the University of Texas. Grattan had first visited Australia in 1927, published his first work on Australian literature soon after, and in 1942 had written *Introducing Australia*, a significant book for its time and for the Americans who were to read it. In 1963 he had published his two-volume work, *The Southwest Pacific*. The Grattan that I ushered from the tea room to Seminar Room D had a fifty-year record of writing on Australasia, was carefully dressed, urbane, and while elderly still had an easy fluency in an accent that came from Massachusetts, Texas and much world travel. He had notes to carry him through the first part of the address, but when he had to speak from memory he lost his certainty of sentence construction, and at times wandered into endless clauses. He had the fluency but he was not conveying the scholarship that he had displayed so easily through a long career. It was very sad. In question time he recovered, and answered adequately. Afterwards one of my colleagues told me I should have stopped the presentation much earlier. I replied simply, 'I couldn't'.

Hank Nelson on Anzac Parade, 2000

In the same room and soon after, I chaired another seminar which was equally embarrassing but the cause less public and more comic. A colleague had encountered an ex-diplomat who at the height of his career had been—and I am now making up these details—the third secretary in the High Commission in Apia where he had been witness to significant events. He was asked to come along and share his knowledge. Unfortunately I had not been able to get a clear idea of what he was going to talk about, and as we sat at the head of the table waiting for casual academics to wander in, tinkling their cups and saucers, I leaned across and said, 'Have you got a title?' 'No', he answered, with fierce enthusiasm. He then launched into an impassioned speech:

> 'Well might you ask. All the other members of the department have been recognised. None of them, I think I can fairly say, have my record of service. I thought that in the last Queen's Birthday list I would have been recognised ...'. It was at this point that I belatedly realised that I had invited him to express his pent up anger about his own lack of a title. That left both of us in need of a title. I commiserated with him, and turned to the audience and gave some lame introduction which went a little like: 'How fortunate we are to have Mr ... with us and, as we all know, he is going to talk about something or other and it probably happened in Apia or nearby ...'.

One of the most tense and productive seminars that I have been involved in took place in August 1991. Gavan McCormack and I gathered together six Australian ex-prisoners of war, a Korean who had served in the Japanese army as a guard of the prisoners, Japanese historians and Australian and Japanese journalists. All the ex-servicemen had been on the Burma-Thailand Railway. Because we were uncertain about what would happen and we did not want to put excess strain on the elderly participants, we had given the seminar no more publicity than the internal reminders that normally circulated within the Coombs for a departmental seminar. We also wanted all the participants to sit around the central table and talk, rather than give formal papers to an audience on the other side of a lectern. Some of the ex-prisoners of war, such as Tom Uren, ex-cabinet minister in the Whitlam and Hawke governments, and Sir Edward 'Weary' Dunlop, already recognised as the heroic surgeon and leader, were experienced speakers, and while all the others were articulate, several were hesitant about speaking at a university at any time, and certainly before an audience including their ex-enemies. We had unwisely used the term 'colloquium' in one of the descriptions of what we hoped was to happen. Hugh Clarke, an artillery man who had worked on the Thai end of the railway and then been shipped to Japan, rang up and asked, 'What's a bloody colloquium? I can't even understand what the dictionary says.'

We wanted the ex-prisoners to be candid and detailed. They had to show what was concealed behind phrases in Japanese histories which referred to 'unfortunate' or 'regrettable' events, but did not say what they were. We need not have worried. The ex-prisoners were determined to say exactly what had happened. Tom Morris had enlisted under-age straight from finishing his New South Wales Leaving, and he was nineteen when he was working on the Burma end of the Railway. Having recovered from sickness, Tom volunteered to work in the 55 Kilo hospital, and at great emotional cost to himself he now carefully, almost relentlessly, described the stench, the overcrowding and the 'putrid cloths that were washed over and over again to cover ulcers'. The only treatment available was crude curettage of the festering ulcers, done without any pain killers or sedatives. Tom said: 'It was not unusual for 80 to 100 patients to have their ulcers scraped and gouged ... each day. It was pathetic to hear the screams of these poor souls, whose shattered nerves could no longer stand the strain ...'. The nearby Japanese hospital, Tom said, was then 'lavishly supplied with drugs and medicines'. The ex-prisoners answered questions from the Japanese historians and journalist without any apparent anger or resentment, and again with evocative, disturbing detail. On that cold day on the shady side of the Coombs I sweated—with the tension and out of sympathy for those suffering from heat and deprivation on the Railway.

The ex-Korean guard, Yi Hak-Nae, was in an invidious position. But as we learnt, much of his life had been spent in difficult circumstance, and the discomfort of speaking in a Coombs seminar in front of his victims' comrades was far from the worst situation he had faced. He too had a story that he wanted told. With single-minded concentration that seemed to add to the narrative, Gavan translated for Yi Hak-Nae. He wanted, he said, to apologise to the ex-prisoners. He had visited the graves of the 6,000 prisoners buried at Kanchanaburi in Thailand, left flowers, prayed and was unable to restrain his anger and tears. He then went on to explain how he had been taken into the Japanese army, beaten every day, and sent to Thailand as a guard. There, he could not avoid 'absolute, unconditional and immediate obedience' to all orders. After the war he had been charged as a war criminal for not providing adequate food and medicines, forcing sick prisoners to work, and failing to control subordinates who ill-treated prisoners. He was sentenced to death, and after eight months' wait, his sentence was reduced to twenty years imprisonment. Released on parole after ten years, he could not return to his 'beloved home country' because he was branded a Japanese collaborator and war criminal, but in Japan he had suffered discrimination and been forced to 'live in extreme poverty'. He had been trying to persuade the Japanese government to recognise that he and his Korean comrades had been compelled to work for the Japanese army, and that they should be given the same aid that the Japanese government has given its own ex-servicemen—including those convicted of war crimes. Yi Hak-Nae also wondered why those at 'the lowest levels' went to prison and so few of those responsible for that 'nightmare period' were punished by the Allies. The ex-prisoners, still with vivid memories of bashings and deaths, may not have been moved to sympathy, but they did emerge with greater understanding.

The book that came out of that seminar, *The Burma-Thailand Railway*, was published in English and Japanese, and remained available ten years later. The Japanese scholars, engaged by Gavan, used their access to living and archival sources in Australia to increase their knowledge and publish further material in Japan. It was interesting to see the trust that developed between the Japanese historians and the ex-prisoners: both sides recognised the mutual desire to get the record straight. On return to Japan, one of the Japanese historians received a death threat from an extreme right wing organisation.

Nearly every week, scholars give seminars in the Coombs in what for them is a foreign language. They win admiration for battling through a written script, struggling with the inconsistencies between English spelling and pronunciation, and trying to interpret questions that come in a variety of accents from the Mallee and Maine to Manchester. On one occasion a speaker came to halt, went red in the face and then emitted a word, a cough or sneeze. He went back to the start of the sentence and again halted and exploded. He tried a third time with the same result. Fortunately, a quiet, humane scholar sitting nearby looked across at the paper and said quietly, 'gonorrhoea'. The speaker had been attempting to begin a list of introduced diseases, and had been ambushed by an impenetrable collection of consonants.

My own experience of giving seminars overseas has scarcely been marked with success. When I spoke at the Cenderawasih University at Jayapura in what was then Irian Jaya, I was pleased to see a crowded hall. At the end of the talk I was given prolonged applause. For a moment I thought I had gained an international reputation. But the presence of uniformed Indonesian solders with pistols obvious in holsters should have alerted me to another explanation. The soldiers had rounded up the crowd to fill the hall, many of whom were probably neither students nor academic staff, few knew any English, the language in which I had spoken, and of course they had expressed their pleasure when I had finished—they were at last going to be set free.

What makes a good seminar is elusive. An elderly actor, asked to say what separated the exceptional actors from the good and ordinary, said he had no idea, but when some actors walked on stage an audience looked, listened, and was provoked to feel and think. It is similar with seminar givers. Some scholars begin to talk and the audience listens: if others were presenting the same material the audience would think about whether they should buy bread on the way home—or mentally or actually begin to write their own next presentation. Those who have given the best seminars that I have heard (among the historians that includes Gavan Daws, Donald Denoon, Ken Inglis and Bill Gammage) spoke without rhetorical flourishes and they used plain English with a sparkling clarity, sometimes investing simple words with grace and power, and they shifted easily between particular cases, shrewd insights and generalisations. They were also saying something significant, evidenced by the prizes given to their subsequent books and the many translations of Daws' work. (Both Inglis and Gammage won premier's prizes and *Holy Man* appeared in seven languages)

It has intrigued me that two of my colleagues can on different days give either a good and mediocre seminar. But most of us probably operate at around about the same level every time. This was brought home to me early in my career when I asked my wife if she was going to hear me give a seminar paper. She said, kindly, 'No. I have heard you.' I think that it is probably true that while I might talk about different people in different places in different events, I always give the same seminar. My wife now says that I either misheard or misinterpreted what she said, and my misunderstanding of that distant conversation comes out of my repetition of the anecdote, not from her words. That raises such complex questions about memory and narrative, indeed about all oral history and autobiography, that it is worthy of a seminar—even in Seminar Room A.

CHAPTER 28

Space Wars

Colin Filer

Dear lords and masters of the Martian Embassy,

You have asked me to submit a report on the 'social relations' prevailing amongst the crew of the Coombs spaceship. Alas, my researches indicate that these things ceased to exist before I came on board. There are still some elements of 'social structure' that might be read as the residue of past social relations, for it is hard to understand them otherwise, but legendary sites of social interaction, such as the infamous 'Snake Pit', have long since been converted into silent 'reading' spaces where nothing can be read at all, except in English. I shall therefore devote the better part of this report to the Space Wars that represent the negative form of sociality now prevailing within the spaceship as it passes into the realm of anti-matter.

As you know, the spaceship is divided into a light and a dark side, each with its own commander. Captain Jim Skywalker, Commander of the Light Side, believes that all spaceships in this galaxy are naturally divided into two or four parts, depending on the time of day. One of his lieutenants has even written a book about 'quadripartite structures'—a book that might have been inspired by the fourfold division of the Light Side under the command of Captain Skywalker and his predecessors. However, the author may be suffering from the same delusions as the Commander, for I am told that the Light Side was once divided into *five* parts, and the memory of this fact has been rigidly suppressed under the present regime. Nor should we forget that the spaceship itself takes the form of *three hexagons*—an undeniable spatial fact which has led me to conclude that the so-called 'quadripartite structure' is a purely cultural phenomenon.

I thought I might be able to test this hypothesis by investigating the brains of the crew members on the dark side of the spaceship. However, when crew members from the Light Side travel over to the Dark Side, the space appears to be empty. I now believe that the two crews are actually invisible to each other, and might even be alternative manifestations of the same force field. Soon after I took up my present position on the Light Side, there were persistent rumours that the Commander of the Dark Side was attempting to invade Our Space.

According to these stories, he was pacing up and down our gangways, looking for cabins that might be vulnerable to seizure by members of his own crew. But I never saw him myself, so I suspend my judgement. If we were all invisible to him, then his own crew may already have occupied our own bodies, while we, in our sleep or dreams, may occupy theirs. In that case, Captain Jim's frequent periods of 'absence' from the spaceship might only be periods in which he takes on his dark and invisible form.

I now wonder whether the rumours were only audible to me, as to any newly inducted crew member, because they are telling us that the true purpose of our 'work' is to fight for space within the spaceship as part of the grand cosmic struggle between the forces of light and darkness.

My own mission, as you may recall, was to penetrate the darkest part of the Light Side, near the waste ejection chamber, and populate it with alien life forms disguised as ordinary crew members. At one stage I thought our cover had been blown, for I was put in control of a 'resource management' unit which is officially treated as an alien body within the quadripartite 'divisional' structure of the Light Side. I thus feared that I and my underlings might soon find ourselves back in the waste ejection chamber through which we had secretly entered.

But nothing is quite what it seems around here. Although my unit is treated as an autonomous and anomalous AOU ('aerospatial organizational unit') for all superficial purposes, like the writing of reports, it is included within the Division of 'Society and Environment' (DSE) for the deeper purpose of our existence, which is the practice of space wars. The reason for this, as I later discovered, is that the quadripartite structure is not really a division of the crew members into teams, but *a cultural partition of the space itself*. The labeling of space even extends to some of the docking stations from which crew members are transported to other galaxies by means of 'seminars', for these contain holograms of dead divisional luminaries staring into (Guess what?) *space*.

Yet these are mere diversions. The fact of the matter is that our space wars are not conducted on a level force field. If we inhabited the distant galaxy of Austronesia, which Captain Skywalker likes to visit in his spare time, then I would now be the head of the most junior lineage in the biggest clan on a small island with *no space left*. By this light, we may be doomed to repeat the fate of the legendary space station of Easter Island—our own space cluttered with the memories of dead ancestors, with barely a patch of ground left for the cultivation of new social relations (as I have previously noted).

Colin Filer, Space Warrior, 2002

The Commander's own reports make persistent reference to 'the house' as the basic unit of spatial antagonism. Since this otherwise makes no sense, I read it as code for the nested hierarchy of cultural spaces erected on the foundation of the solitary cabin in our own spaceship. In the language of the captain's own dreams, the four clans that battle for possession of these 'houses' should ideally be ranked according to the time at which their founding ancestors first entered the spaceship. But this ranking no longer matters very much, because each clan has *become* a space whose boundaries are notionally fixed for time immemorial. This means that the rank of each clan is simply a function of the number of cabins or 'houses' within its territory that are occupied by the ghosts and phantoms of dead ancestors, or by crew members who are no longer engaged in active duties, and whose mortal status is a matter of speculation. More intense, by far, is the struggle for space within each of the four divisions, where crew members can still remember the founding of new teams or 'lineages', and can measure the rate of their numerical expansion or contraction over recent years.

Even the Commander will concede, in his waking hours, that AOUs are the groups that really matter in this game. Once each solar year, this social fact is reaffirmed in the great ceremony of The Budget, in which the leaders of each team troop up to the bridge of the spaceship to repeat their oaths of loyalty and swear to carry on with the mother of all battles.

Of course, the battle can only be sustained if there is no rational set of rules for the allocation of cabin space to members of the crew. That is because all crew members must prove that they are reasonable people when they fabricate their annual 'budgets'. This in turn means that the commander of the spaceship must convince the rest of the crew that he is either insane or else unable to impose his will on this particular aspect of reality. That is why no commander normally lasts more than five years in his post. Some have sought to escape their terrible dilemma by jumping ship before their time is up, leaving those who stay behind to draw their own conclusions. Not Captain Jim. His command has lent the grand cosmic struggle a new lease of life, for most of the crew members *do now believe* that no one has the power to change its course.

The secret of success is something called 'the buck'. This is a ritual object that is 'passed' between individuals in order to deconstruct the concept of power. That is all very well, but rational and intelligent human beings are not so easily fooled—and nor am I. In the present case, the deep secret of disempowerment is to be found in the role of the droids.

The droids are crew members, but they are 'general' members, a subaltern caste apparently dedicated to the service of the expert members who specialize in writing reports about the rest of the universe. The expert members fancy that their knowledge of outer space qualifies them to be the only true subjects of an internal space war. Or do they just pretend?

As one joins the ranks of this expert crew, so it gradually dawns that all of them are actually aliens, like me, pretending to be humans. The 'real' humans—the indigenous people of the spaceship—are the droids, and the droids are the real owners of all space war magic. At least, that is what the Deputy Commander likes to tell me when he comes beaming through our gangway. But should I believe him?

One hypothesis would be that we are trapped (and even reproduced) by a double movement in the control of internal space—a delegation of superficial power from the Commander to the Deputy Commander, which is cross-cut by the reciprocal passage of 'the buck' between the senior and junior moieties in the secret society of the spaceship. Yet this is too simple a view. While some droids are attached to the divisions and subdivisions of the quadripartite structure, and purportedly serve the expert crew members in charge of each component part, many of them are so 'general' as to serve no expert in particular. Whom, then, do they serve? The Commander? The Deputy Commander? The general union of expert crew members (not very evident)? Secret divisions and subdivisions (likewise)? Themselves alone (Why not?)? Or an alien force (aside from our own—and the other ones)?

I must confess, my lords and masters, that I cannot yet provide an answer to these questions. I have only been a permanent fixture in the spaceship for five years or so.

Perhaps there can be no solution to the Matrix. Perhaps the balance of power must always remain in a state of obscurity. But let me point to some notable warp factors.

There are some occasions on which all the droids appear to act in concert to disempower the expert crew members. The so-called 'fire drills' are nothing more than a periodic evacuation of the expert members by the general members when the latter want to ensure that the allocation of space to the former is perfectly irrational. There are other occasions on which a small group of experts will agree that this is a jolly good thing, if only they could do without the fire drills. Most will also tell you that the droids alone have access to the Great Map that shows the actual allocation of space within and beyond the quadripartite structure, and no ordinary expert is allowed more than a brief glimpse of a small portion of this document, for fear that he or she will explode in a puff of smoke. This must also have something to do with the fire drills, but I am yet to fathom the connection.

Despite their hidden powers, there are occasional 'faculty meetings' at which the unattached droids profess great oaths of attachment, and many secret meetings of the most powerful experts at which no droid would dare to speak at all for fear of being blanketed by the Great Hum that envelops the spaceship at 6pm each evening—solar time. So the experts still maintain the semblance of their own power, even if they are all aliens. Yet this power dissolves in the moment of its own imagination—into four bits and several other bits (my own included).

Thus it is that I do not know why it is that I *cannot get more space* for my growing clump of subterranean expert fungus. Even after I had followed the commands of the Commander and the Deputy Commander, or any number of superficially helpful droids, there was no movement to be had. If I have multiplied the population of my team (or bloody 'lineage') by diverse strategies, this is a task dedicated to its own frustration. Even after I have shrunk ten apprentice crew members to a size that enables all of them to be squashed into a single cabin, there is no beam of light at the end of the gangway. For the wall is created at the moment of its own dissolution—and vice versa.

Lords and masters, I must give you a concrete example of my struggles—otherwise, you might not believe me.

There is a cabin at the rear end of 'our' gangway, right next to the waste ejection chamber, that is shaped like a dead Dalek. This was either one of my first conquests or else a Trojan horse granted to me by another AOU in DSE (Remember? 'Division of Society and Environment'?), because the crew member posted to it might or might not have been a member of my own gang once he got inside. How would I know?

To prove his loyalty, he volunteered to relinquish this marginal outpost for another one in the central section of the gangway—one that had formerly been part of the Deputy Commander's 'divisional' domain. One might have thought that the Deputy Commander would then seize control of the newly vacated space under the so-called principle of reciprocity. But no! The cabin door containing the standard perspex porthole was replaced by one containing a magnetic heat shield impervious to all forms of light and radiation, on which was emblazoned the name 'Admiral Wan Kenobi'. From that moment on, the door was firmly locked and sealed at all times of the day and night, and no sentient being was ever seen to pass through it.

To test the possibility of nocturnal use by one of the officers from the Dark Side, I applied small quantities of 'blu-tack' to the tiny gaps between the door and the cabin wall, but these never showed any sign of disturbance. I therefore concluded that the Admiral was either (a) non-existent, or (b) the commander of another spaceship, or (c) entering and leaving our own ship by crawling through the ventilation system or teleporting himself through the computer network. These were not mutually exclusive options, but they did exclude the opinion of one crew member, who was heard to mumble something about a police box that whooshed, gyrated and vanished at the very same moment. This I put down to a long liquid lunch.

After some period of time, I dispatched a series of probes through the droid network with a view to securing the return of this silent space and the restoration of its perspex porthole. But behold! No sooner had I done so than the Admiral's name was removed from the door and replaced by an indecipherable script. I was told that this signified the presence of a being from another planet, but being from another planet myself, this meant nothing to me. One day, an extra-terrestrial creature did emerge from the cabin, declared that he was one of the Commander's secret agents, and promptly vanished into thin air. So this cabin had somehow passed from the domain of the Deputy Commander to that of the Commander himself. Yet no one—not even the most knowledgeable droids in the vicinity—had any idea how this had come to pass.

Shortly afterwards, a team of menial droids, acting on unknown orders, began to excavate a huge quantity of ancient signaling equipment from the cabin directly opposite the one which now lay empty once again. On the door of this cabin was inscribed another mysterious name—one that I dare not repeat in this report, for it is said to be the name of the officer once in charge of the 'lost' fifth column of the Coombs. Some say that his ghost still walks the gangway at odd hours, grumbling about something called a 'test match score', which may be the last signal he ever sent to whatever world he once inhabited. Others say that his body was amongst the items taken from the cabin, his hand still clutching an ancient stone artefact from that same lost world.

In our travels through space, we can only ever see part of the picture. You will remember the rule that senior crew members who become too old and frail to fight in the space wars are normally assigned a cabin in an AOU that is not the one in which they formerly did their business. Well, it turns out that the fifth columnist, his sacred stones and his signaling equipment were all dumped in the waste ejection chamber because his was the space that will soon be the final resting place of the Commander himself when his chieftainship comes to its timely end. What is more, Captain Jim has made it known that he will then become a member of our AOU, and so his new space will be part of ours, a new addition to our trophy cabinet. Now you might think that we shall gain a greater prize than this, because his secret knowledge of the space wars will enlighten and empower the rest of us, and our rank will rise up the hierarchy like a great soufflé. But alas—I fear the Captain's memory banks, like those of all his predecessors, will be erased by the droids at the moment of his last command. He'll walk the sky no more—or not as much; still armed with dreams of structure, but now devoid of magical power to influence the cosmic struggle. Is this what he meant when he said that our AOU no longer feels like a subterranean fungus, but has become the 'dark star' of the Light Side?

Dear lords and masters, I wish I knew the answer to this question, but I don't—and that is how I know that I am still part of the cosmic struggle and the meaning of life. No one can establish who is real and who is not, who is present and who is absent, who is dead and who is alive. What worries me now is that one of my very own crew members claims to have got a copy of the Great Map, and to be working out an algorithm for the rational allocation of cabin space. How mad is that?!? Does he not realize that this could spell the end of our reason for being here? Of course I have tried to tell him that he is putting the life of the Coombs in the deepest, darkest danger. But he simply will not listen to me! We can only hope and pray that he is either a droid disguised as an expert for some unfathomable reason, or else that the droids will foil his ghastly scheme. I cannot believe that 'the buck' will stop. The war must go on. Otherwise we are all doomed!

And by the way, dear lords and masters, when on Earth can I come back to Mars?

CHAPTER 29

Dark Side of the Coombs

Grant Rebbeck, Peter Adams and Andrew Muirden with Allison Ley

Just after two o'clock in the morning. Coombs professors safely tucked up in bed, dreaming of standing ovations at book launches. But outside the Coombs building it's dark and cold. The voices of Grant Rebbeck, Coombs nightwatchman, and his early morning visitor drift over the frosty lawns.

> 'Where've you been?' 'Dunno.' 'Do you know the Coombs building?' 'Where's that?' 'How did you get here?' 'Dunno.' 'Where are you staying?' 'Dunno.' 'Where have you been?' 'Out drinkin' with me mates.' 'How did you get here?' 'Dunno.'

After persistent questioning, Grant determined that 'Dunno', in Canberra for a sporting event, was supposed to fly out at 7.00am, but had somehow arrived at the Coombs building. Grant urged him to phone his mates. He managed to ring one on his mobile, waking him in his hotel room, so Grant sent him off in a taxi in the direction of his hotel.

The Coombs building is an incubator of knowledge during the daylight hours, with researchers busily producing important tomes and giving impressive seminars. But who ensures the building they work in is safe at night? Who are our night watchmen? What special problems do they face?

Grant Rebbeck, Peter Adams and Andrew Muirden guard the building at night. Grant is a no-nonsense avuncular character ready to assist with all manner of requests from mending staplers, to supplying instant coffee and advising on football tips. Peter, originally from New Zealand, loves working at night. He has a ready smile and has the knack of conversing with just about everyone. Although Andrew is a relative newcomer to Coombs, he settled in quickly and enjoys photographing possums in the building at night.

On any given night our watchmen, Grant, Peter or Andrew know who is in the building and exactly where they are. They know the working hours we keep and the state of our rooms. They know how we leave our desks and even what we throw in our bins. But what is it like at night in Coombs?

Navigating the labyrinthine corridors within the three hexagons is daunting enough during the day, but Peter says that when he first came to work, the building was 'like a maze' at night. 'I found myself in the Lab wing and couldn't figure out where I was.' On his first night, Andrew discovered there were no windows at many points within the building, so it was difficult to orient himself. He still keeps a map in his pocket.

Soon all three got to know their way around the building and their work became more routine. Their night time duties involve walking the Coombs corridors on an hourly basis, checking rooms, emptying rubbish bins, and locking the outside doors.

Although the recent trend has been towards swipe cards, identity checks and security procedures becoming more prevalent, the front door of the Coombs building remains open 24/7, with staff, students and visitors coming and going all hours.

Students have exploited the openness of the building especially when they are finishing their PhDs. Andrew observes, 'If students work all night, they are going to get tired, and if they need a couple of hours rest, that's fine … as long as there's not a sleeping bag set up'. Peter and Grant agree 'We turn a blind eye to those working long hours. This is not a dormitory, but we have to be flexible'.

Andrew Muirden, Grant Rebbeck and Peter Adams, 2006

Lost souls gravitate to Coombs at night too. Whether it be the memory of friendly associations in the Coombs or the knowledge the building is always open, the dispossessed come to Coombs. The nightwatchmen deal with these sad, sometimes desperate individuals efficiently, but with great tolerance. Listen to Grant's stories of 'strangers' in Coombs after dark.

> A young lad decided to take two chairs from the Business Manager's alcove and shift them down near the Coombs Lecture Theatre. Near the old lift. I went down there. Three o'clock in the morning in the dark. No light but from the stairwell. Looked in the corner and there was the two-seater moved into the alcove. This young man had a white sheet and cushion and had bunkered down for the night. He was about 17- years-old and fast asleep. I nudged him.
>
> 'What are you doing?'
> 'I had nowhere to go.'
> 'Hmmmm ...'
> 'My mum works here'
> 'Does she? Who's your mum?'
>
> He rattled off some names which didn't ring any bells with me, but knew some people and room numbers. After some discussion we worked out that his mum had worked here about ten years ago. He had just come down from Sydney, been let down badly by his mates, had nowhere to go. He knew the Coombs building was open ...
>
> 'Okay, then. Pack up your bed, I'll put you in the sick room; wake you up at six, but don't come back tomorrow night.'

And the second, the story that became known as 'the tale of the pregnant woman'.

> We noticed her in Economics on the first floor, on the small lounge in the alcove by the window. She could hardly speak any English. She said she was reading the pamphlets and newspapers. And this was the middle of winter and she had a big belly. I didn't worry about her. I let it go. Let her sleep the night. Jo was on next night. He said 'she's up there again tonight. We let it go for one more night. The next night she's there again – said the same things in broken English, she only wanted to read the newspapers and pamphlets. She was helping herself to coffee.
>
> I said 'Look this is all very well. But you can't keep reading the same

> papers over and over again... '
>
> 'No. I just want to read newspapers here.'
>
> 'Well you can't stay here and read every night.'
>
> She sat there in the chair – I went past a couple of times and she was almost nodding off. I rang mobile security. An officer came and suggested he take her to a university residence or to a women's refuge. She wouldn't agree to any of this. Sensing she was about to be taken outside soon, she started to take out some of her warm clothes from the bulk around her middle. What I thought was pregnancy turned out to be her winter wardrobe.

Peter recalls the case of 'a young woman who was intelligent, but got into heroin. We had to be careful emptying her bin because she left her needles there'. She was struggling with her addiction 'we used to pick up the methodone bottles too...' The same woman's face confronted him one night when he was disposing of her rubbish. She had curled up under the desk to sleep. 'I nearly dropped the bin on her head with shock' he said.

Night-time surprises are a feature of the watchmen's work. In a very different sort of confrontation, Andrew turned on the light to empty a bin and a huge huntsman was staring at him about six inches from his face.

No-one likes to confront violence, so imagine how Peter must have felt when one night, on the top floor...

> Suddenly I heard a sound. A wailing noise then a bang. Then it came again. A cry and then a thump. I straightened up and listened and looked around. There were no other sounds. It was pitch black outside I could not see very clearly in the corridors, only about three feet ahead. I couldn't find anything. With small steps, slowly, I entered a room on the top floor and the banging and wailing increased. Gradually, I opened the window, shaking, and discovered a branch whacking the balcony with a possum hanging on for dear life.

Real danger is not something Coombs nightwatchmen face on a regular basis, though they have had to deal with some 'emergencies'. Andrew tells one story which involved workmen installing the sprinkler system for the Coombs extension, 'They dug next to a power junction, and accidentally broke into it. When the sprinklers came on, sparks and flashes appeared outside on the lawn and all the lights in the building were going on and off'.

Peter describes a genuine emergency. Donald Denoon had organized a book launch one evening and half way through the event there was a fire in the building and the alarm went off. Jo Wiggan rushed up the stairs to the fire. He met Donald coming down the steps, agitated, 'Turn off the fire alarm; it is interrupting my book launch.' The retelling of this makes Peter laugh, a characteristic of the watchmen who, whilst diligent in their duties, do not take themselves too seriously. Like their namesakes in the game of cricket, sent in to protect the wicket at the end of a day's play, they are happy in a supporting role.

For Grant the cricket metaphor goes further. He says 'Like the umpires, we have everything in our pockets.' Ministering to the needs of ill-equipped academics may not be on the job description, but it is certainly one of his unofficial duties. 'There are two in Economics for whom I open wine. We have corkscrews, knives, forks, spoons, coffee, tea, sugar …' and 'there was one researcher's wife who was doing her thesis here. She smoked, and when she finished a packet I'd go hunting for cigarettes for her…'

The nightwatchmen have assisted people in all kinds of situations. Some will approach Peter with the question 'Do you know where my bike is?' confident he will have the answer. Andrew was once asked to mind a suitcase for a gentleman who commented 'There's no bomb in it!' and Peter found that 'One gentleman would come out of the male toilets regularly with his fly undone. I had to say each time, "Would you mind doing up your fly?"'

The openness of Coombs leaves it vulnerable to thieves, but with so many people using the building, identifying potential thieves requires special skill. Andrew puts in bluntly, 'Everyone in the building looks dodgy, so how do you pick a thief?' It was on Peter's watch that the worst robbery occurred. He took it personally

> I was really pissed off. We lost $20,000 dollars worth of computers. All taken from one area. We know who did it but because you can't catch them with it … It happened between ten and twelve o'clock at night. They went out through the back lab wing. They were relief cleaners, both young men. They left soon afterwards.

Grant has had to deal with petty crimes. He describes one incident.

> One morning Joan McDevitt came in and said:
> 'There's a lady down the street carrying one of the chairs from Seminar Room A.'
> I had the trailer on the car and took off down the street and found her carrying the chair.

'Where are you taking it?'
'I fix up antiques.'
'That's no antique, that's just an old chair. Thank you very much.'

The distinction between valued item and rubbish is something our night watchmen occasionally redefine whilst emptying our rubbish bins. Peter rescues precious things, 'I kept a Chinese opera mask for Jamie Greenbaum, who translates Chinese Opera'. Coombs rubbish is a reflection of its inhabitants' different cultures and foods. Peter again, 'Chinese biscuits, moon cakes, green drinks. Tea with seeds.' And of differing diets: some bins have 'Three empty packets of chips per day ... and soy bean containers'. Rubbish gives the nightwatchmen a picture of individuals. A woman said to Peter on her way home late one night 'I have been trying so hard to lose weight' but he thought 'Hang on a minute ... I just disposed of four empty Twix packets from your rubbish bin!' Staplers are thrown out with great abandon. Grant rescues and mends them, 'I have a thousand staplers. They usually have only a couple of jammed staples in them.'

But all three night watchmen agree the worst offenders in Coombs at night are smaller fry. Peter says 'Possums sometimes fart loudly while I talk to people at the front desk. I shake my head and say, "It wasn't me", but people just nod and say "Yeah, sure mate."' Do possums tease our nightwatchmen? Grant wonders... 'at the bottom of the door of one of the plant rooms there is a gap of about 3 inches to the floor. Occasionally a tail will pop out and wave back and forward.' They are certainly a nuisance. Grant again, 'I chased one possum around the building for two hours. Started at the front door, but ended in the lab wing getting him out. I was not happy.'

Possums are very untidy and smelly, according to Grant.

> In Pacific History we had a possum locked in the kitchen over the Christmas period. We cleaned up the mess and thought we had gotten rid of him. The next day, exactly the same, possum mess. He came in through the kitchen window, which was wide open in the middle of summer and lived under the sink. I was sick of cleaning up at this stage. After about four or five attempts, one day I found him sitting on the sink. I was not going to go near him unless I had to. There was a timber shelf standing by the door. I put one end of the shelf out the window, got a stick and held the other end into the sink, picked up the broom handle and teased him onto the plank. He moved to the edge of the window. I lifted the plank. Then I shut the window. Goodbye possum.

It is not only possums who snuffle and rumble at night in Coombs, Peter discovered.

> One night it was about 2am, I was in the Human Geography corridors and I heard these snuffling noises in the ladies toilet, I thought 'bloody possums again', opened the door and there was a young lady and a gentlemen in a compromising position ... I knew them. They weren't from RSPAS [Naturally, Eds]. I said 'what are you doing on this side of the building.' They said 'We got lost'.

But late night assignations are a thing of the past. The new breed of student keeps their noses in books and their fingers on the keyboards. Peter says 'The building is much quieter. There are more students who are into their work, conscious they are here for a short time.'

As the watchmen know, that's the thing about the night time; it is not really fun, except, of course, unless you are a possum.

CHAPTER 30

All Corridors Lead to the Tea Room

Sophie (Vilaythong) and Lisa (Alicia Dal Molin) in conversation with Maxine McArthur

If the heart of the research schools are the scholars and the brains are the administrators, then surely the belly—and therefore the seat of the soul—of the Coombs Building is the tea room. The tea room is physically situated as close to a centre as is possible for three linked hexagons, and it is one of the easiest places to find in Coombs. Wherever you start, you are most likely to finish up there. If you arrange to meet someone in Coombs, usually it is 'in the tea room', for the simple reason that you will probably both not get lost on the way.

It is a psychological centre also. The large, airy room, looking out onto a grassy courtyard on one side and a verandah on the other, is lighter than most of the offices by virtue of its floor-to-ceiling windows. The ceiling is two floors high, overlooked by a walkway along one side that gives access from the offices in the building behind. Other doors give access from the building in front, from the verandah, from the courtyard, and from the front lobby. After spending hours hunched over a computer in one's office, it is comforting to enter the open space of the tea room and chat to one's colleagues, or to eat lunch there in solitary comfort while perusing the daily newspapers thoughtfully provided.

But the tea room would not be the hub that it is without certain extraordinary people—the tea ladies. 'Tea ladies' seems an anachronism in today's self-serve society, but at Coombs they provide a service that is irreplaceable. Every day tea, coffee and biscuits are for sale at morning and afternoon tea, at low prices that even struggling PhD scholars can afford. The beverages and bickies aren't just 'for sale', though; you stand in line and hand over your 50 cents, and Sophie gives you a big grin and remembers whether you take tea or coffee, white or black (at morning tea), or Lisa is ready with a smile and greeting (in the afternoon).

What do the tea ladies themselves think about working in Coombs? What does the view *from* the tea room look like?

I spoke with Sophie and Lisa about their work at Coombs and the changes they have seen here over the years.

Sophie

Sophie, you are an incredibly energetic lady. Whenever I see you around the building you seem to be in a hurry. When did you start work here?

I have been working at Coombs for 18 years now. I started in 1988, doing the early cleaning, from 4am to 8am. I'd clean two floors, working with the night watchman. In 1992 I changed to providing other services in the building, and I served the tea when the tea ladies were away. In 2002 when the joint services of the two research schools [Research School of Social Sciences and Research School of Pacific and Asian Studies] split up, I started doing only services for RSPAS. Before that, we worked together.

What does your job entail? We see you once a day in the tea room, but also sometimes in the corridors of the building, carrying boxes and trays.

My job now involves preparing the rooms and morning/afternoon teas for seminars. I also go around the corridors and collect dirty cups that people have forgotten to bring back to the tea room, also cardboard boxes for recycling. Sometimes I refill the water coolers and cups.

I get the morning tea ready and serve it. For morning tea I have to boil the hot water, fill the urn and percolator, load and unload the cups and biscuits etc on the trolley to take into the tea room. Then I clean up afterwards, stack the cups and saucers and cutlery in the dishwasher, mop the kitchen floor and the tea room floor. We don't have a contract cleaner for the tea room, I do it all.

Once a year, after the Christmas Party, I polish the tea room floor. And I refill the Coke machine with the different drinks.

Does the structure of the building give you any trouble in your job? It's a bit of a maze, as you know.

The Coombs Building can be confusing for visitors. Often I have to direct them where to go. But I've been working here so long that I can close my eyes and know which floor I'm on. I know who works on each floor, too, the same way I can remember what everyone has for their morning tea.

I couldn't complain about working in the Coombs Building. Nobody looks down on me because I'm a Level 1. Sometimes things get really busy, like when I'm organising morning teas for many seminars at once, but I manage. If anyone gets impatient, I explain to them and they understand. I get on with everyone. I'll keep going until they don't need me. Even if I married a millionaire, I'd keep working here.

Lisa

Lisa, how long have you been working at the ANU?

I've been working at the ANU since August 1973. My first job was with the Chancelry, Credit Union, Health Centre and Central Store. Then I moved to the John Curtin School of Medical Research. I started by doing morning cleaning—4am to 8am, which was good because I had small children so I could then spend the rest of the day with them. Then I did evening cleaning—4pm to 10pm. When my son was in lower primary, his teacher asked the class what their mothers did at work. When my son asked me what I did at John Curtin School of Medicine, I told him I was a 'mopologist'. Apparently the teacher was impressed, if mystified.

In 1986 I began working as a tea assistant in the Coombs building. This is where I have been ever since.

Has working in the Coombs building presented any particular challenges?

My beginning at Coombs was, I should say, a very tricky experience. It was hard to know where I was and even harder to know where I was supposed to serve tea. I did at times prepare the tea in the wrong seminar room. Very soon I learned that you achieve success with guidance. Feedback from the other staff was crucial to my getting to know physically where the correct seminar room was located. I soon learned that the only way to get my bearings was to leave the building and see where I was located and find my way back to the tearoom.

Have there been many changes over the years?

Yes, a lot of people have been and gone during that time. New faces have arrived and old faces have left. My job has changed over the years. I have seen the amalgamation and the separation of the research schools; overall it has been very rewarding.

When I began to work in the tearoom, a cup of tea was five cents, a cup of coffee ten cents, plain biscuits two cents, and five cents for a cream biscuit. Some people complained when the prices were increased, so I told them they should go to the Salvation Army for cheaper tea and coffee. This remark made me infamous. The word went around: don't complain to Lisa about the increase in the prices, she has the right answer for that.

Do you recall any particular incidents or people?

There have been some interesting incidents over the years, often because people in Coombs can be absorbed in their work to the extent that they forget where they are. Even in their 'break', they are thinking about work or talking about work.

One of the hardest things I had to do was to tell someone they had a fresh 'Do Not Sit Wet Paint' label attached to their jacket from the balcony of the tearoom. I must admit, the stripes of wet paint did look cute on the jacket.

From that day on I learned that the tearoom was a place to breathe and to de-stress, to laugh, to enjoy, to be merry (and on one occasion, to be married!). The Christmas Parties are especially fun. We always try to be helpful in good times and in bad times, but believe me it is not true that tea ladies know all the gossip…Maybe.

I would like to say that it has been a privilege to serve and to know all the students, professors, staff and visitors (from all over the world).

Sophie Vilaythong and Lisa Alicia Dal Molin, 2006

PART VI

Coombs Memories

CHAPTER 31

Work and Play in the Coombs Building 1967–73

Peter Corris

I spent approximately five years in the Coombs Building—three as a PhD student with about nine months out for fieldwork in the Pacific, and another eighteen months or so as a Research Fellow in Pacific History after returning from an ANU post-doctoral fellowship. Without doubt these years were my high point in a brief academic career, not only in terms of achievement, but in fun!

Arriving at the ANU in January 1967 after a stint as a tutor at Monash, I was astonished to find that a doctoral student had considerable status—a shared room in the Coombs Building, full use of telephone and secretarial services, a per diem allowance when travelling to archives interstate, guaranteed funding for overseas fieldwork. And, as a married, childless Research Scholar, I had a comfortable flat on Northbourne Avenue with a minimal rent and like-minded people all about.

The stage was set for some of the most enjoyable years of my life, certainly the most enjoyable to that point. To focus on the Coombs, there was something exhilarating about being in the company of scholars from associated disciplines and being privy to their concerns, ambitions, scandals and gossip. The Coombs was a hive of gossip, some of it malicious. The Professor of Pacific History, the urbane James Wightman (Jim) Davidson, was an inveterate gossip and waspish denigrator of his colleagues. I recall that he condemned the entire International Relations Department as 'purveyors of ephemeral journalism.'

The place was full of eccentrics and anomalies. A fellow in Anthropology was said to have published nothing but an article on fighting beetles. A student had allegedly changed his thesis subject in mid-stream from the 'The role of the Air Craft Carrier in WWII' to 'Children's attitudes to the Vietnam War.' John Barnes, the Professor of Anthropology in the RSPacS, had to travel to Southeast Asia to placate museum officials after one of his staff members had snapped the penises from ceremonial statues. Or so the story went.

We smoked in our rooms and kept alcohol there. I kept a flagon of red wine and a bottle of dry sherry and indulged in both as it pleased me. I slept in the room on several occasions during a rocky period in my failing marriage, and one of my room mates committed adultery there on a regular basis. A close friend of mine, studying the Scullin government for his doctorate, brought a bicycle chain to the building to confront a staff member he suspected of sleeping with his wife.

Peter Corris, 1970

In the days before email, communication was personal and intense friendships and enmities formed. I wore a Jesus beard, my hair on my shoulders and occasionally a kaftan, and incurred the contempt of a senior member of another department. A senior person in Pacific History, who always wore a suit and tie, looked askance at those of us who, like Davidson, Deryck Scarr and myself wore shorts, open-necked shirts and sandals to work.

Returning from fieldwork in late 1968 and farewelling my wife, I wrote my thesis in six weeks. That left me almost a year in which to play and I did. I submitted the work to my supervisor as though it was on-going, and did the required revision. Otherwise I partied, pursued women younger and older than myself, and had a hell of a good time. Coming late to a seminar, I pleaded as an excuse, 'a matter of the heart.' An aggrieved female present said, 'Peter, I didn't know you had one.'

It was a wild, irresponsible time, but I also published a monograph, reviews and articles and formed lasting friendships, notably with the late Roger Keesing with whom I wrote a book, *Lightning Meets the West Wind*, and Jim Allen, later Professor of Prehistory at La Trobe University, with whom I edited an important text in Torres Strait history—*The Journal of John Sweatman*.

As a Research Fellow I continued to publish and supervised doctoral students with only moderate success. I didn't know it at the time, but my enthusiasm for academic work was declining. I wrote Maughamish short stories, a novel based on the thesis (much rejected) and, in the throes of new relationship, a pornographic novella—also rejected by publishers. It surprises me to learn that this hectic piece of writing should be known about. I must have shown it to others but I have no recollection of doing so.

Anyway, such activities were precursors of the career I was later to follow as a fiction writer. The death of Jim Davidson in 1973 changed the atmosphere in the department. Factions developed and contended and I was bored. I subsequently held a couple of academic positions elsewhere, but never felt as suited to the life as I had under Davidson. My time at the ANU gave me confidence and relieved me of the burden of a puritanical Melbourne working class upbringing. I was to draw on Canberra and ANU experiences in all sorts of ways but, as a novelist must, I changed names, place names and dates to protect the innocent (and the guilty).

CHAPTER 32

Recalling the Coombs—Pacific History 1970–73

Kerry Howe

A lovely wrought iron entrance way, but rapid disorientation in the honeycomb maze. After weeks of conscious and unsuccessful navigating I gave up and resorted, successfully, to intuitive direction finding.

In 1970 you could usually park outside the main entrance. But Noel Butlin's massive yank tank always had the prime spot—on the red line directly in front of the door.

The Coombs Building is somewhat elemental—in Canberra's vicious summer, the brickwork glows with heat, water coolers gurgle, and closed wooden shutters vibrate to the hum of insects. In winter the sun sets over Black Mountain early, plunging the place into a freezing greyness. The tea room, outside, is a delightful centrepiece, especially in mid-winter when the sun shines. You can smell the eucalypts, and the sky is such a delicate shade of blue it seems it might crack. In the old days, there were rich slices of year-round Christmas cake lovingly baked by the tea ladies.

It was 24/7 as we would now say. There were assiduous PhD students at work at weekends and evenings. There seemed to be scores of us, from all over the world. There were the PhD starters, nervous and overawed. There were mid-termers, more relaxed and know-it all. There were the finishers and out-of-timers, frantic, often haunted. There was a collective buzz of purpose, expectation, commitment. Within the Coombs there were many staff who wrote books and articles, spoke out on public issues, and some were actively engaged in writing constitutions and preparing infrastructure for new Pacific island nation states. Some of us in our PhD studies were developing 'island centred history', rejecting older imperial approaches to the past. We were engaging in ideas of islander agency, though we did not use that term then. More generally we were all caught up in an intoxicating dose of postcolonialism, though we did not use that term either.

There was, centred in the Coombs, an atmosphere of achievement and an ethos of dedicated and relevant scholarship that burned into our psyches and still drives many of us. It was a time when my youthful generation thought society could be improved through research and rational debate, and that major inequalities between colonisers and colonised might be ended. And Canberra was one place where it all seemed to be happening—increasingly powerful anti-Vietnam War marches, the Aboriginal Tent Embassy was established, and the Whitlam Government swept into power, seemingly offering a boundless future of renewal and hope. Marvellous stuff! And with our new PhDs we would now go forth to help transform the world, enlighten and energise it.

Kerry Howe with wife Marilyn, Canberra, vintage 1970

This mood of passionate scholarship was enhanced by good friends and fun. Throughout the Coombs there was an irreverence of pretentious authority, a casualness in behaviour and dress style, and a vicarious enjoyment of the then nascent ocker nationalism. It was very heady mix for a lad fresh from a rather staid New Zealand. Later Friday afternoons might be spent across the road at the University House garden bar or at the Staff Club at Old Canberra House overlooking the lake. There were always student parties somewhere, with flagons of Kaiser Stuhl, marijuana (though we never inhaled), The Doors, The Cream, Joe Cocker, Leon Russell. The real larrikins and most assiduous party animals in the Coombs were the prehistorians—Jack Golson, who went about calling himself Hydraulic Jack after his successful Kuk excavations, and Les and Rosemary Groube with their manic eyes. There were a couple of momentous cricket matches between historians and prehistorians on the oval.

Presiding over the world of Pacific History was Jim Davidson, invariably beaming from ear to ear, rapidly puffing a cigarette, loose unbuttoned floral shirt, tiny tight shorts and jandals. Merrilyn and I were flattered that a man who wrote books, helped with the independence constitution of Samoa and was now working on one for New Guinea had time to bother with us. He had us stay numerous times with him at his house on the South Coast. When he came to dinner with us in Northbourne Flats he would listen intently to our rock LPs played at numbing decibels. Among his many intellectual influences on me was his emphasis on the importance and experience of place for historians. If you are studying some location in the Pacific or elsewhere, you need to go and live there for a while. His sudden death in 1973 was a real shock. Thinking back now, he was the first of our friends (as opposed to family) to die. His death hastened the division of a relatively homogenous department into its subsequent component bits—the Islandists, New Guineaists, and Southeast Asianists. It's never been the same since.

Among the many other notables in the Pacific History corridor was the impossibly shy and modest David Lewis, a legend even then, in the final throes of putting together probably one of the most important texts in Pacific History—*We the Navigators*—and, almost incidentally, sailing his tiny steel yacht *Ice Bird* around the Antarctic. While we froze and grizzled in the Canberra winter, he would shoot off to the Snowy Mountains and live in a snow cave each weekend to toughen himself up for the voyage. He returned from the Antarctic quite nonchalant, apparently none the worse for wear except for blackened fingertips. A different legend was Peter Corris, and that was due to his supposedly having written up his PhD thesis in six weeks! Most of us took at least 12 months for that part. He wrote the most erotic pulp fiction I ever read, and drank red wine in prodigious quantities. Does the Cliff Hardy of his later novels originate in the Coombs? The indefatigable Robert Langdon immediately regaled me, a total stranger, with tales of Spanish Polynesians. Bob kept up the relentless pressure on me to believe in his lost caravels of Spaniards until the day he died, more than three decades later. I never succumbed. One fellow student (a mid-termer) to whom I am most indebted is Bronwen Douglas. She convinced me to do a thesis on the Loyalty Islands—pristine, outside the malarial zone, and with archival material in Rome, Paris, and London. So, it was off to the islands, then to the capitals of Europe….

For the Coombs was above all a place of arrivals and departures. Staff migrated from Canberra to warm destinations during the winter dog months, and to the South Coast every summer. PhD students arrived, departed for life-changing fieldtrips all over the world, returned, wrote their 100,000 words, and departed with degrees. Many of us have been returning to the Coombs ever since, for sabbatical leave, for conferences and workshops. Though I normally enter the building by some back alley, I still usually go in through the main entrance at least once, just for old times' sake. But I can no longer park right outside. Thirty-five years ago I became a very small part of the Coombs Building, it remains a large part of me. I still find my way about it intuitively.

CHAPTER 33

1970s Coombs Dramas

Grant McCall

What is it that produces great, even good scholarship?

Anybody in the academic game must ask themselves that question from time to time, whether they are just beginning, as a student intending a professional vocation, or a scholar with experience and observation.

I arrived at the Coombs on 23 December 1971, having just come from the United Kingdom by ship, with my wife and seven month-old boy. I had done undergraduate study working part-time to finance it and the same was true for my time as a postgraduate, both in the United States and in the United Kingdom. I assumed that was the way things were.

Although Ravindra Kumar Jain, my tutor at Oxford, had told me that the ANU was a unique institution in its support and respect for PhD students, he could not have prepared me for what I was to experience.

No doubt many others will comment how they discovered to their delight that they were treated with respect and kindness as postgraduates, there being a confidence that we had been selected for our ANU Scholarship to produce great work and that we would do so.

Between 1971 and 1976, when I completed my thesis, including some 21 months fieldwork on Rapanui (Easter Island), in Chile and Peru, my fellow students and I had a study to ourselves, full support from the research library and all costs of our research met. As well, we were provided with a decent living allowance and our rental accommodation, amongst other similar scholars, was subsidised.

None of us could have asked for better conditions.

For myself, I felt that I could afford to experiment and used photography in my research, being provided by ANU with an excellent 35mm camera. When I returned, I played around with using mainframe computer technology for the analysis of my field data, again fully supported and encouraged. A colleague of mine at the time actually wrote his thesis on a computer: fancy that!

Students demonstrating against cuts in funds for tertiary education, 1976

I was not alone in this. Fellow scholars would order books and other materials through the library, which would be delivered in a matter of days, a few weeks, if coming from overseas. If we wished microfilm material from archives, that was obtained for us. If we wished to travel to Australian archives outside Canberra, we were assisted.

Apart from that material support, there was an excellent and professional support staff who assisted us with accomplishing our tasks.

Academic staff demonstrated that confidence in our maturity also. As the Coombs was entirely research oriented during my tenure there, academics there were interested in discussing ideas amongst themselves and with research scholars. We felt that if we had a question about our research or we wished to discuss some puzzling point in our analysis with some staff member, that we were free to do so.

Even the architecture lent itself to collegiality: people regularly attended the tearoom that was located between the two hexagons of the Coombs, Social Sciences and Pacific Studies. Morning and afternoon tea provided the perfect occasion to approach someone you didn't know to discuss some point of (sometimes) common interest.

Very different from my other experiences, the Coombs building was open to us at all hours. If I was writing something I felt that I could just continue: there was no closing time. If I awoke in the night—well, that didn't happen often—I could have walked from my flat at nearby Masson Street to the Coombs and write whatever it was that was on my mind. Weekends and weekday sometimes blurred, especially when a chapter was taking longer than expected to complete.

As research scholars, we were amused when a new traffic sign was erected: 'You are now entering the Australian National University. Slow Down'. Whilst our fellow inhabitants were mostly as diligent as we were, there were some exceptions and all of us knew about them. We would talk about people who had been at the ANU 'for years' and 'done nothing'. We would shake our heads and cluck our tongues. WE never would let such an opportunity, as ANU presented, not be exploited.

The one thing that we rarely discussed was what we would do when we finished our PhDs: academic jobs were not a problem. We were all good and we would get one, easily we thought. As we arrived, others were leaving, taking up good positions. Whilst we did our research and writing, those who had come before us, finished and moved into the academic life that was our goal. Notice boards featured cartoons, book reviews and similar ephemera, but rarely was there a notice for a job; they were just there and we could find one when our time came.

But there were worms in the apple that was the Coombs paradise. People got stymied in the research and their minds wandered. This wandering might take the form of extending the Friday afternoon convivial drink to the entire week. Some let their minds wander from ideas to their fellow students and gossip, the stuff of social anthropology, became an obsession with foibles discussed, sexual peccadilloes enjoyed and personal habits the focus of much discussion.

I recall that a group of us who had been in the Coombs for a couple of years were speaking in the corridor, almost as frequent a place of serious discussion as the seminar room, when a bright, new scholar arrived from the USA. He was sooooo earnest and serious; he immediately started to discuss in considerable detail the intellectual basis for his research as though we were some kind of a selection committee. One—I can't recall which one—asked a question about the new arrival's preparations for his fieldwork. That was enough, as each of us began to suggest more and more outlandish field supplies that our obsessive new colleague should obtain. Each of us, with or with out without tropical jungle experience, would suggest some piece of exotic gear: camouflage, a pith helmet, special boots, a butterfly net, a walking stick, special backpacks and so on. Actually, we were just making up most of it! Our young friend seemed very impressed and the more impressed he was, the more we exaggerated the supplies that he would need. To our surprise (and, of course, cruel delight) the next time we saw him at more or less the same spot—it was the foyer where the old plunger lift brought people to the heart of the (then) Department of Sociology and Anthropology—he was draped with most of the items that we had jokingly suggested!

In spite of our jests, this man went on to become a senior and innovative anthropologist in his home country. Certainly he had no lack of equipment for his first fieldwork!

Most of the Coombs scholars could not do enough for us. Very senior people would remember a question or a point we had raised at a seminar or with them informally, and would pop around (or send a note) with further helpful comments.

The biggest worm in the paradise Coombs experience in the 1970s was a very senior scholar whose own work clearly had not gone as he had planned. We all knew of his eccentric behaviour; there were tales of going berserk in foreign museums. He would lock students in detailed discussion of his latest obsession. Once or twice, although a public non-believer, he would insist that a student pray with him! When I first arrived, the man had invited me to talk over my plans for research, which I was eager to do, although I was unaware that he never had done any research in the Pacific Islands, where I proposed to carry out my fieldwork. He quizzed me on all the people who had done research on Rapanui, asking me about the flaws in their research. He urged me to pick one of them—the most prominent—and to base my research on debunking their work. I found this a puzzling bit of advice at the time since no social anthropologist had ever carried out research on Rapanui; I would be the first. Nevertheless, this man insisted that a focus on debunking was the way to carry out a piece of research. He also was convinced at the time that social anthropology ought to be done as a kind of naturalistic observation and recommended that as well as the camera, that I should take a stopwatch to the field with me to time interactions I might observe.

Upon my return, when I told him that I was not going to debunk anyone famous and that the stopwatch had received little use, he threatened to have my funding terminated and expel me from the ANU!

Unlike most other Coombs scholars, this man had little tolerance for opinions that differed from his own. As 1974 progressed, this man deteriorated and became a very large worm indeed, insulting my fellow students viciously in seminars, carrying out surprise and unwelcome visits to their rooms when they were trying to work and generally making himself unpleasant about the place.

Things came to a head when during one particularly unpleasant encounter, I accused him of being a 'paranoid schizophrenic'. Now, lest the reader think that somehow during my Coombs years, I had acquired power of psychiatric symptomology, I got the term from a black comedy film, 'The Ruling Class' that I had been to see the night before: my accusation was more an off-the-cuff remark, to keep the beast at bay than a serious and insightful diagnosis. It did the trick, though, and the threats to me and others faded as he was diverted trying to demonstrate his sanity.

In spite of that bizarre behaviour—tolerated with the same good sense by ANU as what we as research scholars did—the overall impression that all of us who experienced the Coombs was one of productive scholarship and intellectual integrity. From time to time, for conferences or to visit colleagues, mainly, when I return to the Coombs, my memory of the place with its (still) confusing corridors that seem to be an architectural Mobius strip is one of warm nostalgia. The building and the many positive, helpful people who were in it have fused and I am surprised to look at a study door and not see a familiar name there: they, like me, have moved on.

There was a particular smell in the Coombs that probably was some king of industrial cleaning material that was used; I sometimes come across it in other public buildings, but no more in the Coombs corridors and rooms. Just sometimes too, when I am in a bushy area and there is a large blow fly butting noisily against a screen, that too is a Coombs memory.

But more than that self-indulgence, mixed with memories of youth, of course, are the lessons of scholarship that I learned in the Coombs: support for learning, respect for the work of others (by both example and breach!) and the sense that the best way to promote learning is to just let people get on with it in the best possible conditions that can be arranged.

CHAPTER 34

The 'Catacoombs'

Michael R. Godley

The *Oxford English Dictionary* defines a 'catacomb' as a subterranean place for the burial of the dead, consisting of galleries or passages with recesses excavated in their sides for tombs but does include, among subsidiary meanings: 'a catacomb of books with lettered avenues' or 'a compartment in a cellar for storing wine'. Somewhat less-authoritative works even allow 'labyrithine passageway'. All of the above definitions will evoke fond memories for the readers of this volume. When I paid my first visit to Department of Far Eastern History, the Coombs Building, in the winter of 1979, Bob Hawke, who then headed the Australian Council of Trade Unions (ACTU), had pointed the bone at the Kurnell Oil Refinery and there was no heat on campus. New to this hemisphere, I'd asked Syd Crawcour, Professorial Fellow, to rent me a cheap room at University House with a 'southern exposure'. Cold as the grave it was. I'd heat up one of those ancient porcelain water jugs, empty the contents, and cuddle up close, dreaming of my absent wife who had remained in Hawaii. My new friend Andrew Fraser, Senior Fellow, one of the first inhabitants of the Coombs after he arrived from Oxford as a young PhD student in the 1960s, before Burlèy Griffin was a lake, wasn't joking when he welcomed me to the *'Tombs Building'*. He had stayed on: one of quite a few ANU doctoral students, including Edwin Sydney Crawcour, Igor de Rachewiltz, and Noel Barnard, unwilling to leave what had been comfortable surroundings. 'From womb to tomb' I heard one wag remark.

There was no Thought Police (political correctness had yet to be invented and who, in any case, would have dared say anything sexist to female academics as formidable as Coral Bell, International Relations or Audrey Donnithorne, Economics). However there was still the dreaded Heater Gestapo (from Buildings and Grounds or some similarly powerful, yet secret, organization) to deal with: on the hunt for 'illegal electric fires' as a threatening notice read. A quite distinguished colleague hid in his dark office so that no one might ever suspect that he was the latest culprit, whose added drain on the circuit had blown another fuse. The Coombs Building only warmed up when there was a national summit meeting of chancellors of real vice. Within an hour, University House became a tropical paradise. Perhaps a tanker of heating oil really was hijacked as the rumour mill suggested; but I've always suspected that Anthony Low simply tapped an 'extra-extraordinary' contingency fund to purchase fuel at Fyshwick market. After all, that's where many of my new associates bought coal for their, not quite-modern, Hughes apartments. The ANU was awash with money back then. I was once told how Geomorphology had attempted to buy a helicopter with nothing more than a purchase order! Green as he was, Michael Godley believed everything in those days: including a report that a nest of redback spiders had once been found under a bench outside the tearoom.

I was offered my first 'visiting research fellowship' very much as a consolation prize, after my application for a paid position had, inadvertently, gone by sea. Fortunately, Stephen Fitzgerald and Wang Gungwu kindly invited me for a three month visit. That was my first foot in the door. Although spending most of my subsequent career at Monash University, I soon become a regular visitor. The proverbial bad penny, that's me. I've heard that the Research School has a pretty thick file, including a signed document acknowledging that my long hair could be a hazard around machinery. Fair enough. There were, back then, no personal computers. Although IBM electrics could be heard, those few academics whose fingers knew the alphabet were forced to rely on iron-age machines from the earliest stages of the industrial revolution. No doubt that was why every department had its own manuscript typist. One I was particularly fond of was a prototype for Microsoft Word: automatically correcting my grammar and spelling. She was also witty, attractive, and eventually escaped to become a lawyer.

Perhaps only remembering external appearance, you might reject the allegation that the Coombs Honeycomb is somehow 'subterranean' but you must remember that it was always very difficult negotiating your way down the corridors at night. You quickly learnt where to find the light switches. Come to think of if, daylight really wasn't that much help. Back in the 1970s, there were few signs about the place. One 'old timer' admitted to me that he only knew one way in and out of the structure and, after more than a dozen years in the place, still couldn't find 'Seminar Room C'. No wonder my teenage son, who was with me when I turned up again as a visiting research fellow in the mid-1980s, carefully mapped the entire building to use as an original setting for Dungeons and Dragons. After all, the *Oxford* does acknowledge 'a perfect catacomb for monsters of extinct races' and also includes the act of savouring that smell: 'catacombish.' Always something of an amateur lexicologist, permit me to add 'catacoombs' and 'catacoombish'. It's my way of honouring a building with so many ghosts and memories.

Catacoombs

Everyone who knew him firmly believed that Wang Ling, Professorial Fellow in Far Eastern History, was a reincarnation of Lao Tzu (Laozi), the ancient sage. He took a particular liking to me when I first arrived—perhaps because I helped him start his car (actually Monkey's magic cloud trapize) by striking the starter with a crow bar whilst he turned on the ignition. Quite True! No Joke! What could I say? He was a world authority on Han science. In thanks, he later took Tim Wright, then a Research Fellow, who had gotten the job I had originally attempted to apply for, and me out to lunch at what was then one of the few decent Chinese restaurants in Canberra. We sat in utter amazement as he steered the wheel as if he were driving without having yet bothered to switch on the key. It was the ride of a lifetime! I had lost my job in the States and was pretty down on the world. One evening, after patiently listening for over an hour to my bitter complaints about the unfairness of the academic world, Ling merely advised: 'You need to write more Christmas Cards.' I never thought that he was talking about a religious holiday; his words were more directed at my own lack of warmth and charity.

Such self absorption was, of course, not unknown to the Coombs Building. However what struck me most when I first arrived was not the chill brought on by the refinery strike or my own unhappiness but the warmth displayed by so many of the inhabitants. I remember how, when one of the secretaries had her pay packet (it was cash in an envelope in those days) stolen by an intruder, Tim Wright took up a collection. Everyone on the corridor, high or low, professor or student, helped her out. It was mateship all round. We drank together and played bridge and Saturday night poker. Oh what a feeling! As new friends rebuilt my confidence, I gave seminars that were well attended, praised, and later published. Frankly, the Catacoombs saved my career and changed my life. I'll never forget how, on one visit, Wang Gungwu dragged me away from my desk. He was the big chief, of course, and I didn't really even qualify as an Indian. But he wanted me to meet C.P. Fitzgerald and A.L. Basham: those two original pillars of the Asian Studies field. Both were long retired by then, but they regaled us over lunch with many wonderful stories of the early institution. No, I didn't dare ask if the founding faculty had really been recruited in a pub in Soho. Didn't need to since Andrew and Syd had already told me the gossip: things that no mere visitor ever heard. But even so extensive a briefing didn't save me the embarrassment of introducing 'X' to his former spouse 'Y'. Oh how catacoombish!

The late 1970s—that's now over twenty five years ago—were a fascinating time of transition when most of the original inhabitants still walked the corridors and the next generation had only started to make its mark. I was privileged to met most of them. Canberra, too, was a different place. You could still have a beer at the old Civic Hotel and talk to other pioneering natives. Car parks were all unpaved, the dung beetle had yet to reduce the fly population, and missing tea was socially and academically unacceptable. As a first-time visitor, I was introduced to 'Nugget' Coombs and spoke now and then with Gough Whitlam, who also lived in University House and was extraordinarily competent at dishing out the soup. No, not all changes are for the good but, for better or worse, I've witnessed many things. Saw Bob Hawke, by then prime minister, cry over Tiananmen Square and school directors come and go. I've given more seminars than I can remember on a wide range of topics, drank coffee (wine and beer) with supportive friends and colleagues, and known (even helped or encouraged) dozens of post-graduate students. Quite a few of those are now successful academics. Thanks to all of you for so many memories.

I've come to appreciate that nametags are never thrown out, just recycled. Mine always miraculously reappears on some door or other. I do understand that it is important to keep the director in the dark; he or someday she must never think that any crypt is empty. I've even suspected that some of the names were fictitious. Indeed, I vaguely remember a FAN ROO (finally figured that the 'M' had gone missing though that could have been at Monash) and will never stop wondering just what went on in the infamous IMPREGNATION ROOM (out the back, past school vehicles, on the way to the Cellar Bar). Only one name, 'B.H. ONG', has probably ever been stolen. The mysterious Mr Ong shared a tomb with me in 1999, twenty years after my first internment. Turned out that he was Chin Peng, the once-notorious Malayan Chinese terrorist. Although my wife and I became quite friendly with him, he never did show up at the office. Others never go away. I wasn't at all surprised to see the name de Rachewiltz there on a door when I arrived last month. He had, you know, witnessed the building's construction. However it was still a bit of a shock when out popped Igor. May I, too, long haunt the corridors and meet you all again some day.

CHAPTER 35

The Old Hospital Building

Anton Ploeg

In September 1959 I arrived in Canberra, by train, to take up my Research Scholarship in anthropology. Professor John Barnes met me at the railway station, then a very elementary affair, and drove me to University House. The trip went through quite a bit of bushland. Drawing my attention to various points of interest John told me that the hill to our left, in a savannah landscape, was 'the heart of Canberra'. Later I understood that it was Capitol Hill, destined to become the site of the National Parliament Building. University House, with its courtyard, the common room with its Art Deco furniture, the lofty hall where we had our meals, and the luxury of its accommodation provided an intriguing contrast.

Such contrasts were then common in Canberra. The Anthropology Department was housed in the Nurses' Quarters of the Old Hospital Buildings that had become available after a new hospital was built further south, along the way to Lennox Crossing. They were located on both sides of Mills Road. Our section of the buildings was to the north of that road, on the campus side. It was of utmost simplicity, with wooden, clapboard walls. The only architectural nicety was a neat porch supported by two little columns. It seemed a diminutive building, with one, low ceilinged floor. But it was built on sloping ground; at the back side it had two floors, so it was far more spacious than appeared from the front. Then also there was a tearoom, in another section of the buildings, across Mills road. In that section was also the main library.

The inside of these buildings was as modest as the outside. However, that did not matter to me. On the contrary, it seemed quite appropriate, in keeping with the kind of work carried out there. Most important to me was that I got a room of my own. That was another unexpected luxury. I could straightaway start imagining myself as a member of a research institute. Working there and being in contact with both other PhD candidates and with staff members gave me a first taste of scholarly life. In Dutch universities, in the 1950s, social distance between staff, almost exclusively professors, and students was enormous, in every respect. In the Old Hospital Buildings the distance was, geographically speaking, tiny and contacts were regular, in the corridors, in the tearoom, over meals and during seminars.

Coombs Tea Room under construction 1962

I had become a member of a Department of Anthropology and Sociology, and especially John Barnes was emphatic that that name and that orientation be retained. The department included linguists and, from the early 1960s, also archaologists. Paula Brown's research cooperation with the geographer Harold Brookfield meant that he also often took part in seminars. Moreover, the department was a very international one, both as regards staff and students. Because it was all new to me, I did not see the multidisciplinarity and the presence of many nationalities as so very special, but in retrospect it was. I see it as a boon that I was exposed to it and that it added to my scholarly outlook.

The amount of refurbishing done to transform the building from a hospital into a research institute appeared to have been minimal. The most obvious was that book shelves had been installed. John Barnes' study impressed me enormously, with long rows of books and a large number of cardboard boxes that I presumed were stacked full with field work notes. This may have been a figment of my imagination, but, nevertheless, these boxes made it abundantly clear what task was ahead of me. Heating was just primitive. There were movable electric heaters, but not enough for all rooms. Even though the buildings were patrolled by safety personnel, the heaters must have formed a fire hazard. I cannot recollect the existence of ventilators.

In sharp contrast, however, the seminar room was extensively changed to make it suit its purpose. It must have been a large room to start with, or interior walls had been removed, to make it accommodate a large rectangular table and a number of display cases with New Guinea artifacts. It had windows on at least two sides so a lot of light entered. Off that room was a small departmental library, with on the wall the portrait of the founding professor, Siegfried Nadel, who had died in early 1956. It may well have been the one now in the Nadel seminar room in the Coombs building. Among the books was a field work guide, as far as I remember, typewritten but bound. It seems now lost. It was meant to be a practical guide. As regards food it sang the praises of taro, then quite unknown to me, and provided recipes. Later, while in the field in the west New Guinea highlands, I indeed ate a lot of taro, and liked it.

The emphasis that the seminar room had been given in the refurbishment impressed on me the importance of seminars in getting a PhD thesis written. They seemed to be essential, one had to attend, join in the discussion and could not escape presenting a number of them. In the case of students they were often called 'Work-in-Progress' papers. The size of the department allowed staff, students and visitors to present papers in the same seminar series. The first one I heard was by Derek Freeman, who on this occasion launched a savage attack on Marshall Sahlins' *Social Stratification in Polynesia.*

In the early sixties the ANU campus rapidly changed face, due to building and landscaping. Among the new buildings were the Menzies and the Chifley libraries, the first accommodation for undergraduates, the Haydon Allen building and ... the Coombs building. The supervising architect who lived in University House, told us that it was to be a simple building, in contrast to the more expensive Menzies library which was constructed just a bit earlier. Even so, it looked vast. Twice, we ventured into the unfinished shell, wandering through the corridors, marvelling at the many staircases and trying to guess the future use of all the enclosures. We mistook what was to become the tearoom for a lecture hall, and argued over the spot from where the lecturer was supposed to speak. But when I left Canberra in early 1964 to go back to the Netherlands, the building was still unfinished.

When I returned, for a few months, in late 1967, it had been in use for several years. It still existed as a hyphenated double hexagon, while the Coombs lecture theatre was under construction. To get to the anthropology department, I learnt to enter the building by a back entrance, at the left end of the hyphen, go up a short, straight staircase to the first floor, turn left to go up a winding staircase to the second floor, and then turn left again. From that point the territory was familiar. Also in this new environment anthropologists and linguists, although now in separate departments, were in close proximity. The department extended over three stretches of corridor. Rooms varied mainly in size and the number of quite small rooms—for PhD students?—was definitely larger than in the Old Hospital building. But the seminar room called for disappointment. It turned out to be small and dull, not at all as nicely fitted as the one in the Old Hospital Building.

PART VII

Corridors of Coombs

THE CORRIDORS OF COOMBS

Tessa Morris-Suzuki

"Excuse me,
I'm looking for the way out,"
he said;

an eager-eyed young man
in a hurry,

hair tamed for the occasion,

carrying an armful of books:
I think it was Foucault, Derrida and Negri,
but it may have been Parsons, Myrdal and Rostow…

"Just keep going straight ahead,"
I replied.

I hope my smile did not look malicious.

*****

I think of him sometimes,
over the years and decades,
wondering if he still haunts these corridors,

transfigured by the miracle of being lost.

I've tried to guide myself
by external landmarks –
the dappled bark of gum tree
glimpsed through a window,
a certain pattern of leaves
against the colbalt sky.
But even today, time and time again,
I turn a corner

and find myself in unfamiliar territory.

The doors look the same,
but the names are all unknown.
the masks on the wall speak unheard languages,
the filing cabinets conceal the passions
of wars the newspapers do not report.
Overheard snippets of conversation

pose unanswerable questions.

Me, I've long since given up looking
for the way out,

but what endless explorations,
what doubts, what dreams,
what revelations still wait,
yet undiscovered,

 beyond the next turning
in the mazes of the mind.

The spiral staircase

List of Contributors

Bryant Allen is Senior Fellow in Human Geography in RSPAS.

Gillian Atkin a technical officer Archaeology and Natural History, began work in Coombs in 1982 and left in 2005.

Desmond Ball is a Professor of Strategic and Defence Studies in RSPAS.

Ann Buller is the Administrator of the Division of Society and Environment, RSPAS.

William C. Clarke is a Visiting Fellow at the Pacific Centre in RSPAS.

Peter Corris trained as a Pacific historian in RSPAS and is now the successful author of Cliff Hardy series of detective fiction.

Lisa Dal Molin is a 'Tea Lady' in the Coombs Building.

Colin Filer is Senior Fellow and Head of Resource Management in Asia-Pacific Project in RSPAS.

James Fox is Professor of Anthropology and a former Director of RSPAS.

Ross Garnaut is a Professor of Economics in RSPAS.

Michael Godley a retired Chinese historian at Monash, was a Visiting Fellow in Coombs in 2005.

Jack Golson was the Foundation Professor of Prehistory in RSPAS.

Julie Gordon retired after a long period of service in the Division of Pacific and Asian History, RSPAS.

Niel Gunson retired as Senior Fellow in Pacific History and is now a Visiting Fellow in the Division of Pacific and Asian History, RSPAS.

Kerry Howe is a Professor of History at Massey University, Albany Campus, Auckland, and has been a Visiting Fellow in RSPAS.

Sue Lawrence has been a senior administrator in the RSPAS for many years where she is now Acting Business Manager.

Anthony Low was Director of RSPacS and Vice Chancellor of The Australian National University and is currently Visiting Fellow in the Division of Pacific and Asian History, RSPAS.

Ewan Maidment is the Executive Officer of the Pacific Manuscript Bureau in RSPAS.

Ron May retired as Senior Fellow in Political and Social Change and is currently a Visiting Fellow at the Pacific Centre, RSPAS.

Maxine McArthur is a science fiction writer who presently works as an editor in Pacific and Asian History, RSPAS.

Grant McCall is a professor specializing in Pacific studies at the University of New South Wales.

Tessa Morris-Suzuki is Professor of Japanese History in RSPAS.

Hank Nelson is an Emeritus Professor and Visiting Fellow in Pacific and Asian History, RSPAS.

Anton Ploeg is at the Center for Pacific and Asian Studies at Radboud University, Netherlands, and has been a Visiting Fellow in RSPAS.

John Ravenhill is a professor in the Department of International Relations, RSPAS.

Merle Ricklefs presently a Professor of History at the National University of Singapore, was Director of RSPAS.

Kathy Robinson is a Senior Fellow in Anthropology in RSPAS.

Jude Shanahan worked for many years in the Division of Pacific and Asian History and is now an IT Support Officer in RSPAS.

Claire Smith retired as Departmental Administrator of Political and Social Change in RSPAS.

Oskar Spate was Foundation Professor of Geography and Director of the Research School of Pacific Studies.

Darrell Tryon is Professor of Linguistics in RSPAS and a former Deputy Director of the School.

Sophie Vilaythong is a 'Tea Lady' in the Coombs Building.

Wang Gungwu presently at the National University of Singapore, was Professor of Far Eastern History and Director of RSPacS.

R. Gerard Ward currently a Visiting Fellow at the Pacific Centre, was Professor of Human Geography and Director of RSPacS.

INDEX

Page numbers in **bold** denote photographs.

A

Aboriginal affairs, 79
Aboriginal History, 79-80
Aboriginal man and environment in Australia, 110
Aboriginal studies, 119
Aborigines in the Defence of Australia, 154
Accounts Section, 175
Acting Directors, 51
Adams, Peter, 252-57, **252**
administration, 221-226
    1970s, 173
    departmental, 222
    fieldwork, 223
    technology changes, 225
administrators, 226
Ake, Willie, 184
Allen, Bryant, **80**
Allen, Jim, 112, 114,116, 266
Allen, Michael, 119
Ali, Ahmed, 75
Altman, Jon, 161, 163
Ambrose, Wal, 110, 113, 115
Amyx, Jennifer, 164
Anderson, Robyn, 209
Angau Lodge, 186
Angels of War, 209
Anthropology and Sociology, Department of, 89, 118, 286
    early days, 201
Anthropology, Department of, 5, 36, 202
    artworks in, 64–65
    fieldwork, 123
    gender imbalance, 120
    photographs, 10
appointments, 7–9, 47, 55, 58, 76, 126, 172
    women-only positions, 58
Archaeology and Natural History, Department of, 116
    field work, 215, 216-218
    laboratories, 213, 215
Archaeology *see* Prehistory
archival advocacy, 180
Armstrong, David, 149
Arndt, Heinz, 8, 40,125, 127, **128**, 129, 131-132, 135, 140
Australian student recruitment, 140
Arsenio, Balisacan, 141
art works, 61-66
    Aboriginal art, 64
    bark cloths, 63
    photographs, 64-65
    Tikopian artefacts, 63
Asch, Patsy, 63
Asch, Tim, 64, 65
ASEAN in a Changing Pacific and World Economy conference, 133
ASEAN-Australia Economic Relations Research Project, 135
Asia Pacific Economic Cooperation (APEC), 141-142
Asia Pacific Journal of Anthropology see Canberra Anthropology
Asia Pacific School of Economics and Management (APSEM), 144-145
Asian Financial Crises and the Global Financial Architecture, 106
Asian-Pacific Economic Literature, 138
Asia-Pacific Magazine, 59
Asia-Pacific Security, 106
ASIO, 127, 154
Assistant Business Manager's Office, 174-175
Assistant Registrar, 175
Atkin, Gillian, **214**
Atlas of Languages of the Pacific, 92
Austin, Greg, 105
Australia and the Northeast Asian Ascendancy, 139, 141
Australia South Asia Research Centre, 143
Australia's Regional Security, 107

Australia-Japan Research Centre, 131, 138, 142
Australian Journal of International Affairs, 107
Australian Research Council (ARC), 57
Australian Research Grants Committee, 51
Australia-Western Pacific Economic Relations Research Project *see* Australia-Japan Research Centre
Austronesian Project, 5
Ayson, Robert, 157

B
Baker, John, 83
Ball, Desmond, 128, **150**
Ballard, Chris, 209
Barmé, Geremie, 209
Barnard, Rosemary, 83
Barnes, John, 13, 36, 118-119, 286,
    New Guinea Research Unit, 98
Barrow, Nora, 106
Barwick, Diane, 79
Bastin, John, 5
Batt, Sean, 227-232, **228**
Baumann, Theo, 91
Beazley, Kim, 143, 152, 153
Beckett, Jeremy, 119
Bedford, Dick, 83, 84
Bell, Coral, 155
Belshaw, Cyril, 97
Bensusan-Butt, David M, 8, 125, 140
Bettison, David, 4, 8, 97, 98
Bhagwati, Jagdish, 143
Bienen, Henry, 106
Billerwell, Christine, 93
Biogeography and Geomorphology, Department of (later Archaeology and Natural History), 5, 83 *see also* Geography, Department of
biogeography, 109, 113-114
biogeography: highlands agriculture, 113
birds, xvi, 48, 200, 211, 222
Birk, David, 92

Bjelikov, Vladimir, 90
Black Harvest, 209
block grants, 51, 57, 81 *see also* funding
Blyth, C A, 8
Board of Institute of Advanced Studies (BIAS), 49
Board of Institute of Advanced Studies (BIAS): Vietnam debate, 24, 27, 29–30
boomerang boys (and girls), 74
Booth, Anne, 131, 138
Borrie, Mick, 38
Bowden, John, 92
Bowers, Nancy, 98
Bowler, Jim, 113
Bretherton, Jan, 59, 160
Brookfield, Harold, 8, 81-85, 225, 286
    New Guinea Research Unit, 96
Brown, Colin, 161
Brown, Paula, 286
Bryan, Barbara, 106
budget cuts *see* funding
Bull, Hedley, 149
Buller, Ann, 117, **223**
Bulletin of Indonesian Economic Studies, 131
Bureau of Mineral Resources, Geology and Geophysics, 110
Burgmann, Bishop, 30, 71
Burma Update, 164
Burma-Thailand Railway seminar, 239-241
Burma-Thailand Railway, 241
Burnie, Joan, 91-92
Burns, Arthur, 8, 149
Burridge, Kenelm, 86
Burton, John W, 29–30, 71
Business Manager, 38, 53 *see also* Grimshaw, Peter
Business Manager's Office, 171, 175
Butler, Richard, 39
Butlin, Noel, 48

C

Cambridge History of the Pacific Islanders, 75
Cammack, Floyd, 179
Campion, Max, 215
Canberra Anthropology, 120, 123, 202
Canberra University College, 2
Canberra: in the 1950s, 24, 285
Carrington, Lois, 92
Carron, Margaret, 38
cartography, 91
Caruana, Willy, 64
Chant, Pauline, 92
Chen, Amy, 106
Chey, Jocelyn, 133
Childe, Gordon, 71
China: late 1970s, 133
Clarke, Hugh, 239
Clarke, William, 81, 83
cleaning, 163, 241, 242
Clunies Ross, Anthony, 123
collaborative research *see* cross-disciplinary research
collegiality, 42, 49-51, 67, 108, 253
Collins, Oanh, 194
Coming of the Gods, 66
Committee of Assessors, 12, 13
Commons, Merv, 229-232, **232**
comparative research, 121
computing, 227-232, 280
Connolly, Bob, 209
constitution makers, 75
Contemporary China Centre, 41
Conversations with Mbah Wali, 63
Conyers, Diana, 99
Cook Islands National Archives, 184
Coombs building: early history, 3–4, 6–9, 11–15
    opening, 15, 203
    planning and construction, 10–13
    social life, 9, 265-66, 270
    structure, 1, 16, 38, 194, 195, 203, 204
Coombs, Herbert Cole (Nugget), 3, 4, 6, 127, 128, **190**
    Clifton Pugh portrait of, xiii, 15, 51
Copland, Sir Douglas, 26
Corden, W Max, 8, 125, 128, 132, 136, 137
corridors, 179, 195, 199
Corris, Peter, 73, 76, **266**, 271
Cotton, James, 103
Council on Security Cooperation in Asia Pacific (CSCAP), 156
Couper, Alastair, 81
Craft, Mary, 91
Craig, Jean (Jean Martin), 118
Crawford School of Economics and Government (CSEG), 145
Crawford, Sir John, 7, 8, 16, 36, 74, **89**, 128, 130-131, **132**, 135-136
    approach to research, 127
    New Guinea Research Unit, 95-100
    cricket matches, 115-116, 140
Crocker, W R (Bill), 7, 8, 26
Crocombe, Ron, 8, 13, 72, 96, 130
cross-disciplinary research, 5, 154, 286
    New Guinea Research Unit, 96
Crouch, Harold, 161, 165
Crozier, Dorothy, 180
CSIRO, 106-107
Cummins, Rev Geoff, 72
Cunningham, Adrian, 181
Curnow, Miriam, 91
Cyclone Heta, 184

D

Dal Molin, Alicia (Lisa), **262**
Dalrymple, Billie, 151
Daro, Boio Bess, 98
Dauvergne, Peter, 107
Davidson, J W (Jim), 4, 5, 6–7, 8, 26, 36, 40, 69-72, **70**, 74-75, 265, 266, 271
    planning Coombs building, 12, 13
    Vietnam debate, 29–30
    views on research, 7

Pacific Manuscripts Bureau, 179
Daws, Gavan, 40, 75, 209, 242
Dedman, J J, 3
Dening, Greg, 72
Denoon, Donald, 75, 242, 254-5
Department of Foreign Affairs and Trade, diploma for, 102
departmental secretaries, 117
development economics, 125
Development Studies Centre *see* National Centre for Development Studies
Dibb, Paul, 152, 155, 156, 157
Dick, Howard, 131
Dinnen, Sinclair, 100, 162
Diokno, Jose (Pepe), 162
diplomats, 58
directional diagrams, 16, 47
Director's Office, 47-48, 61
Director's Secretary, 53
Directors, 6, 47-48, 74, 80
Divisions, 52, 225
Documentary Basis for Pacific Studies, 179
Donnithorne, Audrey, 126, **126**, 140, 279
Douglas, Bronwen, 271
Drysdale, Peter, 130, 132, 135, 142
Duncan, Ron, 146
Dunlop, Sir Edward 'Weary', 239
duplicating, 174
Dupont, Alan, 153, 155, 156
Dutton, Tom, 87, 88

E
East Asia Imperilled: Transnational Challenges to Security, 156
Eccles, John, 30
Economic History of Southeast Asia Project, 5
Economic History, Department of, 27
Economics, Department of, 5, 27, 136, 142,
    agricultural development group, 134
    early history, 125-127
    Japan research, 130
    trade and industry policy, 132
    Work in Progress seminars, 125
editing, 196-97, 203
Egloff, Brian, 112
Elek, Andrew, 142
Elephant Stalls, 82
Elliot, Lorraine, 107
Epstein, A L (Bill), 8
Epstein, T Scarlett, 8, 125
Eri, Vincent, **89**
Eteuati, Kilifoti, 73
ethnographic field research, 117
ethnohistory, 72
European Vision and the South Pacific, 72

F
Faculty Board Committee, 129
Faculty Board, 50, 74, 108
Fagan, Bob, 81
Fairburn, Ian Teo, 96
Far Eastern History, Department of, 5, 36
Fegan, Brian, 161
Fele, Nokise, 73
fieldwork, 1783, 215, 216-8
    administration of, 223-4
Filer, Colin, 19, 100, **245**
financial crisis, 1996 and 1997, 56–57, 59-60, 144
Findlay, Chris, 133, 146
Finney, Ben, 96
Finney, Ruth, 96
First Contact, 209
Firth, Raymond, 3, 4, 5, 21, 36, 63
Fisk, E K (Fred), 8, 125, 131, 134, 139-40
Fitchett, Keith, 215
Fitzgerald, C P (Patrick), 8, 30, 36, 40
Fitzgerald, Stephen, 133
Florey, Howard, 3, 4
fly screens, 16–17, 74
Foley, Kevin, 149
Fox, James (Jim), **62**, **119**, 121-22,

164, 175
France, Peter, 72
Franklin, Karl, 87
Fraser, Beverley, **200**
Frazer, Roger, 81
Freeman, Derek, 8, 45, 65-66, 75, 86, 121
    at seminars, 237
    Margaret Mead debate, 121
Fry, Greg, 107, 108, 153
funding, 38, 51, 56-7, 103-04, 137, 157 *see also* block grants

G

Gammage, William, 207, 209, 211, 242
Garnaut, Ross, 98, 99, **128**, 139,
    work on Papua New Guinea, 130
gender imbalance, 8, 58, 120
Gender Relations Centre, 120
general staff, 210
Geography, Department of, 5, 21, 36, 81, 109 *see also* Human Geography, and Biogeography and Geomorphology
geography, quantitative revolution in, 81-82
Gillion, Ken, **70**, 71
Gilman, Judy, 91
Gilson, Richard (Dick), 8, **70**
Girling, John, 200
Glover, Ian, 112
Gollan, Robin, 13
Golson, Jack, 8, 40, 83, **110**, 137, **190,** 271
Gordon, Julie, 194, 207, **208**
Gordon, Sandy, 153
Graduate Programme in Public Policy, 145
Graduate Studies in International Affairs (GSIA) *see* International Relations, Department of
Grattan, C Hartley, 237-238
Gray, Helen, **96**
Grenville, Steve, 131
Grimes, Charles, 92

Grimshaw, Peter, 16, 25, 38, 43-44, 53, 83, 122, 171, 176-78, **177**, 222
    memos, 176
    North Australia Research Unit and New Guinea Research Unit, 177
Groube, Les, 111, 271
Groube, Rosemary, 271
Grounds, Romberg and Boyd (architects), 11–12 *see also* Coombs building: planning and construction
Grubel, Herb, 132
Gunson, Niel, **70**, 207
    Pacific Manuscripts Bureau, 181
Guy, Jacques, 92

H

Half Life, 209
Hambly, Luke, 202
Hamilton-Hart, Natasha, 107
Hancock, Sir Keith, 3, 4, 5, 6, 9
    planning Coombs building, 1, 13
    Wool Seminar, 35
Harris, Stuart, 103, **128**, 135, 142
Hart, Doreen, 81
Harvest of the Palm, 121
Hasluck, Paul, 76
Hassall, Graham, 73
Hastings, Peter, 151
Hatanaka, Sachiko, 96
Hattori, Shirō, 90
Hau'ofa, Epeli, 120
Hawke, Bob, 71, 134
Hawke, Hazel, 71
Healey, Alan, 87
Healey, Phyllis, 87
heating, 279, 286
Hegarty, David, 153
Helgeby, Edward, 53
Henningham, Stephen, 161
Herbert, Mary, 38, 49, 53
Hewison, Kevin, 161
Heyward, Ian, 91
Hiatt, Les, 119
Higgins, Ben, 136

Higgott, Richard, 102, 104
Hill, Hal, 131, 135, 138
hiring practices *see* appointments,
History Society or Club, 69
Ho, Bobby, 82
Holy Man, 242
Hooker, Virginia, 161
Hope, Alec, 26
Horner, David, 147, 155, 156
Horsburgh, Ian, 171
Howard government, 59
Howarth, Barry, 184
Howe, Kerry, 73, **270**
Howe, Marilyn, **270**
Howlett, Diana , 81, 83, 96
Hughes, Ian, 81, 84, 132, 138
Huisken, Ron, 155, 156
Hull, Terry, 161
Human Geography, Department of, 5, 81, 83 *see also* Geography, Department of
Hutchens, Graham, 38
Huxley, Sir Leonard, 15, 203

I

In the Play of Life, 63
Indonesia Project, 160
Indonesia Update conference, 134, 141
Indonesia, politics, 162
Inglis, Ken, 242
Institute of Advanced Studies, 2
Institute of Advanced Studies, Review, 57-58, 154
Institute of Applied Social and Economic Research, Papua New Guinea (IASER), 39, 99 *see also* New Guinea Research Unit (NGRU)
International Crisis Group, 165
International Relations, Department of, 28–29, 101-107
    funding, 103-104
    Graduate Studies in
International Affairs (GSIA), 106
    monograph series, 105
    support staff, 106

intrigue, 60, 75

J

J G Crawford Building, 138
J G Crawford Chair in Agricultural Economics, 142
Jennings, J N (Joe), 8, 24, 74, 81
Jha, Raghbendra, 146
Joe Leahy's Neighbours, 209
Jolly, Margaret, 120
Jones, Rhys, 109, **111**, 112
Journal of John Sweatman, 266
Journal of Pacific History, 72
    manuscripts section, 180
Jukes, Geoffrey, 109, 149, 202

K

Kamenka, Eugene, 44
Karawinata, Han, 92
Keal, Paul, 144, 149, 153
Keesing, Roger, 65, 118, 120-21, 266
Krerkvliet, Ben, 161, 167
Key, Con, 109
Kikusawa, Ritsuko, 92
Kindleberger, Charles, 125
kindred, concept of, 121
Kingdon, Elizabeth, 59
Kipnis, Andrew, 122
Klintworth, Gary, 103
Koentjaraningrat, 120
Krinks, Peter, 81, 96
Kwasik, Mira, 91, 92

L

la Nauze, John, 235, **236**
laboratory wing, 113-114, 213
    1996 fire, 218-219
Lal, Brij, **17**, 75, 208
    Pacific Manuscripts Bureau, 181
Lampert, Ron, 110, 112-113
Land Management Group, 84
Langdon, Robert, **180**, 181, 236-37, 271
    at seminars, 236-37
Langmore, Diane, 73

Langness, L L, 96
Langtry, J O (Jol), 151
Lapita Homeland Project, 114
Laracy, Hugh, 73
Lasaqa, Isireli, 81
Lātūkefu, Sione, 73, 97, 209
Lawrence, Peter, 119
Lawrence, Sue, **172**
Lawson, Stephanie, 105
Laycock, Don, 87-88, **88**
Lea, David, 81,83
Leach, Hilda, 91, 92
Leaver, Richard, 102, 104
Lee, Mei Wah (Mei Smith), 91, 97
Lewis, David, 72, 271
Ley, Allison, 165, **200**
library, 70
Lightning Meets the West Wind, 266
Lim, Robyn, 149
Lindsay, Lord of Birker, 8, 28–29
Ling, Matsay, 91-92
Linge, Godfrey, 16, 79, 80, 81, 82
Linguistic Atlas series, 45, 90, 92
Linguistics, Department of, 5, 90-93, 109
    early history, 87–93 *see also* Anthropology and Sociology, Department of
Lloyd, Peter, 132
Lockwood, Ken, 85
Low, Anthony, 7, **37**, 163
    on New Guinea Research Unit, 99
Low, Morris, 193
Luo Yuanzheng, 133

M
Macdonald, Barrie, 73
MacFarlane, Bruce, 125
MacIntyre, Andrew,146
Mack, Andy, 103, 105
Mackie, J A C (Jamie), 40, 134, 136, 159, 160, 166
Macknight, Campbell, 112
Maidment, Ewan, **182**
mail, 173
Mander-Jones, Phyllis, 180

Manning, Chris, 131
manuscripts, pre-computer, 89
Marck, Jeff, 92
Masing, James, 66
Mason, Nora, 87
Matthew, Shirley, **96**
Matthews, Rae, 70
Maude, Alaric, 84
Maude, Harry, 8, 69, 72, 180
    festschrift for, 76
    Pacific Manuscripts Bureau, 179
May, Ron, 8, **160**, 203
McArthur, Maxine, **195**
McCawley, Peter, 131, 134, 138
McCormack, Gavan, 239, 240
McIntosh, Dorothy, 193, 208
McKibbin, Warwick, 139, 146
McLeod, Ross, 131
McMillan, Don, 153
McQueen, Humphrey, 129
McWilliam, Andrew, 122
'Meditating Buddha sheltered by the Naga King', 61
Melanesia: a Geographical Interpretation of an Island World, 81
Melbourne Cup, 73, 141
Melville, Sir Leslie, 26–27, 128, 136
Menzies, Sir Robert, 27
metal screens, 17–18, 46
microfilm, 181, 183
Millar, T (Tom) B, 150
Miller, J D B (Bruce), 7, 8, 16, 40, 101
Mitchell, Keith, 91
Mockridge, Stahle and Mitchell (architects) *see* Coombs building: planning and construction,
Modelski, J A , 8
Modjeska, Nick, 83
Morauta, Mekere, 130
Morris, Tom, 240
Morton, Kathy, 106
Mosko, Mark, 120
Moulik, T K, 96

Moyal, Ann, 8
Muirden, Andrew, 251-257, **252**
multidisciplinary research *see* cross-disciplinary research,
Mulvaney, John, 111, 112, 114
Mumford, Win, 111
Munn, Nancy, 120

N
Nadel, Siegfried F (Fred), 7, 8, 26, 118, 120
Namaliu, Rabbie, 130
Nash, Don, 96
Nash, Jill, 96
Nation, John, 161
National Centre for Development Studies (NCDS), 39, 138, 142
National Graduate School of Management, 145
National Research Institute, Papua New Guinea, 4, 100
Nawawi, M A, 161
Nekitel, Otto, 92
Nelson, Hank, **17**, 64, 75, 79, 207, 209, 235, **238**
Nemenzo, Francisco, 161, 162
New Guinea Research Bulletin, 97
New Guinea Research Unit (NGRU), 4, 39, 72, 95-100, 130, 131 *see also* Institute of Applied Social and Economic Research, Papua New Guinea (IASER),
    general staff, 98
        cross-disciplinary research, 96
        premises, 97
New Guinea Society, 69
New Guinea: languages, mapping of, 87, 90
New Heaven, New Earth, 85
Newbury, Colin, **70**, 71
Newbury, Trudy, **70**
Ngok, Lee, 153
Nguyen Dang Liem, 92
nightwatchmen, 251-257
Noble, Greg, 105
North Australia Research Unit (NARU), 163. 177

Northeast Asian Programme, 103

O
O'Farrell, Patrick, 10
O'Hagan, Cindy, 106
O'Malley, William, 161
O'Neill, Robert, 150–151
O'Rourke, Dennis, 209
Old Hospital Building, 10, 24, 35, 69, 285
    seminar room, 287
Old Nurse's Quarters, 113
Oliphant, Sir Mark, 3
On the Margins of History, 237
Oram, Nigel, 95, 96
Oruga, 98
Owen-Jones, Barbara, 199

P
pace of research, 18, 275, 283
Pacific and Asian History, Division of, 193, 207, 209
Pacific Community seminar, 135
Pacific Cooperation, 104
Pacific Economic Cooperation Council, 134
Pacific Economic Relations, 103, 104
Pacific History, Department of, 5, 36, 69–75, 271
Pacific in Transition: Geographical perspectives and Adapatation and Change, 81
Pacific Islands Group (PIG), 202
Pacific Linguistics, 91
    printing of, 88
    staff, 91
Pacific Manuscripts Bureau, 72, 179–180, 185
    field trips, 175, 183–184, 186
    funding consortium, 181

management committee, 171, 183
    reformatting method, 183
Pacific Since Magellan, 45
Pacific Trade and Development Conference series, 135

Pacino, Leo, 91
Paniani, George, 184
Papua New Guinea, 83, 98
    highlands, prehistory, 109
    national elections study, 97
Partridge, P H (Perc), 35
Passmore, John, 13
Patz, Gunther, 149
pavilion model, 12–13
Pawley, Andrew, 90, 92
payday, 172–173
Payne, Lynne, 106
Peace Research Centre (PRC), 59, 103
Penny, David, 125
People, Land Management and Environmental Change (PLEC) Project, 84
Perkins, Charles, 76
Philippines After Marcos seminar, 162
Philippines Update, 164
photographs, 64–65, 117,
Pike, Andrew, 209
Ploeg, Anton, 96
Polach, Henry, 111
Political and Social Change Monograph series, 165
Political and Social Change, Department of, 5, 38, 159–161, 162, 164–166
    academic disciplines, 161
    geographic interests, 161
    thematic conferences on the Pacific, 164
    thematic interests, 161
pollen analysis, 214–215
Polomka, Peter, 153
possums, 211, 256
Powell, Jocelyn (formerly Wheeler), 96, 112–113
Powell, Mitchell, 96
Prehistory, 109–111
    Australian and Southwest Pacific, 109
    Cambridge links, 112
    fieldwork, 112–113

Prentice, Jack, 89, 92
Preston-Stanley, Jan, 106
printery, 174
psychohistory, 75

R

Rabuka, Sitiveni, 210
Radiocarbon Laboratory, 111, 114
Rae, Heather, 106
Rajiv Gandhi Chair in South Asian Economics, 143
Ravenhill, John, **102**
Reay, Marie, 117, 119, 120
Rebbeck, Grant, 251–257, **252**
reception staff, 173
Reece, Robert, 76
Regan, Anthony, 100, 162
Regime Change and Regime Maintenance in Asia and the Pacific Project (RCRMAP), 163
research assistants, 199, 202–203, 204
Research School of Pacific and Asian Studies (RSPAS), 51, 52, 204
    archival advocacy, 180
    archival resources, 185
    early history, 2
Research School of Pacific Studies (RSPacS), 2, 50 *see also* Research School of Pacific and Asian Studies (RSPAS)
    directors, 36
    early history, 2, 5, 8, 35–36
Research School of Social Sciences (RSSS), 2, 35, 44
Resource Management in Asia Pacific Project (RMAP), 5, 84
Reut-Smit, Chris, 105
Review of Australia's Defence Capabilities, 152
Richardson, Gordon, 179
Richardson, James, 102, 103
Ricklefs, Merle, **57**
    as Director, 55–56
Rimmer, Peter, 77, 80, 82
robbery, 255
Robertson, Bob, 81

Robinson, Anne, **200**
Robinson, Kathryn, **118**
Ross, Malcolm, 92
Roy, Denny, 153
rubbish, 256
Ruddock, Grenfell, 12
Ryan, Dawn, 96

S
Sadka, Emily, 5, 71
Saevaru, Sylvia, **96**
Salehzadeh, Farnaz, 106
Sawer, Geoff, 26
scanners, 230
Scarr, Deryck, 72
Schemberg, Annegret, 92
scholarships, PhD research, 50
School of Art, prize to, 63
School Secretary, 53
School Services, 171, 172
Scott, Gillian, 181
Seabrooke, Len, 106
seminar rooms, 38
seminars, 73, 84, 110, 115, 125, 141, 162, 202, 235–242, 287
    Burma-Thailand Railway, 239–241
Serjeantson, Sue, 58
Shanahan, Jude, 194, 208, **208**
Shand, Ric, 83, 134, 143
Shineberg, Dorothy, 7, 181
Singarimbun, Masri, 120
Singh, Gurdip, 215
Sinisoff, Sally, 91, 92
Site Development Committee, 11–12
Skipper, Matcham, 18, 47
Smith, Bernard, 74
Smith, Claire, 165, **200**
Smithies, Arthur, 125–126

Society and Environment, Division of, 225, 226
Sociology and International Relations, Department of, 5
Somare, Michael, 98
Sommer, Elaine, 91

Soviet Union: The Incomplete Superpower, 155
Spate, O H K, 3, 5, 7, 8, 9, **25**, 36, 45, 69, 70, 80, 86, 95, 209
    appointment, 21–24
    as Dean, 27
    at seminars, 237
Specht, Jim, 112
Spillius, James, 63
Spriggs, Matthew, 116
Stacey, Diane, 93
Stanner, W E H (Bill), 7, 8, 76, 112, 117, 202
State, Society and Governance in Melanesia Project (SSGM), 5, 162, 167
stationery store, 173
Stone, David, 72, 98
Strategic and Defence Studies Centre (SDSC), 150–152, 157
    Asia –Pacific security, 156
    F/A-18, 152
    northern defence, 152
    post-Cold War issues, 155–156
    regional security, 153
    stragegic nuclear balance, 152
strategic plan, 51, 56, 59–60
Strategy Committee, 51, 56
Strathern, Andrew, 83
Strathern, Dame Marilyn, 98
Sundrum, R M, 137, 140
supercomputer DEC 10, 227–229
Suwandi, Raharjo, 63
Swan, Trevor, 27, 95, 128

T
Tabbart, Christine, 230
Tange, Sir Arthur, 155
Tapp, Nicholas, 122
tea ladies, 174, 259–262
tea room, 37, 44, 74, 135, 174, 186, 196, 259–262, 269, **286**
telex, 175
Terra Australia series, 115
Terrell, Jenny, **17**
Thailand, King of, 27
Thayer, Carl, 163

Thomas, Nicholas, 73
Thorne, Alan, 114, 115
Tie, Jolika, 151
Tirikatene, Whetu, 76
Toner, J B (Jim), **96**, 98
Tow, Bill, 106
Tran Huong Mai, 93
Transformation in Communist Regimes Project, 5
Trendall, Dale, 18, 69
Tryon, Darrell, **89**
Tsuda, Rico, 161
Turner, Mark, 161
Tuzin, Donald, 120
Typing Pool, 171, 173
typists, 230
Tys, Sue, 91

U
Uberoi, J P Singh, 120
University House, 69
University House, opening, 30
Uren, Tom, 239

V
Vaile, Kanny, 184
van de Veur, Paul, 4
Verhaar, John, 91
Vietnam Update, 164
Vietnam War: Teach-in phenomenon, 129
Vilaythong, Sophie, **262**
viruses, computer, 230–231
visitors, 39, 224
Viviani, Nancy, 149
Voorhoeve, Bert, 88

W
Waddell, Eric, 81, 96
Waigani Seminars, 97, 99
Waiko, John, 64
Walker, Donald, 8, 41, 82, 112

Walmsley, David, 81
Wang, Gungwu, 7, 40, **45**, 77
    as Director, 43
Wang Ling, 8, 282
Ward, Marion, 8, 97, 99
Ward, R Gerard, 41, **49**, 83, **86**, 97
    as Director, 50–54, 139
Ward, Robin, 106
Ward, Robyn, 200
Warr, Peter, 138, 142
We, the Navigators, 271
Weekes, Marion, 194, 208
Weir, Christine, 211
West, Francis, 8, 73
White, Hugh, 157
White, Peter, 112
Whitlam, Gough, 43, 160, 189–191, **190**
Wiggan, Jo, 254
Williams, Clive, 155
Wilson, Basil, 89, 92
Wilson, Bob Kent, 96, 130
Wilson, Judith, 120, 201, 202
Winburn, Evelyn, 91
Wise, Judy, 91
work ethic, 73, 269
World Out of Balance: American Ascendancy and International Politics in the 21st Century, 156
Worseley, Peter, 120
Wright, Michael, 99
Wright, Tim, 282
Wurm, Stephen, 8, 40, 45, 87, 88, **89**, 90–91

Y
Yen, Doug, 114
Yi Hak-Nae, 240
Young, Ken, 161
Young, Michael, 123
Youngson, Sandy, 38, 44

www.ingramcontent.com/pod-product-compliance
Lightning Source LLC
Chambersburg PA
CBHW040934240426

43670CB00033B/2977